Quantrill's Thieves

Quantrill's Thieves

By: Joseph K. Houts, Jr.

Quantrill's Thieves

Copyright 2002 by Joseph K. Houts, Jr.

All rights reserved. This book may not be reproduced by any means either in whole or in parts, excluding passages used for the purpose of magazine or newspaper reviews, without the written consent of the publisher.

Although facts and statements in this book have been checked and rechecked, mistakes—typographical and otherwise—may have occurred. This book was written to entertain and inform. The author and the publisher shall have no liability or responsibility for damages or alleged damages arising out of information contained in this book.

ISBN 0-9719929-3-2
Library of Congress 2002111490
First Edition, 2002

Published by Truman Publishing Company
Printed in the United States of America

Editing and Book Layout by James D. Criswell
Illustrations by Suzanne Emery

All correspondence and credit card orders contact:

Truman Publishing Company
218 Delaware, Suite #303, Kansas City, MO 64105
Or call toll free: 1-888-852-3694
www.trumanpublishing.com

Attention: Corporations and Schools:
Truman Publishing books are available at quantity discounts with bulk purchase for educational, business, or sales promotional use. For information, please write to Truman Publishing Special Sales. Please supply: title of book, quantity, how the book will be used, and date needed.

Dedication

To my grandmother, Allie – Alice Kinyoun Houts – a wonderful lady who instilled in me a sense of appreciation for our country's past and heritage.

Table of Contents

Dedication vii
Acknowledgements xiii
Foreword xv
Introduction xix
Roll of Quantrell's Company of Thieves xxiii

Chapter I:
"To Wage War" 1

Chapter II:
"Nefarious Business...Murdering Loyal Men" 28

Chapter III:
"The Many Wild Birds Were Caroling" 41

Chapter IV:
"Company of Thieves" 50

    W. C. Quantrell 53
    Wm Hallar 1st Lieutenant 61
    G W Todd 2nd Lieutenant 63
    W H Gregg 1st Sergeant 65
    John Jarrette 2nd Sergeant 68
    J L Tucker 3rd Sergeant 70
    Andrew Blunt 71
    F M Scott Commissary 73
    Richard Madox Quartermaster 74
    Henry Acres 76
    U L Anderson 77
    Sylvester Atchison 78
    Wiley Atchison 79
    John Atchison 80
    H Austin 81
    J D Brinker 82
    Jas H Bowling 84
    Richard Burns 86
    W M Burges 88
    W A Baker 90
    W H Butler 92
    G N Burnett 93

QUANTRILL'S THIEVES By: Joseph K. Houts, Jr.

James Barnett	95
O. S. Barnett	96
Lee Ball	98
W M Bledsoe	99
W C Bell	101
J Bowers	102
James Cunningham	104
A L Cunningham	106
W Collesure	108
Thomas Collesure	109
Kit Chiles	110
Samuel Clifton	112
Wm Chamblin	113
Syrus Cockrell	114
W F Cheatham	117
W H Campbell	118
J J R Dejarnatt	119
Robert Davenport	120
N F Doke	122
J N Dickers	123
M H Doors	125
J F Doores	126
Noah Estes	127
J G Freeman	128
J H George	129
Mike Houx	131
Mat Houx	133
Robert Houx	138
W Hally	140
John Hampton	143
O Hampton	144
G N Horn	145
J J Hall	146
M Houston	147
A Harris	148
U Hays	150
Robert Hall	154
J A Hendricks	156
W F Judd	158
J W Koger	159
C A Longacre	162
B L Long	164
James Lyon	165

B. T. Muir	167
James L. Morris	169
George Madox	170
Ezry Moore	173
J N Olliphant	174
J Owings	175
Harry Odgen	176
F M Ogden	178
Otho Offutt	179
T D Perdee	182
J R Perdee	183
D M Pool	185
H C Pemberton	189
F M Robinson	191
J W Rider	192
George Rider	193
Robert Stephenson	194
William D Tucker	195
John Teague	196
T F Teague	198
A B Teague	199
Thomson	201
Wm Vaughn	204
James Vaughn	205
C T Williamson	207
Coal Younger	208
Richard Yeager	217
J. H. Terry	220

Chapter V:
"Micah"	221
General Order No. 2	234
General Order No. 9	235
General Order No. 10	236
General Order No. 11	238
Endnotes	239
Bibliography	272
Index	280

Acknowledgements

Any heartfelt expression of gratitude should always begin with one's family. I would never have completed this project without the patience, understanding, and support of my loving wife, Noreen, and our wonderful children, Joe III and Katie. I must also thank my father for his constant listening, helpful comments, and just always being a special friend, along with his dog, Whiskey.

In the academic world, I thank my former college history professor at Westminster College, Dr. William E. Parrish. Bill was always there to encourage and review my manuscript, as it slowly progressed. He gave countless hours of advice in directing me on the right path. He was never too busy to answer my many questions. Bill, you are a true gentleman of the old school. You were always the one who said, "Don't give up." Thanks, Bill.

Without question many other individuals aided me in this endeavor. Early on in my efforts, Margaret Bardgett, Joanne Chiles Eakin, and Donald R. Hale offered me invaluable information and insight into the guerrilla war in Missouri. In addition, my thanks go to Kay Russell of the Confederate Memorial State Historical Site at Higginsville, Missouri. She opened the door to the story of many of William Clarke Quantrill's original guerrillas. She has truly been a friend to a friend in need during this undertaking.

Many people shared information with me from their family files about various men who rode with Quantrill. Others provided me material simply as a volunteer or researcher. All of them I thank, but in particular: Amos Vannarsall on George Maddox; Michael Burgess, on W. M. Burgess; Judge Frank W. Koger on John Koger; Stephanie Young on W. F. Judd; Randy Senor and Calvin W. Hawkins of the Clay County Archives and Historical Library, Inc. on Robert Stephenson; Holly Beall and Angie Murray on James A. Hendricks; A. Pauline Houx Hall on Michael Morningstar Houx; Anne Houx on Houxes in general; Marilyn Bailiff King on George McKinley Barnett; Virginia Metheny on David Poole; Carolyn M. Bartels and Mary Rainey of the Johnson County Historical Society, Inc.; Anne Clark of

QUANTRILL'S THIEVES By: Joseph K. Houts, Jr.

the Clay County Historical Society, Inc.; Jan Toms on Boone T. Muir; Barb Crader on Dr. W. M. Doores; Verna Gail Johnson of the Mid-Continent Public Library, Genealogical & Local History Branch, Independence, Missouri; Homer Jarmen and Karol at K. W. Archives on J. W. and George Rider; Bob Bledsoe on W. M. Bledsoe; Barbara McCormick on C. A. Longacre; Becky L. Horvath on J. J. and Robert Hall; Bella Hughes on Syrus Cockrell; Ralph E. Church, Cemetery Administration, Jefferson National Cemetery Barracks; William T. Stolz, Manuscript Specialist, Western Historical Manuscript Collection; Clifton D. Cardin, Official Bossier Parrish Historian; Vicki M. Hardin, Bossier Parrish Historical Center; the New Orleans Public Library, Louisiana Division, on Harry and F. M. Ogden; Jerry Russell, Heaton, Bowman, Smith and Sidenfaden Funeral Home; the St. Joseph, Missouri, Police Department; and Dee Matthews on W. Halley.

    Numerous other individuals have also assisted me and if by chance I have forgotten or overlooked your help I apologize and thank all in return. Of special significance there is one very important group of people who have helped and encouraged me—my friends. My thanks go out to Major Mark Martsolf, Randy Schultz, Robert Sanders, Pat Cargill, John Josendale, Mac Burns, Madeleine Verssue, Max Wyeth, Gregg Larson, Sheridan Logan, Suzanne Emery, and many others who have expressed an interest in my book. Again, I apologize to those I may have omitted. Lastly, I thank my old friend, Jim Criswell, who was kind enough to publish my manuscript.

Foreword

Almost everything in life is merely temporary. Friends come and go. Children grow up and leave the home. Loved ones, unfortunately, pass away. Our economic circumstances fluctuate. Any of our physical possessions—a house, a car, a suit of clothes—is only a part of our life for a short time. The enthusiasm and vitality of youth gives way. The only things, really, that we are allowed to retain with any semblance of permanence are our memories.

Biology dictates the predetermined cycle of our species; we are born, we live our lives, and eventually we die. Many of us have fulfilling lives, whether raising families, finding success in our work, or in simply helping others; but all of the activities, endeavors, and achievements of life have their conclusion. Many of us strive for social accolades, accomplishments, or status within society. It could be said that all of the things that we strive for represent the human spirit's need for self-actualization; to find self-fulfillment, and realize our potential. Still, the truth is that we will all be left with nothing of this earth when the end comes.

There remains one exception though, the ability to possibly remember those experiences of life which have brought us to any given point in our existence. Whether consciously, or simply through our daily routine, we record our life experiences in the form of letters, dairies, and formal texts, or through the many manifestations of the new electronic media. Through this process we create a collection of memories, which after the passage of time we call history. The word *history* means our story.

Having grown up in the era of America's Centennial Celebration of the Civil War, I had many special memories from this period. On numerous occasions my parents would take me to Civil War museums and battlefields. I eventually became enthralled with these outings, relishing each new visit. However, one event in particular has stood out among all of the others. Actually, it was a classroom lecture by my 3rd grade teacher, Miss Virginia Gardner, while I was attending Noyes School in St. Joseph, Missouri. It was towards the end of the year in 1962 and

QUANTRILL'S THIEVES By: Joseph K. Houts, Jr.

she was explaining those local and regional happenings that occurred during the war. Her presentation immediately sparked my interest because I never considered this part of the country having much in the way of a Civil War connection.

My understanding and perception had been limited to those battles transpiring east of the Mississippi River. On that day she pointed out how the most violent and savage parts of the war had taken place in Missouri and Kansas. In particular she spoke of a man named Quantrill as being the most vicious of all the bad guys during this period, and quite probably in the annuls of American military history. Worse yet was her telling the class he was a Missourian of sorts. I was horrified by the thought that someone from my own backyard was considered by most scholars as the epitome of terror, destruction, and death. Miss Gardner elaborated in great detail how this individual with his gang of henchmen raided the small town of Lawrence, Kansas in 1863, murdering in cold blood every unarmed man and boy unfortunate enough to fall within their path that day. I could not fathom a more vile and disgusting deed. I stayed awake most of that night reviewing the truth I had just learned.

Within a week or so, I was in Kansas City visiting my grandmother, who was without question the family historian. I asked her about what Miss Gardner had told the class and she responded, yes there was a man named William Clarke Quantrill who was the leader of a gang of partisans in Missouri during the war. Grandmother stated though that he and his men were not necessarily bad as my teacher had said, but that they had been misunderstood and misplaced by time and events. She explained that much of what happened at Lawrence was true. I questioned her as to why such an act did not make this man and his men evil. Going beyond my question, she related that many of our ancestors had been on the same side of the war as Mr. Quantrill, or put in a more refined fashion, several members of the family had supported the Confederacy and fought for the South, including both of her grandfathers.

I was amazed by this revelation and began to think the worse of the family. Sensing my misgivings, grandmother went on to explain how horrible things happen in war and that men and women often times cannot escape their surroundings and become caught up in events leading to abnormal behavior with tragic consequences. She also stated some of the clan had fought for the North. Even with this said, she acknowledged the horror committed at Lawrence, but pointed out men supporting the Union had committed equally terrible acts. Our conversation ended and I was left in a great state of confusion. Fortunately, at my young age she had spared me the real truth about the family, something I would not totally learn about until many years later.

As the Centennial passed, so did my interest in the Civil War. However, my appreciation for history and its study increased through high school and college. I knew upon entering college my major would be history. Of course my parents were somewhat dismayed and thought a degree in political science or business would be far more practical in the real world, especially if I planned on studying law after graduation. I dreaded that thought, which may have explained my persistence in the pursuit of history. Of some sad irony though, my majoring in history did not save me from law school. Another reason for deciding upon this course stemmed in part from the departmental slogan, which read, "He or she who forgets their past is bound to repeat it." For some unexplained reason this phrase had a profound effect on me and its words have stayed with me to this day. I guess it revealed and instilled in me the true purpose and meaning of history.

Later, after my school years, friends and family would razz me about my interest in history, saying it was about as useful as studying Latin. I remained silent on this statement, since I had four years of Latin in high school and one in college. I always felt these individuals misunderstood the importance of both subjects.

Several years ago, I was rummaging through a box of old books my grandmother had given me when I was much younger. While sorting the contents my eyes caught the title of one in particular. It was captioned <u>Gray Ghosts of the Confederacy</u> by Richard S. Brownlee, a noted Missouri historian. At first glance I thought maybe it was just another book with a catchy title, but on flipping through the pages I discovered its real value. To my surprise it dealt with the guerrilla war in Missouri. Of further interest, there was a list in the back of the guerrillas known to have ridden with Quantrill. I scanned those pages looking for any familiar family name, but found none. I proceeded to read the book and once again became interested in the Civil War,

QUANTRILL'S THIEVES By: Joseph K. Houts, Jr.

especially Missouri's role in the conflict. The more I read though, the more I learned how bitter and passionate the war had been in this state.

With this renewed infatuation, my family again proceeded to poke fun at my efforts, questioning the point of reliving the past. At times I wondered myself about the importance of this pursuit, until one day I uncovered an unsubstantiated recent bit of history which confirmed my beliefs.

It must be understood that my generation grew up under the dark clouds of the Cold War. Through my readings, I discovered how an Asian revolutionary had studied the Civil War in this state, concentrating in particular on the guerrilla war and the tactics of William Clarke Quantrill. As a rising partisan, he employed this new knowledge to wrestle control of his country from the French. Although a communist, he even asked the United States for assistance against this foreign intruder, but America shunned him due to our European alliances and the fear of communism. In time our country would pick up the cause abandoned by the French, only to be outwitted by this man and to suffer even a worse defeat than theirs. Unfortunately, our own history books had trained this man all too well in the mistakes of our past, for his country was Vietnam and his name was Ho Chi Minh.

It can be said Quantrill and his followers eventually lost in their efforts to win a war. However, it could also be said that Ho Chi Min and the Vietnamese people won the war that he lost. Whether or not the study of Quantrill and his guerillas was pivotal in shaping Ho Chi Minh's tactics and strategy will remain a mystery, but it is possible. There are numerous examples throughout civilization's past of one leader borrowing and building on the tactics of another.

The point is that the lessons of history are not always found in antiquity, or in far away lands. Sometimes the greatest lessons of history originate in our very own backyard.

QUANTRILL'S THIEVES By: Joseph K. Houts, Jr.

Introduction

The purpose in writing this book was founded upon several premises. First, the objective was to set forth how the guerrilla war in Missouri evolved from a series of ill-conceived Union orders and decrees and their misinterpretation by the predominately Southern based population within the state. Second, the author wanted to recount an old family Civil War story, concluding with a portrayal of the battle of Pleasant Hill, Missouri on July 11, 1862. Third, the goal was to produce a short biographical sketch of William Clarke Quantrill's original documented 93 riders. Lastly, the intent was to relate how the war in Missouri progressively advanced in its brutality and destruction—showing how a conflict, of relatively confined proportions in the beginning, turned extremely ugly by its end.

The source that revealed Quantrill's partisans was discovered after the fighting at Pleasant Hill when Union troops found his muster roll on one of the dead guerrillas. Two copies were made of the original, one by a Captain Henry J. Stierlin of Company A, 1st Missouri Cavalry, and the other by the author's great, great uncle Major Thomas W. Houts, of Company A, 7th Cavalry, Missouri State Militia (MSM). The original and Captain Stierlin's copy were forwarded to Union commander Brigadier General John M. Schofield. The major retained possession of his copy of the roster.

Many accounts have traced those individuals riding with Quantrill. Upwards of 2,500 men have been said to have participated in some form of guerrilla activity in Missouri between 1861-1865. Estimates have established that approximately 600 men rode with Quantrill during the course of the war. His band started with seven in October 1861, shortly growing to fifteen by December, and by late March 1862, had reached 120 men.

The reader may notice some missing guerrilla names within the text, such as Jim and John Little, Ed Koger, Fletch Taylor, Harrison Trace, Joe Gilchrist, William "Bloody Bill" Anderson, Archie Clement and Frank James, to name just a few. Without question each of these individuals at one time or another rode with Quantrill. However, none of them were on the muster

QUANTRILL'S THIEVES By: Joseph K. Houts, Jr.

roll, attributed either to their not being present when the list was made or because they joined later, as is the case with Anderson, Clement, and James.

Some minor variances have surfaced among the three lists, the most prominent being in the spelling of the names. In all likelihood the two officers wrote their separate lists simultaneously while another soldier read off names from the original. In other words, the names transcribed on their copies were based on the age-old practice of phonetics. The main element to this technique has been to sound out letters, syllables, and words, before committing them to writing.

Another consideration affecting their spelling was the obvious application of phonetics to the original. Literacy was slowly emerging in mid-19th century America. Since most of Quantrill's riders were farm boys or laborers, there was in reality an overall lack of educational refinement among them. The individual drafting the original roll was in all probability relying on phonetics in its composition. Compounding the matter further, some of the riders may not have known the correct spelling of their own name, again due to the fact that they had little formal schooling.

Therefore, many conflicting elements have presented themselves in analyzing these rolls. For the most part though, they have a correlation to the original. In form, the documents have a distinct similarity. At the top a chain of command is set forth, comprising nine men and their ranks, representing Quantrill's officer corp. Following this section there is a semi-alphabetical listing of the riders.

Each list, of course, has a title. The original is captioned "Quantrell's Muster Roll." Whereas Captain Stierlin's list is dubbed "Quantrell's Gang of Outlaws", and Houts' has the more eloquent inscription of "Roll of Quantrell's Company of Thieves."

Concerning the name Quantrill, on all three lists it is misspelled as "Quantrell", with an "e" instead of an "i", which was not an uncommon practice, even in more modern times. This interesting error means that the original was probably not drafted by Quantrill himself. Quantrill was literate, having graduated from the equivalent of high school by the age of 16 and also having been a teacher both in his home of Canal Dover, Ohio and later in Kansas. Odds would be against Quantrill misspelling his own name. Probably, one of his chosen officers transcribed the roll, being basically literate in order to draft the document, but understandably lacking when it came to the spelling of proper names. Even today, the spelling of names has its own rules, outside most of the formal and standard principles in the English language. However, in light of this misspelling, the author has chosen to title this book with the proper spelling of "Quantrill." Although, from a historical standpoint within the confines of this book the spelling of "Quantrell" has been used in place thereof.

    Another peculiarity in comparing the three lists is in the number of names. The original has 92 names, whereas the two copies each have 93. The additional name is that of F. M. Ogden who was included on both Stierlin's and Houts' copies for some unknown reason, perhaps due to a vendetta, or perhaps based on hearsay evidence.

    In light of these dissimilarities, the author has formatted a basis of interpretation. As to each biographical sketch, the original spelling of the rider's name from Major Houts' list has been used as the title. Discrepancies or alternative spellings to the first, middle, or last name of the rider appear in parenthesis immediately below the subject title. From this grouping the author has correlated each rendition to the most logical historical version or reference to the name, starting each sketch with the most probable spelling. In most instances, the final selection has a strong connection to the list's. The only exceptions have been the last names of Brinker, Hays, Vaughn, and Younger.

    Concerning Brinker, the original has J. D. Bicker and Stierlin's has J. A. Bucker. There was a guerrilla named John Brinker as set forth on the Houts copy. Possibly the major was aware of the true name, or the original's was merely misspelled. Stierlin's has a harder explanation, which might be attributed to a misunderstanding of its pronunciation.

    Hays was correctly spelled on the original and Houts' list. Obviously, Stierlin's was a misspelling attributed to phonetics. "Haise" has the same sound as "Hays."

    The Stierlin and Houts copies have the name James Vaughn, whereas the original has only Vaughn, absent a first name or initial. It appears that Stierlin and Houts may have been familiar with Mr. Vaughn and were consequently able to include his first name.

QUANTRILL'S THIEVES   By: Joseph K. Houts, Jr.

Finally, there was not a Richard Younger, but a Richard Yeager – sometimes spelled Yager. In this case, Yeager was mistakenly substituted for an otherwise apparent variance, beyond the explanation of phonetics. The reason for concluding the name was Yeager, stems from a comparison between it and that name corresponding on the original and Stierlin's copy. On both of these documents, the name was listed as Richard Yeager. Younger and Yeager have a faint semblance when sounding out, so it became obvious the major mistook the pronunciation.

As pointed out, the purpose of this project was to condense much of the large amount of material already written about the guerrillas. In comprising the sketches, an extreme amount of material was utilized in their development. The idea was to amass basic facts about each of these 93 riders, and where possible to document their date of birth and death, along with those character traits which defined the individual. Some of the sketches may seem more genealogical in nature than others. Further, the sketches include an account of their military activities.

The portrayal of Quantrill is expanded in order to set forth a general narrative overview and time line for the guerrilla war in Missouri. The intent was to create a reference point when reading about the others.

Outside of these items the goal has been to set forth opinions and descriptions by others. Unfortunately, there is not an abundance of information available about many of the riders, making their sketch somewhat brief.

As a point of reference, the author uses the words "Roll" and "Roster" in discussing and referring to Major Houts' list throughout the text. In a few situations, the author may have made the wrong analysis in determining who was in fact the real guerrilla as to the name on the Roll. Simply, a best guess had to be made in order to complete this project. In cases of mistaken identity, an apology will always be present, with the sincere hope those knowing otherwise would so inform the author. Hopefully in the end though, the reader will be left with a sense of why these men became guerrillas and how they affected the war in this region of the country. However, above all else, the intention is to present history in its often raw and explicit form, to be educational, yet entertaining.

QUANTRILL'S THIEVES By: Joseph K. Houts, Jr.

Roll of Quantrells Company of Thieves
W. E. Quantrell   Capt.
Wm Haller   1st Lieut.
G W Todd   2   J M Scott   Commissary
W H Gregg   1st Sergt. Richard Madox 2 Lt.
John Jarrett   2
J S Tucker   3
Andrew Blunt   4

Acres Henry	Clifton Samuel
Anderson W S	Chamblin Wm
Atchison Sylvester	Cockrell Syrus
Atchison Wiley	Cheatham W S (Dead)
Atchison John	Campbell W H
Austin H	Dejarnett J J R
Brinker J D	Davenport Robert
Bowling Jas H	Doke N J
Burns Richard	Dickus J N
Burgis W M	Doores M H
Baker W A	Doores J F
Butler W H	Estes Noah
Burnett J N	Freeman J G
Barnett James	George J H
Barnett O S	Houx Mike
Ball Lee	Houx Mat
Bledsoe W M	Houx Robert
Bell W C	Hally W
Bowers G	Hampton John
Cunningham James	Hampton O
Cunningham A L	Horn J N
Collusurs W	Hall G J
Collusurs Thomas	Houston M
Chiles Kit	Harris A

Muster roll made by Major Thomas W. Houts (Front Side)

xxiii

QUANTRILL'S THIEVES By: Joseph K. Houts, Jr.

Hays, W.	Robinson, J. M.
Hall, Robert	Riden, J. M.
Hendricks, J. A.	Riden, George
Judd, W. T.	Stephenson, Robert
Koger, J. M.	Tucker, W. D.
Langacre, C. A.	Teague, John
Long, B. S.	Teague, J. H.
Lyon, James	Teague, A. B.
Muir, B. T.	Thomson
Morris, J. L.	Vaughn, Wm.
Madox, George	Vaughn, James
Moore, Eyry	Williamson, C. T.
Olliphant, J. N.	Younger, Coal
Owings, G.	Younger, Richard
Ogden, Harry	Terry, J. H.
Ogden, T.	
Offutt, Otha	
Purdew, T. D.	
Purdew, J. R.	
Pool, D. M.	
Pemberton, H. C.	

Muster roll made by Major Thomas W. Houts (Back Side)

xxiv

QUANTRILL'S THIEVES By: Joseph K. Houts, Jr.

Chapter I
"To Wage War"

The word guerrilla has its origin from the old Germanic term "guerre", meaning war " . . . to wage war." Present day spelling has been derived from Spain. On a broader scale, the term guerrilla has always meant some type of irregular combat or military order, mainly arising from locals or more particularly those known as partisans.

Centralia

Of all the savagery committed that day, one act alone stood out as the most appalling among all the other atrocities. One can only imagine the horrid nightmare witnessed by one particular soldier who had previously betrayed the guerrillas. It has been said the victim was still painfully alive when he was seized and his pants torn from him.

Wander his inner thoughts as the cold steel of a Bowie knife was placed upon his genitals and with a vicious lunge was thrust about until these elements were removed from his body. Piercing screams for mercy rang from his lungs as blood gushed from his groin with the guerrillas grabbing the genitals in hand and pulling them from his body, fondling them as if a slippery fish, fresh of water. They watched in amusement as fluids poured from the hole, pouring out onto the ground. As if rhythmically linked to the beat of his failing heart, opened veins wiggled like newly unearthed worms spewing blood at a slow, but even pace.

The final act of this wretched ceremony was the most sickening, for his severed penis and testicles were shoved into his wailing mouth. The mind can only be left to wonder what would encompass a greater cruelty than this sadistic act of

QUANTRILL'S THIEVES By: Joseph K. Houts, Jr.

barbarism. One can only surmise how a segment of a once predominately peaceful, gentle and neutral populace had become the epitome of terror, oppression, and revenge.

Within the context of the countless misdeeds and horrors to occur during the American Civil War, the battle of Centralia, Missouri on September 27, 1864 was without question the worst. The fight had started innocently enough, never planned, but emerging out of a mere scouting endeavor by those guerrilla forces under the command of William T. "Bloody Bill" Anderson and the combined forces of George Todd and John Thrailkill.

Anderson's men had entered the sleepy little village searching for information, or specifically a newspaper, which might pinpoint the whereabouts of Confederate Major General Sterling Price. Price had recently invaded the state from Arkansas. His hope was to pull Union Major General William T. Sherman's advance through the Deep South away from Atlanta, Georgia. Additionally, Price was in hopes of once again trying to wrestle Missouri into the Confederate fold, much as he had previously tried in the summer and autumn of 1861. Knowing the military prowess of the guerrillas, the general had sent word to them to assist in his invasion. Over the past few months, Anderson and other guerrilla henchmen had reeked havoc throughout the middle of Missouri, disrupting Union forces, stealing from and terrorizing at will that citizenry unfortunate enough to be in their path.

Before the day was out Anderson and his cutthroats had killed, more pointedly murdered, one hundred forty-nine Union soldiers. At first, twenty-three unarmed Union troops were removed from a locomotive that was entering the town, stripped to their underwear and then summarily executed. The town was ransacked and, upon finding a barrel of whisky, the guerrillas indulged themselves to inebriation. In time, the horde left and journeyed two to three miles to the south, where it joined up with Todd and Thrailkill's bands. All total, nearly 250 to 300 guerrillas were now assembled as one group.

Within an hour a contingent of one hundred forty-seven Union troops arrived, known as the 39th Missouri State Militia, under the command of Major A.E.V. Johnson. The unit was newly formed and at best could be considered "green" in its lack of training, experience, and supplies. Their mounts consisted of former plow horses and instead of carrying carbines and revolvers the troops possessed single-shot Enfield rifles. The best of soldiers, let alone raw recruits, could only reload and fire a rifle three times in a minute. They were facing experienced guerrillas carrying three to six 6-shooter revolvers with a firepower of thirty-six shots in a minute.

Upon inspecting the carnage in the town, Johnson decided to pursue and confront Anderson's forces. His orders had been to hold and wait for additional support, but the scenes of slaughter and destruction transformed his thoughts into a thirst for immediate vengeance, which eventually would beckon he and his men to their ultimate demise.

Believing the long range of rifles would stand the foe's challenge of close range revolvers, he went forth with his troops in search of retribution. Several townspeople begged him to wait, but unfortunately his mind was set.

Anderson had learned of his approach and laid a trap by sending a handful of his men under Archie Clements to entice the major towards their ranks. The guerrillas had hidden themselves in a half circle of trees, further camouflaged by the terrain. Upon seeing a contingent of ten guerrillas, Johnson pursued them with one hundred twelve of his men, leaving thirty-five behind to guard Centralia.

After a short chase and upon seeing the bulk of the guerrilla forces, he ordered his men to dismount, leaving every fourth man to hold horses. The Union troops were successful in discharging one round but before a second could be loaded the guerrillas were upon them, killing all in sight and pursuing those who fled back to town and even some to as far away as Sturgeon, Missouri.

A reign of butchery was then cast upon the vanquished. It was not enough that there was a standard of "no quarter" in Missouri between Union and guerrilla forces. It was also not enough that they were dead, the utter substance of their existence had to be ravaged if not obliterated. Limbs, torsos, and heads, soon took on the appearance of broken parts of a child's doll scattered about the floor. The scene which was to befall the fallen became an orgy of mutilation, where human remains became some sick symbol of victory, as if prized trophies.

The guerrillas severed many of the dead soldiers' heads placing them on stakes, or the point of their rifles, while others were tossed about, resembling a uniquely perfected new form of kickball. Seventeen of the victims were scalped, including Johnson. After cutting off their victims legs and arms, the well-intoxicated guerrillas proceeded to rearranged various other body parts. Placards were made and placed around the severed heads, many being obscene in their language. In addition to the scalps, heads were hung from the pommels of saddles. Others were spiked and paraded around gleefully, as if ornaments in some pagan ritual. While several more were stuck upon fence posts and their faces configured so as to be conversing between themselves. All of the victims were shot in the head and one of the victims was missing his nose.

Centralia Atrocities
Illustration by Suzanne Emery

Afterwards, the guerrillas again got drunk in celebration of their great victory. A woman was raped as part of the night's merriment. Noted guerrilla David Pool decided to count the dead by walking on the bodies. In order to make sport of it, he tried not to touch the ground by jumping from body to body. A comrade commented on his method of arithmetic. Pool responded, "If they are dead I can't hurt them. I cannot count them good without stepping on them. When I got my foot on one this way I know I've got them."

Veterans of Centralia were later asked about the bloodshed. In response they said it was because thirteen guerrillas had been killed earlier at Fayette, Missouri. Upon hearing of the tragedy, some folks said it was the alcohol that day which caused the butchery, but others knew it was the war—in particular the war in Missouri.

The Cause

As the war grew out of proportion across all regions of the country Missouri, being a border state, was to become extremely ravaged. Remaining in the Union while at the same time being a slave state became very trying and stressful for its predominately Southern based population. Over a short course of time, and the occurrence of several consequential events, Union military officials would soon inflict their wanton will upon citizens of questionable loyalty. Believing theirs the right way of the law, they began to exact punishment with frequency. The result of this conduct was to further alienate an already uneasy and distrustful populace.

As the fight for control for Missouri deepened and dragged on, partisan groups or guerrilla outfits began to emerge to defend Missouri against the acts of aggression and atrocity committed both by Federal troops and by warring Jayhawkers from Kansas. In time it became a case of virtually trading dreadful blows, with each seeking vengeance upon the other.

Historian William E. Connelley probably characterized the true demeanor of the prewar Missourian by referring to them as "kind, hospitable, generous, tolerant, (and) open-minded." Other descriptions included "charitable...general intelligence... always of a high order...thinking people...sane and safe...." However, as Connelley pointed out, such traits were ironically the cornerstone of what was to come. He stated, "It was these qualities of her people that made the Civil War a carnival of blood in Missouri. Every man stood upon his own convictions... a man may be ruined, despoiled, slain, but he will not be false to his sense of right and justice." As the war grew beyond excess, nothing could better explain the situation that evolved in Missouri.

    The Missourian was far removed from the Eastern Theater of the conflict. Representing the western border of the nation, the state had long been settled, and in large part was self-contained and content within itself. Established state and local governments were in place, but due to the vastness of this part of the country, other ways than those of a legal nature dictated the ways of everyday life. People were neighborly. They cared for their families and homesteads, giving aid to those around them in need. Law and order was commonplace, but at the same time there was still a higher authority than that of government. Overall there was a natural order of self-preservation, kinship, and openness to the less fortunate.

    Courts could not always offer justice; sometimes justice required a greater degree of immediacy as dictated by the situation. True in their spirit, true in their convictions, and true to their God, the Missourian was hard working, disciplined, and of a mindset not to harm unless harmed. In particular, they were of a passive nature accepting matters at face value, even as events initially unfolded against them. They were of an opinion to let things go, such as the ultimate result of Kansas emerging as a free state by the end of the 1850's. However, as Connelley so noted, there was a line that defined the limits of their tolerance. Once breached, that line could never be crossed again.

    As the storm clouds of national discontent continued to swirl, the citizens of Missouri were not prepared for the ensuing calamity about to envelope them. With this said, the origins of war have always been traceable. Although at first unrecognized, the vortex of such events will always be remembered by those who were caught in its devastating sweep.

    In the case of the American Civil War, it evolved over many years, having as its backdrop the question of slavery, compounded by the issue of state's rights. More importantly, it focused on a national conscience wrestling with the question of how a country that embodied personal liberties could still hold others of a different race in bondage.

To this day these questions have continued to haunt the land, even as we have now advanced into a new millennium. The question being: "Will the American Experiment continue to transform and define freedom with humility, inclusiveness, and equality?" The same stirrings that will affect America's future affected its past.

Although the opening events of Fort Sumter and Bull Run have many times been inscribed as the beginning of the Great War of Rebellion, scholars of Western history have more frequently pointed to the Kansas-Nebraska Act of 1854 as the opening salvo. In all probability this single piece of legislation did more to cause the Civil War, and in turn the guerrilla war in Missouri, than any other preceding event.

In essence, the measure became a rallying point for both Northern and Southern interests within the country. From this legislation arose a calliope of fanatical individuals and deeds both vile and virtuous, and a form of mass hysteria in the border region that would forever transform and scar the land. In particular, the grit of all Missourians would be tested, not only as to individual loyalties and convictions, but as to each individual's view of life itself.

The Kansas-Nebraska Act was intended as a compromise between the country's pro- and anti-slavery factions. Although being so devised it was in many respects a victory for the pro-slavery proponents.

The Missouri Compromise of 1820 had admitted Missouri to the Union as a slave state, but simultaneously banned future expansion of slavery north of the 36° 30° parallel running across the continent. This line was the southern border of Missouri. In 1820 the nation's western boundary ended several hundred miles from the edge of the Missouri River and accordingly there were no vast western and northern territories. Continental expansion did not occur until 1848 with the conclusion of the Mexican War, the annexation of Texas, and the Oregon Treaty.

Now, with the stroke of a pen, these western regions were open to slave settlement—abolishing the previously long standing Missouri Compromise. The Act was a simple proposition of majority rules in those territories petitioning to become states. At the outset, however, there were two assumptions about the legislation. First, it was assumed Kansas would enter the Union as a slave state and second, it was assumed Nebraska would enter as a free state. Unfortunately, these assumptions did not hold weight in the eyes of Easterners, especially among those fire-breathing abolitionists of New England.

By the tens, the hundreds, and then the thousands, Yankees packed up and moved to Kansas. They were called "free staters" and "free-soilers." These were people determined to see the state enter the Union as a free state. Virtually within days of its enactment, Northerners issued the rallying cry to save Kansas from the clutches of slavery. New York Senator William H. Seward became one of the more prominent advocates among the abolitionists. Organizations sprung up to assist Easterners in their journey to Kansas. One in particular was the New England Emigrant Aid Society, this society was formed by Eli Thayer and Amos Lawrence. The settlement of Lawrence, Kansas would be named after the latter.

In time, as the dispute and control for the territory expanded, arms and heavy ordnance were sent West. Rifles were shipped to Kansas marked "Books." Light artillery was sent under a similar disguise, but stamped as "machinery."

Missourians found themselves dumb founded by the change in the course of events brought about by the Kansas-Nebraska Act. In their opinion, Missourians should settle the territory, not New Englanders.

Although, Missouri was a slave state, only 12% of the population owned slaves. The main slave areas were located throughout the middle of the state, paralleling the Missouri River and also in that area northeast of the "boot-heal" region. Compared to other slave states its Negro population was relatively small, only approaching 10% of the total. However, 75% of the population was of Southern heritage. The remaining 25% traced their roots from Ohio, Indiana, and Illinois; states that had also been settled predominantly by Southerners. Although the institution of slavery was of a lesser degree of importance than it was in other Southern states, there was still a strong tie to their Southern brethren by family and by nature. Even Missouri's economy, excepting St. Louis, was by and large agrarian, as was the economy throughout the South.

At first the concept of "popular sovereignty" seemed to guarantee that Kansas would join the Union as a slave state, protecting the interests of Missouri and the South, since two-thirds of its population in 1854 were of Southern origin. However, the North felt betrayed by the Kansas-Nebraska Act. What right in their minds did Missourians have to Kansas? The Missouri Compromise had long ago ruled out any entitlement to the territory as far as any Southern claims. Of further merit, there was barely a slave within its boundaries. In the eyes of the Northern abolitionist, Missouri was not going to reap this ill-gotten gain simply because it adjoined Kansas.

All arguments aside, there was one final issue which weighed upon the Kansas question. It was the fact that Kansas represented three things to the slaveholding South. First, if Kansas became a free state it meant that the South would lose its parity in the United States Senate with the Northern free states. Second, Missouri represented the front door to the West and the further expansion of slavery. Third, and more importantly, if Kansas became a free state, then Missouri became not a door, but the back wall of the South, forever enclosing it as a minority territorial and political bastion within the country. Knowing this full well and the possible ultimate consequences of secession, Kansas turned into a battleground, the first of many such scenes yet to occur in the American Civil War.

In time, the state was aflame. Missourians invaded the state as squatters, staking claims to tracts of land, but never intending to become permanent settlers. Their purpose was to be counted as part of the population and guarantee them the right to vote in the Kansas provisional elections. Hundreds of Missourians flocked to the Kansas polls in its elections of November 29, 1854 and March 30, 1855. Stuffing ballot boxes at the point of a gun was a common voting practice. Upon tallying the results, one county had more ballots cast than population. The election was a landslide for the pro-slavery proponents, and they went to work setting up a pro-slavery provisional government at LeCompton, Kansas.

The "free staters" were appalled at the Missouri election invasion and in turn set up their own "free soil" government in this period. Both sides committed numerous outrageous acts. Eventually murder became a common course of conduct, causing the death of upwards of 200 individuals between late 1855 and December 1856. Property damage was estimated at $2,000,000 during this period.

The Northern press called the Missourians "Border Ruffians" or "Pukes." Whereas, the Kansans were called "Jayhawkers," or "Niger Stealers." All these epitaphs were meant to purely belittle the other side. Border ruffians meant a Missourian who crossed the Missouri-Kansas border and was rough in appearance. "Pukes," again referring to the Missourian, meant "poor Southern white trash" or "losers in (the) cultural evolution." "Jayhawker" referred to a blue jay and a chicken hawk, whereas "Niger Stealers" referred to the practice of Kansans stealing Missouri slaves.

Leading the Missourians were such noted politicians as former United States Senator David Rice Atchison, future Missouri Governor Claiborne F. Jackson, and future Confederate General Joseph O. Shelby. On the Kansas side were future United States Senator and Union General James H. Lane, Dr. Charles R. "Doc" Jennison, James Montgomery, and the infamous abolitionist John Brown.

Raids were common, the most notable being the burning of Lawrence on May 24, 1856, by Missouri border ruffians. Three days later John Brown, accompanied by a few of his sons, murdered five suspected pro-slavery settlers on the Pottawatomie Creek near Osawatomie, Kansas in revenge for the raid.

By 1859 the contest was over, the Northern infusion had prevailed and Kansas was to become a free state. The South, but more particularly Missouri, had lost. Scars remained though on both sides, which as time would show would become the basis of the Civil War between Missouri and Kansas and within Missouri itself.

As 1859 drew to a close, John Brown attacked Harper's Ferry, Virginia hoping to arm himself and others and cause a slave revolt which would sweep throughout the South led by a 200,000 man Negro army. Such a possibility had always terrified the South, especially since Nat Turner's slave insurrection in 1831. Nat was a Negro slave preacher, born in Southampton County, Virginia. He and sixty to seventy of his followers had killed fifty-one whites in their rebellion, resulting in his own death by hanging upon his capture.

Brown's action further polarized the nation leading to the abolitionist Republican Party's victory in the November 1860 presidential race and the election of the party's candidate: Abraham Lincoln. By December, South Carolina had seceded from the Union, soon to be followed by ten other states. Within six short years of its passage, the Kansas-Nebraska Act of 1854 had catapulted the nation to the edge of civil war. So much for the concept of majority rules and "popular sovereignty." The nation was now to contest its will internally through violence, turning aside its once proudly cherished democratic form of government.

The Controls

Even with the loss of Kansas and the erupting Civil War, most Missourians were opposed to secession. In January 1861, the newly elected governor, Claiborne F. Jackson, delivered his inaugural address. During the campaign he had disguised his true sentiments. He was in fact a strong supporter of the South and eventually encouraged secession. His address was pro-Southern in its tone. In defiance of his stand, Union sympathizers and strategists like Frank Blair and General Nathaniel Lyon had other plans for the state and set in motion certain measures which led to open confrontation with Jackson's forces.

Jackson commissioned former Missouri Governor Sterling Price to establish a home guard to defend the state from all outsiders. Although there was little doubt that Price's

QUANTRILL'S THIEVES By: Joseph K. Houts, Jr.

Missouri State Guard, as it was formally named, was directed at Union political and military maneuverings in the state.

Within a few short months, the situation in Missouri escalated into full-scale war with Price and his forces defeating Lyon and his troops at the battle of Wilson's Creek, Missouri on August 10, 1861. General Lyon would be killed, making him the first Union general to die in the Civil War.

Prior to this engagement, Union and Confederate troops had fought at Carthage, Missouri on July 5, establishing it as the first major battle of the war. After the victory, Price marched north and began the siege of Lexington, located strategically on the Missouri River. Unable to hold the town, however, he retreated south for the remaining portion of the year. On March 7-8, 1862, Price and his troops were beaten at the battle of Pea Ridge, Arkansas. This defeat marked the end of any major formal military assault on the state, until Price's invasion in the autumn of 1864 and his ultimate defeat at Westport, Missouri, October 23-24, 1864.

It was in these beginning months of the war, between the spring of 1861 and 1862, that a convergence of three events occurred, which in fact led to the guerrilla war. All of them were not necessarily of a spontaneous nature, but one fed upon the other, which would eventually evolve into a single cause or, more importantly, a single course of events.

First, as will be recalled, the Kansas-Nebraska Act opened up a waive of bloodshed and retribution between Missouri and Kansas, until Kansas was admitted to the Union as a free state on January 29, 1861. Missourians by 1860-01 had long recognized their failure in Kansas. Although the issue was resolved, the conflict was far from over and in effect spilled over into the subsequent Civil War.

At this point, it could be said that nature intervened and caused a continuation of the Border War between these states. The problem once again arose out of Kansas, for during this period the state experienced a devastating drought. A climatic event which left many of its citizens destitute and starving. Crops would not grow, livestock died, and babies cried for sustenance. On the other hand, as if by some form of magic,

QUANTRILL'S THIEVES By: Joseph K. Houts, Jr.

Missouri was as green and as lush as the Garden of Eden. Through some mystery, the boundary between drought and bounty was at the Missouri-Kansas border. In this context, Kansans felt it was time for revenge, to now intrude in Missouri for the transgressions of Missourians in the previous decade.

Many of the former Jayhawker bands were still intact so all they had to do was saddle up, which they did in great numbers and with great frequency. Their plunder shocked the Missourians; nothing was sacred in their wake. Livestock, crops, even household furnishings, were stolen from Missouri homes. A special prize of their raids was to steal slaves— setting them free in Kansas. In other cruel instances, Jayhawkers, or a far lesser group called "Free Booters" would steal slaves, only to sell them back into slavery to either the original owner or to another buyer at a pure profit.

The most devastating Jayhawker raid was on September 22, 1861, at Osceola, Missouri. While pursuing General Price on his northward journey to Lexington, General Lane advanced on the town. In the process of their pillage many troops became drunk and turned even more violent, killing ten of its citizens and burning much of the city to the ground. Osceola was a wealthy port on the Osage River and consequently was a prize waiting to be plundered. The raid would long be remembered by Missourians, in particular future guerrillas as they marched on Lawrence, Kansas two years later. It was said "these were the men who would start the guerrilla war on the Western border." This statement was in reference to Jayhawkers—Lane, Jennison, and Montgomery.

The second element that set the stage for the eventual guerrilla war was General Price's actions before and after the battle of Pea Ridge. Prior to this clash, his troops had been bottled up in Southwest Missouri, ever since their victory at Lexington. Price decided to employ guerrilla tactics in order to disrupt interior Union lines. He ordered that telegraph and railroad lines be destroyed. One hundred miles of track were torn up and in addition numerous bridges were burned. The civilian courts usually freed those guerrillas that were apprehended.

QUANTRILL'S THIEVES By: Joseph K. Houts, Jr.

After Pea Ridge, there no longer was a standing pro-Confederate army in Missouri. Those captured or wanting to return home took an oath of allegiance to the United States, promising never again to take up arms against the government. However, as they soon found out, in many instances Union officials did not respect the oaths. If anything, it marked them as traitors and led to continual suspicion and harassment. In time, these now reformed and repentant citizens would forsake these oaths and go underground to fight against the growing atrocities directed at them and their families.

Noted guerrilla John McCorkle had served with Price and returned home under his oath. Eventually, he joined Quantrill saying he could not be left in peace as a neutral and he was determined not to fight against his home and state. Frank James was placed in the same predicament, upon being wounded at Wilson's Creek and giving his oath thereafter. He too was bullied and could not lead a normal life. Consequently, they all took to the bush and became guerrillas.

It has been stated that "jaykawking, however was not the sole cause of the guerrilla war in Missouri; in fact, perhaps it was not even the main cause." Supporting this statement was the fact that guerrilla activity had taken place in the southern and northern regions of the state. With this said, the third element in the guerrilla equation was nothing more than those acts by Missouri Unionists perpetrated against Missouri secessionists. Guerrilla bands sprang up where individuals did not want to be governed by the Union military. Unlike any other state in the Union, the citizens of Missouri were confronted with an especially unique situation. Theirs was a slave state, a slave state not officially joining the Confederacy but desperately trying to remain neutral, while at the same time wanting to stay in the Union.

In those states that did secede, they and their citizens were looked upon as hostile, as if from another country. Non-slaveholding states were cast similarly, whereby they were viewed as a separate nation battling a common enemy or front. Whereas, Missouri was in many respects viewed as both a Southern slave state, but also as a member of the Union.

Accordingly, those citizens bearing arms for the South within the state were not looked upon as Confederates but as traitors, unlike captives from the Confederate army in the eastern sections of the country who were considered prisoners of war.

Since Missouri was still in the Union, all of its citizens were expected to honor this position. In other words, those acting disloyal would not be regarded as prisoners in the ordinary sense of the word. By this dilemma, both Missouri Unionists and those sympathetic to the South found themselves immediately at odds. With Price's army vanquished and driven from the state, and a new pro-Union governor named Hamilton R. Gamble in place, Union military authorities embarked upon an extra legal form of conduct in dealing with the situation. In simple terms, Union authorities began enacting laws and issuing decrees in hopes of controlling the crisis or more importantly controling that portion of the population suspected or known to be sympathetic with the South.

As Missouri citizens rebelled against military control and Kansas Jayhawkers, guerrillas became ever more prevalent. In time, most all of these extra legal measures were directed in some way at curtailing guerrilla activity or imposing a punitive standard upon those violating the Union standard. Major General James C. Frémont issued the first of these orders on August 30, 1861 whereby he imposed martial law in the state. Specifically all of the property, real or personal, of those in opposition to the government was to be confiscated and their slaves to be freed. Further, those men in rebellion caught between Fort Leavenworth, Kansas and Cape Girardeau, Missouri would be subject to court martial and a firing squad.

Following this directive, President Lincoln authorized Major General Henry W. Halleck to suspend "habeas corpus" thereby allowing the imprisonment of individuals based on mere suspicion, without formal charges. Finally, on December 22, 1861, Halleck issued General Order No. 32, which was aimed at those guerrillas sabotaging the railroads. Within the decree it stated those "caught in (the) act ... (will be) immediately shot." In addition, any individual suspected of a crime will be arrested

QUANTRILL'S THIEVES By: Joseph K. Houts, Jr.

and incarcerated until the matter can be reviewed by a military commission. If found guilty, the party was to "… suffer death."

Even more injurious and infuriating to the citizenry was Halleck's General Order No. 24, issued on December 12, 1861. It could best be described as an "allowance decree". It mandated reparation of clothing and the maintenance of those individuals displaced by guerrilla acts at the expense of the disloyal. Coupled with the order was a $10,000 levy to be assessed on a party's personal property, which could be sold as a means to raise said amount. The consequence of this directive was that it led to wholesale stealing and looting of private property under any pretense. Union border cavalry viewed its scope to include arson and summary execution. Censorship also was imposed on the media. Union authorities were empowered to shut down any pro-Southern newspaper or those critical of the military administration. In January 1861, Halleck sent a letter to General Price clarifying his previous summary execution order. He explained the order only applied to those rebels out of uniform or acting as guerrillas.

The importance of General Order No. 24 was that it represented one of the first rulings usurping the authority of the civil courts. In effect, military rule was gradually replacing the state's once democratic framework. The right against unlawful quartering of troops in civilian homes, the protections of due process and of unlawful search and seizure were disappearing. These once guaranteed liberties as set forth in the Constitution and the Bill of Rights were vanishing in very short order.

As a new year dawned, General Halleck established military commissions on January 1, 1862 by issuing General Order No. 1. Union military officers were granted authority to preside over civilian courts where warranted. In effect, this created a "Kangaroo" form of justice, whereby the military could impose its sense of justice, absent long-standing legal precedents and procedures. The measure was also intended to harass those in support or sympathy with the South and the guerrillas.

In order to stop and control the free flow of munitions and supplies to the guerrillas, Halleck also mandated the requirement of permits or license passports. Union troops could now inspect all commerce in transit and confiscate those goods that were being transported without a permit. The purpose being to make sure local Southern sympathizers were not arming rebel units and guerrilla bands. By the end of 1862, St. Louis alone had issued 85,000 of these special passes.

By the early spring of 1862, events were unfolding rapidly in Missouri. Price had been defeated at Pea Ridge in the first week of March and many of his troops scattered or returned home. Halleck was losing patience with the war. Unfortunately, every time an order was issued, it agitated the citizenry more, further compounding matters. Confronted with the ever-growing guerrilla movement, mainly as a result of his bungling decrees, and those of others, he proceeded to issue his famous, or more pointedly infamous, General Order No. 2 on March 13, 1862. This decree became knows as the "no quarter" order. It stated that those individuals enlisting in partisan groups would henceforth be considered outlaws and be subject to summary execution.

The outcome of this ill-conceived edict was that it left few, if any, alternatives for either faction. As previously mentioned, the order had been drafted as a result of the widening guerrilla movement, and because of Price's troops returning home at the end of their enlistment following their defeat at Pea Ridge. Of primary concern was that these retiring and now displaced troops might further swell the guerrilla ranks. Adding to this dilemma was upon returning they were now to be confronted with the raging conflict on the home front orchestrated by Missouri Unionists and warring tribes of Jayhawkers. However, aside from the obvious reasons for the order, probably the real motive behind Halleck's decree may be attributed in large part to the activities of guerrilla chieftain William Clarke Quantrill.

By this time in the war, Quantrill had become the most notorious guerrilla leader. He had gone on the offensive in Western Missouri, attacking the mail service and raiding Union military posts. On March 7, he and his gang raised the ante by raiding Aubry, Kansas. It was the first time Quantrill had taken the offense and it was the first time that Kansas had been attacked by Missourians since the days of the border ruffians. Without question, this intrusion alone had convinced Halleck that General Order No. 2 was necessary in hopes of deterring other pro-Southern citizens and Price's returning troops from joining the ranks of the partisans.

The dye was now cast and Quantrill in particular would pick up the cause and face the challenge, persisting until the final days of the war in 1865. For a while the order went untested, but eventually Union officials would kill one of Quantrill's initial recruits, Perry Hoy, and from then on there would be no quarter left for the most part by the parties on either side.

Following the issuance of General Order No. 2, the Union military set about securing loyalty oaths and performance bonds from citizens of questionable background. In 1861, captured Missouri State Guard troops were required to give a loyalty oath or oath of allegiance in order to secure their freedom. However, in April 1862 these obligations were extended to civilians. Once again those suspected of aiding, abetting, or sympathizing with the Southern cause could be jailed and held until such oath and bond were tendered to the satisfaction of Union authorities. Again, due process and equal protection under the law had been abrogated.

As time would demonstrate, the situation in Missouri was only to worsen. On April 21, 1862 Confederate President Jefferson Davis signed into law the Confederate Partisan Rangers Act. This legislation granted the president authority to commission officers in the field for the purpose of recruiting partisan bands. In other words, civilian military units or partisans would be recognized as legitimate units of the Confederate armed services. The law was intended to supplement the Southern forces by raising armies west of the Mississippi River. Davis believed it important to resist all Northern invasions on Southern soil. The problem was that the North had the ability to wage war on multiple fronts, whereas the South could ill afford to be spread too thin.

Aware of the implications of the Confederate Partisan Rangers Act, Major General John M. Schofield issued General Order No. 18 on May 29, 1862. This ruling was an extension of

Halleck's earlier "no quarter" order. Guerrillas were now to be "shot down on the spot." Following this directive, Schofield issued General Order No. 19 on July 22, 1862, better known as the "Mandatory Enlistment" order. It stated "every able-bodied man (was) ordered to ... report for duty." Each man was also to bring his own weapon and horse. General Order No. 19 became the linchpin to Halleck's "no quarter" order. It implied that any man not enlisting in the Union army was therefore in sympathy with the South, and thus either a rebel, or a guerrilla and could thereby be executed as a traitor. The decree nullified prior oaths of allegiance and for all intents and purposes outlawed neutrality.

The question became—which side should one take? Many joined the guerrillas, in particular Quantrill and his many orbiting bands. The foolishness of this order was that it only increased the guerrilla ranks and ultimately resulted in even more bloodshed. Without this mandatory enlistment order there may have been slightly fewer blue coats in Missouri, but there also would have been far fewer partisans, and less conflict in the state. This order was an attempt to dictate by regulation an individual's convictions—a ridiculous idea on the face of it. Now each man had to choose a side, and for too many it was the last measure of their tolerance.

To those who subsequently joined the guerrilla ranks, the answer was simple. The ideals expressed in the Declaration of Independence—the right to life, liberty, and pursuit of happiness—no longer applied for those living in the military district of Western Missouri. From an historical context, Missourians faced the same sort of tyranny that their colonial forefathers stood up and opposed in the Revolutionary War four score before. It had become a question of the fundamental human right to resist oppression.

Schofield issued one other directive, on August 12, 1862, entitled General Order No. 9. The measure dealt with subsistence. It allowed Union troops to take what they wanted from those citizens in sympathy with the South. This order granted soldiers the right to enter any household without a warrant, in effect abolishing the Fourth Amendment to the Bill of Rights. Widespread foraging and robbery occurred as a result,

QUANTRILL'S THIEVES By: Joseph K. Houts, Jr.

leading to its repeal on September 22, 1862. Chaos was beginning to accompany every decree issued by the Union command.

In late 1862 and early 1863, Major General Samuel R. Curtis issued a series of orders, all directed at strengthening military control. His first order, on December 1, 1862, reorganized the Provost Marshal offices maintained throughout the state. Provost Marshals were given unlimited power in rounding up suspected sympathizers or guerrillas. The civilian courts and local law enforcement were turned over to the military. Union officials were granted the right to arrest individuals "at their will."

On December 24, 1862, he enlarged the Provost Marshal's authority as set forth in General Order No. 35, only to have it rescinded by President Lincoln. However, Secretary of War, Edwin Stanton, reinstated the measure. The consequence of the order was that it led to false arrests. Further, defendants were required to post a large bond which was split between the lawyers and the military commissioners. Also, within this decree was a banishment clause, whereby any suspect could be removed from the area without committing what was termed a "specific act." Lastly, Curtis issued General Order No. 30 on April 22, 1863, which further broadened the definition of guerrilla under Halleck's "no quarter" order.

As demonstrated by Curtis and his ordinances, the military continued to tighten its authority over the everyday citizen. Early on in the war, the majority of Missourians were what was termed "conditional Unionists". The people wished to remain in the Union, but desired a peaceable solution to the slavery question. Because of Halleck's, Schofield's, and Curtis' edicts there was little choice left for slaveholders, or for the friends of slaveholders. They were automatically branded as Southern sympathizers, or worse, supporters of the guerrillas.

Others acted in accordance with the times. General Benjamin Loan issued General Order No. 24 in April 1863, which applied to his jurisdiction. The order prohibited disloyal men from any type of commerce. They were not "allowed to raise crops, sell goods, or carry on business." It was an extremely punitive measure, which would lead to possible starvation unless the individual removed himself and his family from the region where the order applied. In essence, it represented a prohibition against gainful employment and caused self-banishment by the effected party.

On May 24, 1863, General Schofield was placed in charge of the Department of Missouri, replacing General Curtis. In appointing him, President Lincoln had advised him to be firm, but not over zealous in administering the region. In other words, he was to create a balance in his authority among the diverse elements under his command. With this said, in June, Schofield issued what would be known as a "bounty order." This was a highly unusual measure. It required a $5,000.00 bounty to be paid for the killing of a Union soldier from the county in which the crime had taken place. Additionally, a $1,000.00 to $5,000.00 bounty would be assessed for the wounding of a Union soldier, with the amount varying depending on the wound's severity. The levy was to be paid to the family of the victim. To enforce this order, Assessment Boards were established in those counties where such a crime had arisen.

Probably the two most controversial and punitive rulings ever decreed by Union authorities were General Orders No. 10 and 11. The stage for their issuance had been set when General Schofield had established the Border District by way of General Order No. 48. Brigadier General Thomas J. Ewing, Jr., the brother-in-law of Major General William Tecumseh Sherman, had been placed in charge of the district and would become the author of these two onerous decrees.

Upon assuming command, he realized that blame for the guerrilla war could be attributed as much to Jayhawkers on the Kansas side as to the Missouri guerrillas. Ewing also knew that the guerrillas controlled the countryside, whereas Union forces were to some extent bottled up in the cities throughout Missouri. One of the main reasons for the guerrilla's success was because of the local support for their actions and in particular that aid and assistance provided by the family and friends of these partisans.

Of special importance was the role that women played in supplying and protecting these men. These were the men's mothers, sisters, wives, daughters, and sweethearts. The general had had some of these female cohorts rounded up and placed under arrest and incarcerated. One particular group of detainees consisted of Josephine, Mary, and Jeanie Anderson, Mrs. Charity McCorkle Kerr, Mrs. Susan Vandever, Mrs. Armenia Crawford, and Selvey and Nannie Harris, all of whom were related to members of Quantrill's gang. The Anderson women were the sisters of William T. "Bloody Bill" Anderson and Christie McCorkle Kerr was the sister of John McCorkle and the cousin of Cole Younger. These women, along with many others, had been placed in a dilapidated, broken down, old building at 14th and Grand Streets in Kansas City, Missouri.

Almost simultaneous with their imprisonment, Quantrill on August 13, 1863, had pitched a plan to his men proposing that they raid Lawrence, Kansas. His men initially balked at the idea believing it too far away and too dangerous. Quantrill had long wanted revenge on Lawrence because Sheriff Samuel Walker ran him out of town in late 1860. Also, Lawrence represented the "Mecca" for abolitionist. It was in essence the capital or pillar of the country's anti-slavery movement.

Fate intervened, as it often does. The building holding the women captive, collapsed on August 13th. Union officials had been previously warned countless times about the unsound condition of the structure, but had chosen to ignore the situation. The result of this tragedy was the death of five women, specifically, Josephine Anderson, Charity McCorkle Kerr, Armenia Crawford Selvey, Susan Crawford Vandever, and a Mrs. Wilson. Mary Anderson was severely injured and "crippled for life." A new chapter was now to begin in the annuals of the guerrilla war.

Following this disaster, Ewing issued General Order No. 10 on August 18, 1863. The order was a partial banishment directive. It stated, any man, woman, or child found to be in support of the guerrillas would be removed from the western border area and eventually out of the state. Those banished would eventually be sent to Arkansas or some other Southern state. The combination of these two events, the Kansas City building collapse and the issuance of this new order, led directly to the raid on Lawrence.

Several days after the accident, Quantrill's men heard of the tragedy and swore revenge, especially since many of the victims were related to, or known by, the guerrillas. Once again, Quantrill approached his men and argued a raid on Lawrence could be the only true measure of retribution. Many of the guerrillas believed the building had been intentionally undermined by the Union military. Coupled with the further insult of banishment of their families and friends, Quantrill had little problem in selling his Lawrence proposal.

Sadly, on August 21, 1863, Quantrill and 450 of his raiders slammed into Lawrence killing upwards of 200 men, looting and burning the town, causing damage estimated at nearly $2,100,000. The brutality was devastating, if not sickening. Unarmed men were killed in cold blood and others were burned alive. Those attempting surrender were cut down with a bullet where they stood. The course of the war changed that day. Henceforth unarmed, innocent civilians would be marked for death.

Tragically, the outrages committed at Lawrence awakened the whole nation's conscience to the continuing crisis of the Civil War still before them. Although, the recent Northern victories at Gettysburg and Vicksburg indicated the end at long last might be in sight, the raid on Lawrence demonstrated the war was far from being won. As the next two years would demonstrate, the country would continue to wash itself with the blood of its sons.

The repercussions of Lawrence were immediate. Ewing had been thrown off guard and the Kansas radicals, such as James Lane, were hysterical for revenge. Lane issued a command to invade Missouri, which would have started a war within a war. Generals Schofield and Ewing eventually tamed him to some extent by promising to issue a new directive aimed at the Missourians. After in part negotiating the matter with Lane, General Order No. 11 was issued by Ewing on August 25, 1863. The decree mandated the evacuation within fifteen days of <u>all</u> citizens from the countryside in the counties of Jackson, Cass,

Bates and half of Vernon. Those citizens who could prove their loyalty would be allowed to remain in the county, but they were required to reside within one mile of a Union military outpost.

Of striking irony, Captain George Caleb Bingham, a painter who was destined to become a celebrated 19th Century artist, was also Missouri State Treasurer and the owner of the collapsed building in Kansas City. Bingham left Jefferson City, Missouri upon hearing of the proposed plan and traveled to meet with Ewing at his headquarters in Kansas City. In their meeting, he went as far as to threaten Ewing by promising to create a vivid depiction on canvas of the horror yet to come, if he persisted in implementing the decree. Ewing ignored the threat and proceeded to enforce the measure with the assistance of the likes of Jayhawker Dr. Charles "Doc" Jennison and other rogue elements from Kansas.

Within two weeks, Cass County went from a population of 10,000 to 600. Union troops destroyed or confiscated everything not taken by the evacuees. Many men were killed in the process, simply because they were Missourians. Crops and livestock were seized, personal items stolen, and the houses and farmsteads were put to the torch. Nothing that the guerrillas could use was left standing or in tact. The region became known as the "burnt district" for many years following the war. The only remaining structures within the area were darkened skeletal remains of chimneys, known as "Jennison's chimneys."

The effect of the order had also spilled over into Lafayette and Henry counties. Years later, Ewing would be personally haunted by his now infamous order. True to his word, Bingham painted an emotional scene depicting the order, setting forth a caricature of Ewing sitting next to James Lane and showing the plight of the victims and the burnt hollow image of smoldering farms. In the years following the war, the general aspired to political office, but every time he sought office Bingham would produce his now famous painting entitled "Martial Law" and distribute it widely in those districts where Ewing was campaigning. Ewing failed to win election on several occasions.

The citizens of Missouri would remember Order No. 11. For years the physical devastation to the land would remain highly visible. In many respects, the order was more costly in lives and dollars than the raid on Lawrence. The adverse sentiments generated by both the raid and Order No. 11 would be far reaching. For one thing it showed to what lengths the Union military would go in pursuing its course of controlling the population. Unfortunately, as the remaining two years of the war would prove, its effectiveness in controlling the guerrillas was at best minimal. If anything the treachery, brutality, and bloodthirstiness of the partisans would escalate beyond all recognized boundaries of civility. Scalping and mutilation would become commonplace. The only blessing a victim could pray for was to already be dead before commencement of the atrocity.

Other orders and decrees would follow, further limiting and infringing upon what civil liberties remained for the average citizen. General Schofield further trampled on these rights by his issuance of General Order No. 96 on September 17, 1863. This new order curtailed freedom of speech. Offenders were subject to a fine or imprisonment.

By this point in the war, little was left of a free and democratic society. Freedom had succumbed by now to the many dictates of the military. What is important to remember is that although the guerrillas were fighting for their sense of justice, so were those parties supporting the Union. On numerous occasions the guerrilla had been cast as the "bad guy" in the conflict. However, Union troops were equally brutal in enforcing these orders and were simply acting based on sheer strength and power. The guerrillas in many cases were merely reacting to the over zealous conduct of their foe. It can be said that the mentality of both sides was affected by the war that they waged.

Because of Schoefield's "mandatory enlistment order," upwards of 150,000 Missourians joined the Union army, also known as the Missouri State Militia, whether they wanted to or not. In comparison, relatively few men became guerrillas or part of the Confederate ranks. Estimates have placed the entire state's guerrilla force at only 2,500 men, with only 600 of this number being at one time or another associated with Quantrill.

QUANTRILL'S THIEVES   By: Joseph K. Houts, Jr.

Concerning Confederate enlistment, estimates have placed the number around 50,000.

One thing the guerrillas did accomplish, and accomplish well, was to tie up Union forces in the state. At one time 50,000 Union troops were scattered throughout Missouri because of partisan unrest. These soldiers could have easily been used in other parts of the war and could have brought about an earlier conclusion to the struggle. Therefore, these overbearing measures probably inflicted more harm than good to the Union cause. If anything the military's usurpation of the law left lasting scars and a land drenched in the blood of its best and youngest.

In the end the Union military could never really defeat the partisans. Without question countless numbers of guerrillas were killed or captured because of martial law. In addition, many of the guerrilla leaders were killed during the war. But one thing has remained clear, the military in the end had to ask for their surrender, even long after General Robert E. Lee's surrender at Appomattox Court House, Virginia on April 9, 1865. The guerrillas in large part had remained undefeated and were fierce fighters and adversaries up to the final days of the war.

General Lee was said to have contemplated transforming his remaining army into a guerrilla band and continue on with the war in the Appalachian Mountains. With the conflict concluding back East, local Union military authorities conjured upon a solution to the guerrilla problem. Earlier in March 1865, General John Pope and Missouri Governor Thomas C. Fletcher finally rescinded General Frémont's original martial law order. Next, the military offered the guerrillas amnesty, if they would surrender. The guerrillas knew that from their perspective the war was played out and the "Southern Cause" was lost. So given the opportunity to return to their homes, they elected amnesty and slowly hostilities subsided.

Unfortunately, the animosity created by war often persists long after the fighting is over. This has been true throughout history. Many times a war's ultimate outcome depends greatly on the generosity, or the harshness, of the peace imposed on the defeated. The 1919 Treaty of Versailles marked the end of

World War I; and at the same time it laid the groundwork for World War II.

Likewise the stage set in post-war Missouri foretold continued conflict and hard feelings. The passage of the Drake Constitution is a notable example of the hardships imposed upon Missourians even after the war. The Drake Constitution was a revised Missouri Constitution adopted on April 8, 1865. It was named after it's main author and proponet, a radical Republican lawyer named Charles D. Drake. The Republicans feared that returning Confederate soldiers would probably vote the straight Democratic ticket. The Drake Constitution was harsh and punitive upon former Confederates and partisans, seizing their property, causing disenfranchisement, and in some cases leading to incarceration, trial, and punishment. Fortunately, the Democratic Party regained control of the civilian government by the 1870's and life and politics began to return to a sense of normalcy.

One post-war mistake though would linger and terrorize the Midwest for many years. A young guerrilla by the name of Jesse James, who had ridden with William T. "Bloody Bill" Anderson, would attempt to surrender in 1865, only to be shot down and almost killed by rogue Union elements to whom he was surrendering. James would never forget this double cross and consequently would never surrender. He would become the most noted outlaw in the country's history, robbing banks and trains with the remnants of his former guerrilla brethren. He was killed eventually, not by those in pursuit, but by one of his own men. The dirty little coward Robert Ford shot Jesse James in the back on April 3, 1882 in St. Joseph, Missouri. Ford was interested in the $10,000 reward for Jesse. With Jesse dead, the guerrilla war was said by some to be finally at an end.

From the perspective of time and events, Missouri had been in conflict since the passage of the Kansas-Nebraska Act of 1854—a period of almost 30 years, until the death of Jesse. On further retrospect though, Missouri had been at war with either its neighbor or within itself for almost half its existence as a state. In time, the wounds would heal and even be forgiven. However for the most part, the enormity of the encounters and the tales of human suffering during this period would not be forgotten.

QUANTRILL'S THIEVES By: Joseph K. Houts, Jr.

Chapter II
"Nefarious Business... Murdering Loyal Men"

With the war's conclusion, countless stories about its participant's experiences began to be handed down to surviving generations. The more compelling and tragic of these has involved families on opposing sides. The underlying composition of this great conflict was far from being merely a schism between the North and South. In the border states, it had turned into a regional, or more importantly a local fight amongst the inhabitants. Sadly, it had become a personal war between neighbors, and worse, between brothers.

In the deep South and far North there was a greater sense of unity among the citizenry. There was a well-defined sentiment of unanimity of opinion. Missouri citizens, on the other hand, were plainly divided. Hard feelings lingered among partisans on both sides of the conflict. Whole communities would find themselves totally divided in their convictions, creating a leadership vacuum and creating an atmosphere of suspicion and apprehension. Loyalties were frequently mistaken. Even apparent agreement was only built on sandy soil. This schism of emotions was to cast ever greater wounds and scars upon the populace. A situation evolved in which no one could be trusted. Everyone was fearful of their neighbor, and at the same time feared by their neighbor.

Living in the shadows of the struggle for Missouri were ten ancestors. Of this number, eight fought for the South and two for the North. Actually, there were only three groups representing this figure, and both were not directly related until the 1880s. Long before the war they had settled in Johnson County outside Warrensburg, even prior to Missouri statehood. Grandmother, who had been a genealogist with the Daughters of the American Revolution, developed the basis for this information. She traced many of the family's lines and in the process uncovered an abundance of material as to their history. On many occasions, she would recount numerous stories, in particular those adventures experienced during the Civil War.

Of special interest was the tale concerning one of grandfather's Northern relations capturing and almost killing a member of her clan. Frequently, she would comment that had this fact been known beforehand, her marriage would have been to someone else. The story was always entertaining, if not a little humorous and she was proud to repeat it with glee at the slightest prompting. Unfortunately, many of the details of the story were lost upon her death.

Because of her background, various items in testimony to the family's history have been saved. Within this preserve were photographs, real estate deeds, and newspaper clippings, as well as the more personal effects such as garments and old letters. Upon her passing, these articles were further handed down among the family. While searching through the assortment a discovery was made which brought back to memory her often told tale. The find originated out of a tightly bound stack of papers concerning great great uncle Major Thomas W. Houts, one of the family's Union participants. The bundle comprised several documents regarding the war and his receipt of an honorable discharge twenty-six years later. Such an untimely dismissal seemed very unusual, arousing a curiosity to explore deeper.

After examining that material regarding the major, a lone envelope was found at the bottom of the pile. On its surface was what appeared to be some scribbling in faded pencil. Inside was a neatly folded sheet bearing at first glance a double list of names on the front and back. Above the columns was a separate section, setting forth an additional nine individuals followed by apparent ranks and resembling a chain of command. The top was captioned "Roll of Quantrell's Company of Thieves" (sic). Turning again to the cover the handwriting now became legible, reading "Roll of Quantrell's Company Guerllars" (sic). At once the realization occurred that this single piece of paper might be a missing link to the past. To much further surprise, it contained three names of individuals that would become family members in the future: Mike, Mat, and Robert Houx, all great great great uncles.

Finding this roster caused an awakening, not only in the meaning of its discovery, but in uncovering a part of history. Even with these considerations, a direct connection between it and the story was lacking—leaving to conjecture as to who among the family's' Confederates had been apprehended by a Houts. Both of grandmother's grandfathers had served the South, but each was removed from the conflict in Missouri. Therefore the tale was not about either of these individuals. Nor had there ever been an inkling of the Houx role in the war, until stumbling upon the papers of Major Houts. Undoubtedly, it was about the major and his pursuit of Quantrill and the Houxes. After examining each family's origins and the uncle's service records, the substance of the story began to further unfold and show signs of foundation.

Regarding the Houts family, they had migrated into the territory from Pennsylvania. The head of the household was George Wilson Houts, who had been an early advocate of the preservation of the Union. A prominent and influential citizen of Johnson County, George would serve as a pro-Union state representative, although he had been a slave owner. The family's Northern stance was attributed to several factors. Of foremost significance was the fact great uncle Christopher G. Houts had been one of the forty-one representatives to Missouri's Constitutional Convention in 1820. Another consideration

Houts Family Coat of Arms

was that George Houts had been a Whig and professed the ideology of Henry Clay. He had even freed his slaves before the war, however they stayed on for years out of their respect for him. George had ten children with his two oldest, William L. and Thomas W., serving in the Missouri State Militia (MSM), or Union army. Thomas had been a prosperous merchant at a young age, with both he and his brother openly supporting the North before the war. Nevertheless, they had gone to Fort Scott, Kansas as part of the Johnson County delegation during the border wars, to vote slavery into Kansas. In effect, they had been "border ruffians" a term applied to Missourians during this period, who interfered in Kansas' political struggle over slavery. Obviously they were steadfast in their convictions supporting the Union.

The Houx side of the family originated from Jacob and Susan Morningstar Houx. Although, Susan would die early on in the marriage, Jacob would later remarry and father eleven children in all between the two marriages, two of whom, Matthias and Michael Morningstar, would fight for the South, and of particular note for Quantrill. Jacob had moved to Missouri from Kentucky in 1816, bringing some of the first slaves into the territory. The Houxes owned three slaves and in 1860 son Matthias, or Mat as commonly called, was himself a slave owner.

Houx FamilyCoat of Arms

In earlier times, Mat had joined a company organized and commanded by his future father-in-law during the Missouri Mormon uprising in the 1830s. When Mormon founder Joseph Smith was captured, he was part of the apprehending party. Following this experience, he served in the Mexican War. Responding to the beckoning call of the West, Mat next went to California as a '49er, amongst the country's gold fever, returning home in 1851 with $2,000.00 worth of the precious metal. Several years later, he married and settled down as a farmer. At the war's outset, Mat was acknowledged as "a Confederate in sentiment, but not in activities."

In addition to the two brothers, a nephew, Robert Washington Kavanaugh Houx, would join his uncles as a Southern partisan. Robert's parents were Philip Simons and Margaret Hutchison Monroe Houx, who had also migrated to the state from Kentucky. Phillip was the first born of Jacob and Susan Morningstar Houx. The family had first settled in Lafayette County. Eventually, they moved to Johnson County, where Phillip built "a one room log cabin" located northwest of Centerview. In the early 1850s, Phillip served as the county sheriff. Besides Robert's service as a guerrilla, brothers Jacob Edwin and George Washington "Tip" Houx would fight for the South. Jacob would be killed during the battle for Vicksburg, Mississippi.

Unfortunately, each family experienced a terrifying encounter at the beginning of the war, which forever solidified their respective stances. The Houts household was to be visited by two such trespasses. On the first occasion, apparently, some of their pro-Southern neighbors had become angry over them being slaveholders and at the same time supporting the Union. One night a rancorous crowd of local rebels awakened them from sleep. The group chastised and threatened the family before departing. Because of this confrontation, Thomas and William would subsequently enlist in the Union army.

The other incident occurred after the regular Confederates had been driven out of the area. Because of their sentiments, the Houts homestead had been singled out by a bunch of

George Houts Up Against the Barn
Illustration by Suzanne Emery

bushwhackers. The names were never recorded of those involved, but they happened to be well known by all the participants. After stealing his stock, the guerrillas stood George up against the barn and readied their guns at him. Right at the moment of discharging their weapons a rider came dashing upon the scene mounted astride a heavily lathered horse. The intruder was Thomas Dawson Houts, often called Uncle Daws, who was a second cousin of George, but favored the South. He would openly boast about his being a rebel. Prior to this incident the two cousins had been described as "bitter enemies." Even though foes, blood relationships prevailed over political disagreement in this case. In Uncle Daws' own words, "I whipped up hell and down hell," once learning of his capture in hopes of rescuing him. Supposedly, the bushwhackers "put three point blank questions" to Uncle Daws concerning everyone's allegiance, who in response "gave three point blank answers." Later, the revelation would be made that all the "point blank answers" had been point blank lies, but luckily were good enough to dupe the guerrillas and save the elder Houts.

  By coincidence, Mat would encounter a similar type of affair early in the war. Residing approximately eight miles northwest of Warrensburg, he had been arrested by Union troops and charged with murder. He was tried by a court martial at Lexington and found guilty based upon circumstantial evidence. His sentence was that he was to be shot at dawn a few days following the trial. Two days prior to the execution, Shanklin Gilkeson, a friend living in Warrensburg and having contrary information of Mat's guilt, approached Colonel James D. Eads as to Mat's impending fate. Gilkeson recalled for Eads that he had Mat under arrest and in custody, when the alleged crime had taken place. The colonel did recollect the incarceration, and on the day before imposition of the sentence, set out for Lexington to save the life of this innocent man. Upon departure, Gilkeson advised Colonel Eads against wearing his Federal uniform in that the countryside was full of guerrillas. Eads responded that he would go as dressed in uniform or not at all. Besides, he was unarmed and attempting to save a friend of these bushwhackers. On their way, guerrillas surrounded the two men, having the obvious intent of killing the colonel. Gilkeson explained the circumstances of their journey and the bushwhackers released them. The colonel and Gilkeson completed their trip and saved Mat's life. Afterwards, they would learn that the guerrillas had positioned guards on both sides of the road, insuring their arrival at Lexington.

Of some irony, both families had many similarities. Both had been early pioneers in the state, and both had been slaveholders. Of further significance, they lived in the same general area, making them in effect neighbors. Unfortunately, the dark side of war had touched them, when in truth their desire was to avoid involvement. As their separate run-ins demonstrated, outside aggression had precipitated a call to arms in self-defense. In reality, neither family probably could have escaped the oncoming conflict. It was bound to consume all of those in its path. Because of the course of events, Houts and Houx were to go in opposite directions, which would eventually thrust them into several head-on confrontations.

Thomas Houts was the first to draw up sides. In the spring of 1861, he enlisted in what afterwards would become the 27th Infantry Missouri Volunteers as one of the first recruits. He was formerly mustered into service on July 4, and shortly thereafter was made quartermaster, a likely advance in view of his merchant background. In January 1862, Houts resigned and re-enlisted as a private in Company A, Seventh Cavalry, Missouri State Militia, with the first battalion being formed by Major Emery S. Foster. On January 11, he was promoted to captain and on February 16, 1863 rose to the rank of major in the regiment's Second Battalion. Throughout the early war years, Major Houts was dubbed exemplary of those officers considered the best of their grade in the state. Others would refer to him as "a very gallant and dashing Cavalry officer. Always ready for any sort of desperate service, great zeal for the cause, and unflinching loyalty to his friends."

Portrayed also as "essentially a man of action," the major was known to exact vengeance upon his foes. Captain J. D. Thompson of the First Iowa Cavalry in a statement dated March 30, 1862 regarding an encounter on the Blackwater River, spoke disapprovingly of Houts' eagerness to destroy the enemy: "Captain Thomas W. Houts while out with a party of some 50 men killed one, Mr. Piper, and burned five dwellings, turning the families out of doors and destroying everything in the houses." The dispatch went on to say that another officer refused to allow his troops to engage in the "nefarious business." Thompson further commented such conduct would likely cause retaliation by the bushwhackers and between the two, Union and Southern sympathizers, the whole country would lay in ruins. Although this disapproval was reported, nothing apparently came of the incident.

The war years proved to be a busy period for the major. His first important battle was at Lone Jack, Missouri on August 16, 1862, where Union forces suffered a narrow defeat. In October 1863 he chased Confederate General Jo Shelby across the state after his loss at Marshall. Within a few days, the major abandoned the pursuit, much to the disfavor of General Schofield in allowing Shelby and his raiders to escape. Thereafter, throughout the rest of 1863 and much of 1864, he regularly sought out guerrilla factions. During the process his travels would extend as far south as Arkansas. On one occasion, a guerrilla by the name of David Vaughn was known to have taken a couple of shots at him. Vaughn's wife would later recall that the major was the equivalent to a redleg, notorious for his pilfering and murderous ways. She would always comment there was nothing good about the man.

Major Thomas W. Houts

In the fall of 1864 the major participated in the campaign to stop General Sterling Price's advance into Missouri at a confrontation on the outskirts of Jefferson City. He was again cited as serving with distinction. Yet, in December 1864 a

QUANTRILL'S THIEVES By: Joseph K. Houts, Jr.

misunderstanding would take place, leading eventually to his dismissal from the army. The whole affair had arisen from a change of command upon the regiment's return to Warrensburg, following the victory over Price. Colonel John F. Philips was placed in control of the district and Lieutenant Colonel Thomas T. Crittenden was made head of the post. By this maneuvering, Major Houts became the highest ranking regimental officer. As the Provost Marshal was Captain Ferguson, supposedly and enemy of the major's, who unbeknownst was technically in charge because of his position, though lower in rank.

 On December 13, Private William Higgins of the 15th Kansas Cavalry visited Warrensburg with Major Houts' brother William under the pretense of it being a personal visit. Actually, he was on a special mission to uncover the circumstances surrounding a purported shooting involving a man referred to as "Colored Tom." Higgins had the appropriate passes for the assignment from his commanding officer, Brigadier General James B. Blunt of the Department of Kansas.

 During this period, Union officials of the Kansas and Missouri Departments did not always cooperate with each other, due to regional mistrust. A feeling probably shared by officers of lesser levels. Over the course of a few days the private had visited the house of the major's father several times. Captain Ferguson suspected him of being one of "Jennison's red-legs." The 15th Kansas Cavalry was under the infamous Jayhawker Dr. Charles R. "Doc" Jennison. Because of his hunch, he arrested Higgins on December 18 and placed him in the county jail. Higgins repeatedly requested that the captain verify his pass with General Blunt or Major Houts, however the captain ignored the requests. The major looked upon this as a personal insult, since being directed at a friend and guest. On this day, Colonels Philips and Crittenden had taken leave with no one appointed to command in their absence. Major Houts erroneously believed his rank outweighed the captain's authority, even as the Provost Marshal. Based on this assumption he led a detachment to the jail, freed Higgins and, under civilian escort, returned him to his unit at Paola, Kansas. Consequently his career ended in court martial on February 7, 1865.

36

Following the war, the major became a farmer and was elected to the Missouri House of Representatives. For reasons unclear, he declined the seat. There may have been some bitter feelings towards public service because of the court martial. His father, already being a legislator, served the term in his place.

Concerning the dismissal from the army, various efforts were initiated in the late 1880s trying to achieve a reversal. On March 14, 1891, as a result of numerous requests to the President, other elected officials, and from previous army associated including Kansas Secretary of State William Higgins, Major Emory S. Foster, and retired Missouri Governor, Colonel Thomas T. Crittenden, the court martial was overturned by a joint resolution of Congress. Among the more notable petitioners was Missouri Senator Francis M. Cockrell; general of the Missouri State Guard, commander of Matthias Houx, brother of Syrus Cockrell and a former law partner of Colonel Crittenden. The appeal for this redress crossed all former boundaries of the conflict. Major Houts, now blind, was given an honorable discharge without any back pension, but he did receive and allowance from that date forward. "Tardy Justice" was the headline bestowed by the <u>St. Louis Daily Globe-Democrat</u>, in its article describing the event.

Of the three Houxes, Mat's experiences were the best-documented and most revealing as to wartime adventures. Following his near fatal experience at Lexington, Mat took a hardened position towards the war. He joined Price's army as a private in Colonel Hurst's division and was assigned to Company G under the command of F. M. Cockrell. The company was attached to Marmaduke's Cavalry unit. Serving as a regular, he fought at the battles of Wilson's Creek, Lexington, and Pea Ridge. After these engagements, he and the rest of the family's association with Quantrill probably started and lasted off and on until war's end.

Shortly after Pea Ridge, Mat's first official mention as a guerrilla was reported on March 13, 1862. Major Emory S. Foster, in a dispatch to Brigadier General James Totten, commanding the District of Central Missouri, referred to him as a leader of 300 guerrillas. Foster wrote that Mat had sent a messenger asking under what reasonable terms, if any, they could be permitted to return home. In addition, he had issued a caveat concerning his inquiry by stating "in case they are to be treated as outlaws they will ruin the country, burning houses and murdering loyal men." Continuing in the report, Foster pointed out these irregulars were scattered into small groups of 10 to 15. He advised that his present troop strength would be wholly inadequate in adverting any attempt to "enforce the threat." Apparently, the basis of Mat's request was in response to Major General Henry W. Halleck's issuance of General Order No. 2 in early March, declaring that guerrillas would now be considered as criminals or traitors. Because of this decree and its likely consequences, Mat was probably trying to avoid further bloodshed through some arrangement or compromise. Regrettably, an agreement was never reached, and he remained as previously cast. A now once internal conflict was starting to grow beyond all boundaries, with the result being a further spiraling escalation of an already hostile climate of revenge, retribution, and death.

Although he was an active guerrilla early on in the war, sometime between 1863-1864, Mat resided in Texas. With the war's conclusion, he returned to Missouri and was subsequently captured and then paroled. Though paroled, the war was not soon to end for Mat. On May 30, 1866, an action was brought against him entitled The United States vs. the Real Estate and Effects of Matthias Houx. The proceeding was the 159th brought against former guerrillas, confiscating their property under a Presidential proclamation dated July 17, 1862. The purpose of the proclamation was "...to suppress insurrection, to punish treason and rebellion, to seize and confiscate the property of rebels, and for other purposes...." Obviously, the suit had been brought for "other purposes" or as a punitive measure, since the war was over. The petition seized all of his 560 acres. Mat's daughter, Miss Mary Houx, raised $4,000.00 for his bond from several neighbors, one being Nathan W. Perry. Eventually, with the election of 1872 the power basis shifted and the use of this wartime measure was prohibited thereafter.

QUANTRILL'S THIEVES   By: Joseph K. Houts, Jr.

Concerning the wartime experiences of William L. Houts, Michael Morningstar, and Robert Washington Kavanaugh Houx, little information has been found highlighting their military service. William was a captain in the Battalion Loyal Militia of Missouri and he survived the war. Michael and Robert both rode with Quantrill and ended the war in Texas. As later revealed, Robert was at the battle of Pleasant Hill, Missouri on July 11, 1862. In addition, there has been evidence indicating their presence at the raid on Lawrence, Kansas on August 21, 1863, along with Mat Houx. However Major Houts and Mat Houx were more directly aligned against each other, giving the best credence to the theory that they were the participates in grandmother's story.

In support of her tale were two reports establishing that the major and Mat had confronted the other in battle. The first encounter was on March 26, 1862, at the east fork of Post Oak Creek involving 85 guerrillas. On learning their whereabouts, the object of the Union command had been to capture the band, purportedly riding under the notorious Mat Houx. After a spirited chase and several vaulted attempts by both sides to obtain a superior position, a brief fight ensued. The culmination being the guerrillas' rapid retreat, when confronted by a charge from an attached reserve of Union Cavalry. In the communiqué of Brigadier General Totten and Major Foster concerning the skirmish, reference was made of Major Houts providing reinforcements. Of special interest was Mat's reported death. Though being set forth by both officers, casualty accounts happened to be not always accurate, because in this case he lived until 1900. Being only of slight mention, this initial engagement may have been the origination of grandmother's story. Equally of value was its placing the uncles as adversaries. Further, their statements may have constituted a different version of her claim, that of a relative having been captured and almost killed by a Houts.

The more important of these confrontations, which would also include Robert, occurred several months later in the first half of July. Although subsequent battle accounts would be somewhat sketchy as to their individual roles. Nevertheless, they

QUANTRILL'S THIEVES By: Joseph K. Houts, Jr.

were present at the engagement. The fight would involve anywhere from 300 to 600 men depending on wide ranging reports. The conflict would result in hand-to-hand fighting before it was over, with both sides of the family participating. Luckily, all would survive the clash and the family would go on. Other near run-ins most likely occurred between the Houts and Houx clans, even though nothing formally has been found documenting any further associations from this point on in the war.

    This final official encounter would be known as the battle of Pleasant Hill, Missouri. It would be the first and last fight by the partisans, whereby they would openly confront a Union command in a pitched battle. From this point on, except for their involvement at the battle of Independence, Missouri on August 11, 1862, they would only conduct hit and run raids. However, as the aftermath of Pleasant Hill would eventually bring to light, the true identity of Quantrill's original gang of guerrillas would finally be revealed, forever marking these men in not only their struggle for Missouri, but for their own personal survival.

    Regarding the relationship between the families, they came together through the wedding of Nathan Washington Perry to Robert Houx's sister, Catherine Elizabeth Houx, a niece of MiKe and Mat. The only child from this union was Susan Elizabeth Perry, who married Dr. Joseph James Kinyoun. Dr. and Mrs. Kinyoun were the author's grandmother's parents. Grandmother completed the connection by her marriage to Grandfather Hale Houts, whose father was a brother of Major Houts.

Chapter III
"The Many Wild Birds Were Caroling"

The Battle of Pleasant Hill, Missouri on July 11, 1862 was the culmination of a series of escalating events and incidents, the object of which had been to secure the demise or capture of William Clarke Quantrill and his band of guerrillas. Since late spring, the pace of events had steadily increased; due in large part to a tightening of control by Union authorities over Missouri's Southern based population.

At this point in the war, Quantrill had established himself as the premier guerrilla leader. A frequent target of his gang, as well as other gangs, was the Federal mail run between St. Louis and Kansas City, Missouri. The disruption of the route had become a passion of these rural partisans. In like respect, the uninterrupted operation of the line had become cornerstone to the Union command's policy in controlling the state. Without the mail and regular communication with the East it was their opinion that administration of the region would be impaired significantly. Regardless of Union efforts, the guerrillas continually managed to breach the service.

The final straw in this ongoing tug of war occurred when Quantrill and his men raided the Missouri riverboat Little Blue. On board were forty sick and wounded Union soldiers. The guerrillas harassed the troops and seized a large quantity of military supplies. Outraged over the affair, Major Eliphant Bredett detached one hundred ten men from the Seventh Cavalry Post at Lexington, Missouri to hunt down Quantrill. Within a week, Bredett traveled one hundred miles capturing one hundred seven suspects, of which fifty-four were from Wellington and twenty-five from Napoleon. During the course of his roundup, the major recovered much of the stolen ordinance, which had been stashed in various towns along the river. Surprisingly, only two or three of the prisoners were guilty of any treason, with none being guerrillas.

On July 8, Colonel Upton Hays entered the state hoping to raise a Confederate cavalry regiment in Jackson County. At this time, the countryside was full of Union troops searching for partisans. As a result, Hays convinced Quantrill to leave the area, so as to draw off the Federals. In turn, he would then be able to form a regiment. The colonel traveled with him for several days. At the end of their association Quantrill broke out thirty men under the command of George M. Todd, in order to escort Hays back through the county for his recruitment mission. This depleted the guerrilla force to sixty-five men.

Major James D. Gower of the First Iowa Cavalry of Clinton, Missouri learned on July 8 that Quantrill was camped on Sugar Creek near Wadesburg. He sent out a patrol of ninety men from Companies A, G and H, of the First Iowa Cavalry under the command of lieutenants Reynolds, Foster, Bishop, and Wisenad. On July 9, without waiting for the rest of the units to join him, Bishop accompanied by Reynolds attacked the guerrillas' position and was quickly beaten back. The lieutenants reported their casualties as ten dead and three wounded, with one guerrilla killed and several wounded. They returned to Clinton believing the enemy had a far superior force. Upon learning of the skirmish, Gower became infuriated over being dealt a defeat at the hands of Quantrill. He immediately sent out for reinforcements from the Union posts at Butler and Warrensburg, Missouri, directing them to rendezvous on July 10 at the Lotspeich farm near the guerrilla encampment.

At 5:00 a.m. on July 10, Major Gower set out for the farm with four officers and seventy-five enlisted men from Companies A and G of the First Iowa Cavalry. The major arrived at 11:00 a.m., where he met a detachment of sixty-five troops of the First Iowa Cavalry commanded by Captain William H. Ankeny and another sixty-five from the Seventh Missouri Cavalry, led by Captain William A. Martin from Warrensburg. Later, a third contingent, numbering sixty-five, arrived belonging to the First Missouri Cavalry, under the charge of Captain Martin Kehoe, composed of Companies A, C and D. Kehoe was also from Warrensburg, which increased Gower's troop strength to around two hundred sixty-five men.

Quantrill's force was estimated by some at two hundred fifty, purportedly comprised of his own men plus two additional bands, Colonel Upton Hays' and another guerrilla chieftain named, Matthias Houx. Although, other sources have confirmed the guerrillas' strength never exceeded sixty-five men. Gower split his force into groups of four and instructed each to seek out Quantrill. Within a short period, Kehoe picked up his trail at Lincoln Ford on Big Creek, leading east to Rose Hill in Johnson County. From Big Creek, the path led to the Hornsby farm, where he and his gang had eaten and rested earlier. The guerrillas moved on to the Sears farm, owned by a Union man and camped for the night, with Kehoe close behind. They had planned to burn the Sears house that night, but it rained, thereby preventing its destruction. Quantrill posted Hicks George and Robert Houx as rear guard pickets.

After traveling fifty miles, Gower stopped for the night allowing his exhausted men and their horses a much-needed rest. Before dividing his command, he had ordered each unit not to engage the enemy, until all the troops could be brought forward in a combined assault. The next morning Captain Kehoe decided to disobey the order. According to Captain Henry J. Stierlin though, Kehoe had sent a dispatch to the major advising of his position and that he was readying the companies for attack. Gower later disavowed receiving any notice and insisted that if Kehoe had waited Quantrill could have been captured, or better yet annihilated.

The morning of July 11 was described as "bright and lovely." In addition it was said, "the many wild birds were carroling (sic) in the woods." In spite of that poetic description it was stated that the morning was clear and blistering hot. At 10:00 a.m., Kehoe saddled up and started towards the enemy's position. They fired on the two pickets, driving them into the campsite. The guerrillas fainted surprise in order to draw Kehoe and his men into a trap. Quantrill positioned his men behind a corral, which bordered a lane. Blankets had been taken from the house and thrown over the fences, disguising the now low-lying bushwhackers. Men were placed on both sides of the road, as well. William Gregg was placed at the head of the lane as the bait. He later commented, although the wait was only for a few minutes "it seemed to be an hour."

Kehoe led the charge toward Gregg with sword in hand, waving his men on amongst their cheers. The guerrillas opened fire within 40-60 feet of the advance, killing seven and wounding nine. The captain was wounded in the shoulder and had his horse shot out from under him. Gregg motioned Quantrill to open the corral gate, letting the riderless Union mounts run in, thereby falling into their possession. The guerrillas stripped the fallen of seven carbines, six Colt revolvers, seven Colt Navies and seven canteens full of whiskey. In the assault, guerrilla John Hampton was killed with George Maddox, and William Tucker wounded. Maddox had been shot in both lungs. Quantrill commandeered a wagon and two mattresses from the Sears, in order to remove his dead and wounded riders. Meanwhile, Kehoe and his men retreated, dismounted and began firing at long range. He maintained this position, until Gower and the other Federal units arrived in support.

During this brief period, Gregg would later recall a humorous incident. After Kehoe's withdraw, Quantrill had sent David Pool and another man into a nearby pasture to observe the Federal's next move. While waiting, a jackass became spooked by the advancing Union troops and made "a dead run" at them, with its tail straight up, ears laid back, and braying at every leap. Pool later claimed to have been doubly

Pool On the Run
Illustration by Suzanne Emery

scared of both the jackass and the oncoming enemy. Unfortunately, he had been left in charge of the reserve ammunition, which became lost during the fracas.

Although, momentarily a light moment, Quantrill pulled his men back to a ravine with the onslaught of Gower's newly arrived units. The sides of the ravine were 5-7 feet deep with the width between the walls varying between 40-60 feet apart. Upon his arrival at 11:00 a.m., the major dispatched Lieutenant McIntyre of Company L, First Iowa Cavalry with fifty men by way of the Independence Road to a wooded area. He was instructed to position his troops on the west side of the timber, in Quantrill's rear behind the ravine.

Gower's advance guard under Lieutenant John McDermott, commanding Company G of the First Iowa Cavalry, along with Captain Martin's Seventh Missouri Cavalry, then slammed into Quantrill's force inside the ditch. The guerrillas thereupon scaled the back walls of the trench and headed for the woods, only to find McIntyre's men. Turning about, Quantrill charged toward McDermott, Martin, and Kehoe, only to meet with their stiff resistance. For upwards of an hour and a half the combatants engaged each other. The guerrillas, out of ammunition, used gunstocks, rocks and branch limbs as their weapons, because of Pool's earlier loss of the reserve in the jackass incident.

They noted among themselves that the Yankees were fighting fiercely, due in large part to their being drunk. Quantrill realized they must escape, so he ordered Gregg to take twenty-one men with horses and break out through the front. The rest of the command would follow Quantrill on foot in a different direction. Upon mounting up, Ezra Moore was shot, as was Jerre Doore. Later Doore's injury would prove to be fatal. The guerrilla leader himself was wounded in the right leg below the knee, barely missing the bone. Falling to the ground, he told Gregg not to say anything so as to concern the men. Purportedly, Gregg pulled his gun on the man who shot him, placing it to his ear yelling, "Pray!" The soldier closed his eyes and bowed his head, upon which "Gregg blew his brains out."

QUANTRILL'S THIEVES   By: Joseph K. Houts, Jr.

Quantrill and his men, although badly bruised, managed to escape and headed northward toward the Blue River. As a bit of irony, the guerrillas' earlier seizure of the Little Blue riverboat on this river had been the catalyst for the Union campaign, ending at Pleasant Hill. Gower did not pursue the vanquished due to the weariness of his troops and the jaded condition of the horses. Casualty reports varied to a considerable extent. Union casualties were placed at six to eleven dead with from nine to twenty-one wounded, three or four of which being officers. Reports of guerrilla losses ranged anywhere from ten to twenty-six dead and twenty-five to thirty wounded. Commenting on the enemy's dead, who had been taken in the brush by their comrades when retreating, Captain Stierlin remarked somewhat pointedly, "they may not, perhaps, be found until the crows and buzzards hover over them." Other guerrilla casualties included William Gregg, John Koger, David Pool, Cole Younger, James Morris, John Brinker and William Haller. Afterwards, one report noted that those captured by the Federals were treated well, being one of the few times compassion was ever extended to these partisans during the war. Of interest, the <u>Liberty Tribune</u> reported signed loyalty others were found on five of the dead guerrillas.

Following the battle and after the Union forces had returned to their posts, Major Gower and Captains Stierlin and Martin submitted official reports of the engagement to their commanders. Contrary to Gower's initial criticism of Kehoe, he also commended him. Stierlin exulted a more favorable slant of Kehoe's actions, even in light of his obvious blunder. This would only have been natural, since Stierlin too was attached to Kehoe's unit. In each of their accounts, the officers gave honorable mention to the many commissioned and non-commissioned soldiers participating in the fight. Of sad, but well deserving recognition was C. H. Lathrop of the First Iowa Cavalry and W. W. Baily of the First Missouri Cavalry, both assistant surgeons, working laboriously to mend the day's carnage. Captain Martin commenting on his own conduct stated, "I was the first that entered the brush, and everyone of them (his men) was ready to stand by me in the warmest part of the most deadly conflict, according to numbers engaged, that has been fought in Missouri."

Considering the fact that many of his troops were drunk, it would have been small wonder to judge their actions, if they had been sober. What was unquestionably accurate, as set forth by Martin, was that his troops upon returning to their post had been on the march for sixty-nine hours. During this period they had partaken of only three meals and had been in the saddle, all but ten of these hours. Five having been spent trying to sleep in the rain, with the remainder in pursuit or combat. Martin concluded his report by stating "It was enough for them to know that in these days they had many times routed and finally cut to pieces this lawless gang of marauders."

As for the guerrillas, there was to be another day. Although scattered and dismayed, they had survived their first real confrontation. They had fought with perseverance and determination against four-to-one odds. Quantrill in particular proved himself. Repeatedly, he had been quick to respond to the conflict's many changing faces. At the outset, he had laid a trap, followed by a rapid redeployment of his forces once surrounded and finally, realizing their fate could be sealed, devised a plan of escape. Fair to say, not many a commander could have operated that effectively. Quantrill had no formal military training, but he was smart. After all, he had become a schoolteacher at the age of only sixteen. More importantly though, he had become an able marksman and horseman at a young age. In addition, he was accustomed to close calls and getting out of tight spots ever since leaving home in 1855. Experience had taught him to avoid open battles. The guerillas learned to carefully monitor the enemy and to never engage a superior force. For them, the best tactic was to remain a "hit and run" force avoiding the entrapments of open conflict. Years later, the guerrilla veterans of Pleasant Hill would refer to it as their toughest fight.

It was a sorted victory for the Union army on July 11, 1862. Although they won the battle, they failed in their objective to capture Quantrill. Possibly, they prolonged the war by teaching him a sorely needed lesson. Henceforth, he and his men would play by their own rules and not those of the Union

QUANTRILL'S THIEVES By: Joseph K. Houts, Jr.

command. If anything was gained for Gower in this campaign it was found among the dead. After the battle, those guerrillas that lay fallen upon the field were searched and stripped of their possessions. Numerous spoils fell into the winner's hands, not to mention saddles, blankets, guns and even a lone mailbag - the symbolic prelude to the day's task. Quantrill's personal spyglass was also uncovered among the debris.

Of all the finds though, the most important was the company muster roll, which with some formality set forth a chain of command and a listing of 92 riders. If ever a prize could be given to the victors it was this official self-made accounting by their foe. Now, Union authorities had before them a true tabulation of this heretofore hidden and elusive enemy. Of special value was that three of the named guerrillas were already dead as a result of the fighting.

Two copies were apparently made of the original, one by Captain Stierlin and the other by Captain Thomas W. Houts of the Missouri Seventh Cavalry. Upon its discovery, Captain Stierlin sent a copy to Major General John M. Schofield at his headquarters for the Central Division of Missouri in Jefferson City. At the top of Stierlin's copy he wrote "I have the honor to submit also a copy of a roll of Quantrell's (sic) gang which was found on one of his sergeants who was killed in the action, to wit." Of interest was the fact that none of Quantrill's sergeants were killed at Pleasant Hill. Houts captioned his copy "Roll of Quantrell's (sic) Company of Thieves".

Apparently, General Schofield failed to follow up on the roll. Without question many of those names inscribed on the document were already known guerrillas. However, others were not and represented an opportunity for the Union. Schofield could have sought these men out, especially since martial law and the suspension of habeas corpus had become a common Federal practice in dealing with Southern sympathizers, let alone guerrillas. After imposition of the "no quarter" order by General Henry W. Halleck on March 13, 1862, action could have been taken against these men. The record though shows that little or no effort was made to track them down. The real bounty at Pleasant Hill was this roster, but it was to be for naught.

- Tragically, by inaction, the guerrilla activities in Missouri would increase and intensify, becoming some of the most brutal and worst bloodshed of the war.

This battle would be remembered for many things, the least of which would be a victory for Gower and the Union. As later stated by Quantrill biographer, William Elsey Connelley, the conflict was one of the first engagements of "Missourian against Missourian." Unfortunately, it was only the beginning of many such encounters, where Missourians fought and killed fellow Missourians. If only Captain Kehoe had restrained himself, and General Schofield had not, the war in Missouri might have had a more rapid conclusion.

QUANTRILL'S THIEVES By: Joseph K. Houts, Jr.

Chapter IV
"Company of Thieves"

    Personal embellishments have always been the makings of great titles. Being no exception to the statement, Major Thomas W. Houts and his characterization of Quantrill's men as "thieves" has just such a distinction. By this time in the Civil War tensions along the Missouri-Kansas border were running extremely high. As previously noted these hatreds had emerged long before the war, arising out of the struggle over whether Kansas should become a free or slave state after passage of the Kansas-Nebraska Act in 1854. By 1860 the citizens of both states viewed the other with contempt and lingering suspicion. Of corresponding consequence, the same type of sentiment was present among Union and Confederate sympathies within Missouri. It could be stated the border hostilities of the previous decade simply concentrated itself in the state as the national question of unity and loyalty erupted after the election of Republican presidential candidate Abraham Lincoln. Obviously, the major by his title amplified this overall bitterness, not only towards Kansans, but those of traitorous intent and action within Missouri. Kansas did not have this duel problem of hating its neighbor and itself at the same time. Its residents were decidedly pro-Union in their convictions.

    It should be understood though, that the guerrilla war was just beginning to unfold in early to mid 1862 when Quantrill's muster roll was discovered. The conflict would soon grossly widen, paling those events and atrocities committed during the border wars. Most of Quantrill's original 93 riders were far from being "thieves". Major Houts' chosen title was a slander on their character. For the most part they were nothing more than young farmers and laborers trying to eke out a new and better life on the American frontier. Probably all of these men would have remained in large part non-combatants during the war, if only they had not been pushed or betrayed by some event or person, leaving them nowhere to turn except to the guerrillas. Unfortunately, society has frequently acted on mere suspicion, prejudice, and stupidity when assessing grave situations, rather than honestly examining the totality of a state of affairs. Often this leads over time to volatility and eventually civil unrest.

    The men described in this chapter were truly casualties of war. Although many of them would happenstance into the conflict, many too did become bloodthirsty killers as the war progressed, leaving their actions to be described as demonic. It should be understood; these men were termed as "irregulars" as to formal military training, organization and command. Even those officers who led these partisan warriors had little or no military experience or indoctrination. Afterwards, when confronted about their conduct during the war, guerrilla veterans stated they all believed their actions, even their most brutal actions, were an acceptable mode of warfare shared by their brothers-in-arms fighting in the Eastern Theater of the country. These men did not necessarily view war as a purely civil conflict defined by rules of engagement and tradition, but merely as an advanced course in killing and bestowing death upon the enemy, regardless of any measure or degree of restraint in its infliction.

    Of similar importance was the demeanor of their foe. Several historians have claimed the Union soldier and his commander were not of the highest pedigree either. All of the better soldiers had been sent east to fight in the larger war. Those left behind to guard and control Missouri were devoid of high qualities and morals themselves. Granted such a generalization cannot be attributed to every "blue coat", but for those it did speak to, their actions would ring the loudest. Coupled with the fact Missouri was basically under Marshal law, these soldiers had the weight of the law on their side, easily leading to excess and to punitive measures.

    Remember, Missouri was the western edge of America in 1860, the refinements and civilities associated with the country as a whole were present in most places, but lacking to some degree in other places. It was still a land in the process of being settled

QUANTRILL'S THIEVES By: Joseph K. Houts, Jr.

and experiencing growing pains long overcome by the earlier inhabited regions east of the Appalachian Mountains.

As Major Houts also so pointedly tagged, it was a "company", or unit comprised of roughly 100 men or less. However, this company had been formed not as a formal unit of the Missouri State Guard or the Confederate Army, but as a partisan unit having the common purpose of fighting tyranny as seen in their eyes. Because of these partisans, and the several hundred who would eventually join their group, their actions by 1863 required the Union Army to station 50,000 troops in and about the state as a method of containment. A strategy known as military positioning, where there are no open battles, but only endless patrols of seek and destroy missions, constantly confronted by the hit and run tactics of the adversary.

During most of the war the Union forces were boxed up in the numerous urban centers, being unable to dislodge the guerrillas from the countryside. So although the major spitefully referred to them as "thieves", these few men of unsophisticated military background and supply literally dictated the course of the Civil War in Missouri, even after General Robert E. Lee's surrender to General Ulysses S. Grant at Appomattox Court House, Virginia.

As the following illustrated life experiences will reveal, these men were far from being "thieves" in the true sense of the word and in later years proved to be honest, productive, and ordinary citizens, until their dying days. This "company" and those individuals who joined the group later would also demonstrate in subsequent years that they were a proud group united in solidarity as made evident by the annual Quantrill Reunions that were held for thirty years between 1898 and 1927.

One would dare say that there was no more determined group of men fighting on either side during the American Civil War, nor was there any other group more fervently dedicated to their cause. Yes, they were only a "company" as characterized by Major Houts, and yes some of them could be classified as "thieves" or more pointedly murders, but what a profound effect this lot of 93 had on the war in Missouri and on the fate of so many.

QUANTRILL'S THIEVES By: Joseph K. Houts, Jr.

W. C. Quantrell
(William Clarke Quantrill, Charley Hart, Captain Clarke)

William Clarke Quantrill was born on July 31, 1837 in Canal Dover, Ohio. He was the eldest of eight siblings, four of whom died in early childhood. His parents were Thomas Henry and Caroline Clarke Quantrill. Thomas was initially a tinsmith, writing a book on the uses of tin in the American household. Eventually, he became the principal of Union School. Caroline took care of the home as a housewife. By age 16, William graduated from high school and became a teacher.

The Quantrill family had a few black sheep. Two of his uncles were men of low repute, one being a pirate in the Gulf of Mexico, purportedly with French buccaneer Jean Laffite, and the other simply described as a "scalawag" who was arrested

William Clarke Quantrill
Used by permission, State Historical Society of Missouri

for the attempted murder of his wife. Even Quantrill's father found himself in some trouble. While a trustee, he embezzled school funds to finance the publication of his book. Subsequently, he almost killed his accuser in the case, Mr. Harmon V. Beeson. The incident quietly faded from public notice.

Although one authority has asserted that Quantrill was a normal child as a boy, there are some sorted tales about his behavior that lead one to wonder. He supposedly committed acts of cruelty, such as nailing snakes to trees, tying cats together by their tails and then tossing them over a fence to watch the two cats claw each other to death. Some stories have also stated that he liked to throw snakes on girls and would shoot pigs through their ears, demonstrating his prowess with a gun.

On December 7, 1854, Thomas Henry Quantrill died from consumption. Ironically, his death occurred the same year that Congress passed the Kansas-Nebraska Act. This statute led to open conflict in Kansas over the national issue of slavery, culminating in the American Civil War. With Thomas' death, the Quantrill family was thrust into an economic tailspin. William, along with his brothers and sister had to take on odd jobs and Mrs. Quantrill had to take in borders. A family that was once of above average means was now clinging to the near fringes of subsistence. Young William was greatly troubled by their plight. Years later some individuals claimed this experience instilled in him a sense of bitterness and resentment which he carried throughout the remainder of his life.

In 1855, he left the family, and went to Mendota, Illinois in search of better opportunities. He taught school and worked in a lumberyard, where it was said that he committed his first murder. Next, he went to Indiana where he again taught school, but shortly returned home. In 1857, he went to Kansas with his father's old antagonist, Harmond C. Beeson, and Colonel Henry Torrey. On reaching Kansas, because Quantrill was a minor, Beeson and Torrey staked a land claim for him at Stanton, on the Marias des Cygnes River, although Quantrill never worked the land or perfected his claim.

After a while, Quantrill had a falling out with Beeson and became what they called in the Old West a "drifter". He ventured to Utah with Brigadier General Albert Sidney Johnson (later a Confederate general of Shilo fame), who was setting out to enforce government rule over the polygamist Mormons. Leaving Johnson, he sought fortune in the Colorado gold fields, where his efforts went "bust." By the fall of 1859, he returned to Kansas and lived among the Delaware Indians, north of the Kansas River outside Lawrence. He began using the name "Charley Hart" as his alias. Quantrill started associating with men of questionable character, and while occasionally teaching school, would raid settlements to steal cattle and slaves. In November 1860, the Douglas County court issued a warrant to Sheriff Walker for his arrest, based on various charges of stealing and arson.

Quantrill left Lawrence barely escaping arrest by Sheriff Walker. He joined several of his cohorts and concocted a plan to steal twenty slaves that were the property of a farmer named Morgan Walker in Blue Springs, Missouri. At the farm he betrayed his accomplices to the potential victim and as a result several of the would-be slave thieves met their demise.

Afterwards, the Walkers and other neighboring Missourians expressed their suspicions about this now self-proclaimed former Jayhawker and proposed that he be hanged. After all, he had shown up in Blue Springs in the company of a band of thieves, reason enough for the town folk to consider a necktie party. Quantrill saved himself by spinning a protracted fabrication. He told them his home was the sister slave state of Maryland. In 1856, while crossing Kansas enroute to California, Jayhawkers had ambushed he and his brother. They killed his brother and left Quantrill himself for dead with a severe gunshot wound. He would have died but for the assistance that he received from a Shawnee Indian named Golightly Spiebuck. Once recovered, he sought out the perpetrators of this crime and systematically killed them. The crowning embellishment to this yarn was that those men that he betrayed at the Walker farm were the last of the lot to be avenged for his brother's death.

The Missourians were slow to believe this story, but they allowed Quantrill to return to Kansas where he was jailed because of his outstanding warrant. He managed to secure release through a writ of habeas corpus, however another warrant was issued. Quantrill fled the state and crossed back over into Missouri near Paola, Kansas.

With the war in full swing, he enlisted in the Missouri State Guard (MSG) under the command of General Sterling Price. After participating in the battles of Wilson Creek, on August 10, 1861 and Lexington, Missouri on September 18-20, 1861, he left the army, returning to the Morgan Walker farm.

QUANTRILL'S THIEVES By: Joseph K. Houts, Jr.

Since Quantrill's last visit, Morgan's son, Andrew, had formed a local home guard unit to protect area residents from warring Jayhawkers. Quanrtill joined the outfit and assumed its command when Andrew retired in order to help his father with the fall harvest. From a core of seven, the gang would grow to fifteen by December 1861. It was composed of Joe Gilchrist, Perry Hoy, John and Jim Hendricks, Joe Vaughn, Ed and John Koger, Harrison Trace, "Ol" Shepard, Fletch Taylor, George Maddox, George Todd, and William Gregg. All of them were from Jackson County, Missouri, except Todd, a transplanted Canadian.

By early March 1862, the band had increased to one hundred. On March 7, Quantrill took the war to Kansas for the first time by raiding the border town of Aubry. Following this bold strike, Major General Henry W. Halleck, on March 13, issued his infamous "no quarter" order, dictating that all subsequently captured guerrillas would be henceforth subject to summary execution. This decree did little to turn the ever-growing tide of guerrilla factions. If anything, it may have contributed to their numbers.

Quantrill experienced three narrow escapes from Federal troops. These skirmishes were at the David Tate farm on March 22, 1862, the Clark house on March 30, 1862, and the Jordan Lowe house on April 15, 1862. After the last of these three near-capture events his gang would never be taken by surprise again, until the gang's demise in 1865. On each occasion, they had confined themselves indoors, without posting adequate pickets.

At the battle of Pleasant Hill, Missouri, on July 11, 1862, the guerrillas experienced their first significant battle, and they were nearly annihilated. Luckily, Quantrill's cool headedness under fire prevented a disaster, although he was wounded. Afterwards, Union troops would find a copy of his muster roll on one of the dead guerrillas, which set forth 92 names.

Regrouping, the guerrillas captured Independence, Missouri on August 11, 1862. Colonel Gideon W. Thompson officially commissioned Quantrill and his men into Confederate service on August 15, pursuant to the Partisan Rangers Act enacted on April 21, 1862. Thompson was acting on orders from General Thomas L. Hindman, commander of the Confederacy's Trans-Mississippi Department.

Quantrill struck Olathe, Kansas on September 6 in retaliation for the execution of Perry Hoy. Infuriated over the news of this deed, Quantrill was quoted saying "we are going to Kansas to kill ten men in revenge for poor Perry." Quantrill also ordered Andrew Blunt, 4th Sergeant, to execute Union Lieutenant Levi Copeland. Colonel Upton Hays had entrusted Lieutenant Levi to the guerrillas for safekeeping in the event of a future prisoner exchange. A month later, he again raided Kansas, sacking Shawneetown.

In the winter of 1862-63, most of the gang wintered in Northwest Arkansas or Southwest Missouri. Accompanied by Andrew Blunt, Quantrill went to Richmond, Virginia seeking a colonel's commission from the Confederate government. They met with Secretary of War, James A. Sheldon, and Texas Senator, Louis T. Wigfall. The request was apparently denied, although later in the war it has been documented that General Price referred to him as Colonel Quantrill.

In the spring of 1863, the guerrillas returned to Missouri, but remained relatively low-keyed. At some point during this period, Quantrill married Kate King of Blue Springs, Missouri.

In mid-summer, General Thomas W. Ewing, Jr. (brother-in-law of William Tecumseth Sherman) was given command of the military district over Kansas. As a means to curtail guerrilla activity, he imposed several mandates targeted at those individuals, in particular women, who were aiding and abetting the guerrillas. Based on this measure, several women had been incarcerated in an old unstable building at 14th and Grand in Kansas City, Missouri. On August 13, 1863, the building collapsed killing five of the women, in particular the sisters of William T. "Bloody Bill" Anderson, John McCorkle and the cousin of Cole Younger.

This tragedy, coupled with Quantrill's longing for revenge at being run out of Kansas, became the catalyst for the Lawrence Raid on August 21, 1863 where upwards of 150 male inhabitants were massacred by the guerrillas. Responding to the raid, Ewing issued his famous General Order No. 11, which removed all suspected Southern sympathizers from the Missouri counties of Jackson, Cass, Bates and the northern half of Vernon.

In early October, the guerrillas headed south to Texas for the winter. While enroute on October 6, they stumbled upon a partially constructed earthen fort outside Baxter Springs, Kansas. They charged the fortification, sustaining moderate casualties. Upon reforming, they spied Brigadier General James G. Blunt approaching with his musical band. The guerrillas attacked the column, almost capturing Blunt. Following the battle, numerous mutilations were performed upon the dead. Afterwards, Quantrill exalted, "By God, Shelby could not whip Blunt; neither could Marmaduke, but I whipped him." According to William H. Gregg, 1st Sergeant, Quantrill was drunk when he made that pronouncement.

Upon their arrival in Texas, the guerrillas set up camp at Mineral Creek, located approximately 12 miles northwest of Sherman. While in these quarters, Quantrill and his men assisted the Confederacy by fighting Comanches and rounding up deserters. However, the bushwhackers began falling into disfavor with Major General Henry McCulloch, who commanded this section of the state. These guerrilla's had indeed become a seedy group by 1864, often behaving like nothing more than drunken thieves intimidating the local population. Eventually, the general arrested Quantrill for the gang's misdeeds. Quantrill managed to escape and moved his men north of the Red River, outside the general's territorial authority.

Besides tangling with regular army officials during the winter of 1863-64, Quantrill's command started to splinter, in time disintegrating into several camps. The first unraveling occurred when William Gregg sought a leave of absence in response to a disagreement with two of George Todd's henchmen, Jim Little and Fletch Taylor. Todd's popularity among the guerrillas was growing. Quantrill encouraged Gregg's departure because he feared for his safety.

The final split took place in March 1864 after the company returned to Missouri. Following a heated argument over a drunken card game, Todd thrust his revolver into

Quantrill's face demanding he admit to being afraid of him. Quantrill acknowledged the challenge and backed down. Todd pulled back his gun. From this point on, Todd and Anderson operated mostly independent of their former chieftain. They conducted numerous raids throughout the middle of the state, culminating in the grotesque slaughter at Centralia, Missouri on September 27, 1864. Within a month, Todd and Anderson would be dead. Quantrill remained somewhat reserved in his activities during this period, making only a faint appearance at the battle of Westport in late October.

Sensing the war was over in Missouri, he gathered together thirty-one members of his old gang in early December and started towards Kentucky. Upon reaching Pocahontas, Arkansas, several of these men spun off and went to Texas. Led by "Ol" Shepard, the group consisted of Babe and Rufus Hudspath, John Koger, and Jesse James. On New Year's Day, 1865, Quantrill and the remainder of his gang crossed the Mississippi River at Devil's Elbow fifteen miles north of Memphis, Tennessee. Within a few days they had made their way into Southwest Kentucky. Quantrill assumed the alias of "Captain Clarke" and disguised his troops by stating they belonged to the 4th Missouri Union Cavalry.

Several reasons have been advanced explaining why he went east. One account has stated he was going to Washington, D.C. in order to assassinate President Lincoln. Whereas, another source has claimed he wanted to surrender with General Robert E. Lee's Army of Northern Virginia in hopes of securing an honorable discharge for he and his men.

Regardless of the reason for heading east none were fulfilled. On May 10, 1865, while resting in Kentucky farmer James H. Wakefield's barn, Quantril was shot in the back and mortally wounded during a surprise attack by Captain Edwin Terrell. Quantrill was taken to the Louisville prison hospital, where he died on June 6, 1865. While languishing in the hospital, prior to his death, he was converted to Catholicism by Father Michael Power. His body was interred in an unmarked grave at St. Mary's Catholic Cemetery in Louisville .

QUANTRILL'S THIEVES   By: Joseph K. Houts, Jr.

    Years later, in December 1887, Mrs. Quantrill went to St. Mary's Catholic Cemetery, accompanied by her son's boyhood friend, William W. Scott. The two convinced the Sexton, Bridgett Shelly, to let them unearth Quantrill's body so it could be reburied in a zinc-lined box. Later Scott apparently stole the remains, comprised of Quantrill's skull, a patch of hair and an assortment of other bones. He was acting upon the instance of Mrs. Quantrill, who wished to see her son reburied in Canal Dover, Ohio, Quantrill's birthplace.

    Scott kept several of the famous bones and later tried to sell them to the Kansas State Historical Society. Failing to perfect a sale, he eventually gave the society two shinbones. William Elsey Connelley, a Quantrill biographer, bought the rest of the bones along with the hair patch, which in time also ended up with the society.

    Sometime after 1910, William Scott's son Walter gave Quantrill's skull to the Alpha Pi Fraternity, Zeta Chapter, in Dover, Ohio (formerly Canal Dover). The skull was purportedly was used in the fraternity's initiation ceremony. When the fraternity disbanded in 1942 the skull was purchased by one of the fraternity's trustees, an individual named Nelson McMillan. Mr. McMillan stored the skull in his basement for many years. In 1972, he gave the skull to the Dover Historical Society, where it was kept inside a 1929 General Electric refrigerator until 1992. On October 24, 1992, Quantrill's Kansas remains were reburied in the Higginsville Confederate Home Cemetery. Less than a week later, on October 30, his skull was also reburied in Dover, Ohio's 4th Street Cemetery.

    Quantrill was described as "one of the coolest and deadliest men in a personal combat." He was called "a forbidding monster of assassination." But it was more pointedly said many years after his death, "How his audit stands, Who knows save Heaven," (sic)

Wm Hallar 1ˢᵗ Lieutenant
(William M. Haller)

    William M. Haller was born on May 5, 1841. He lived in Independence, Missouri, where his father, a mason, had built a mill. His mother's name was Jane. She was born in Pennsylvania. The family was described as wealthy and in 1860 owned one slave. At age nineteen he became Quantrill's first recruit. An individual named George Washington Haller also rode with Quantrill for a short while. It is unknown whether George Washington Hallar was William M.'s brother or his cousin.

    William M. Haller served in many of the early guerrilla skirmishes and was at the battle of Pleasant Hill, Missouri, July 11, 1862, where he was wounded. He was also at the battle of Independence, Missouri on August 11, 1862. Following Independence, Quantrill had ordered him to hold his post outside the town, but a large battle developed at Lone Jack, Missouri on August 16, 1862. Confederate Colonel Upton Hays made repeated requests for reinforcement, but Haller refused. After further appeals, and the urging of William H. Gregg, Quantrill's 1st sergeant, he advanced on Lone Jack only to find the battle over. However, he did manage to capture 150 fleeing Federal troops.

    Haller was second in command of Quantrill's guerrillas. Colonel Gideon W. Thompson commissioned him a 1ˢᵗ lieutenant upon the company's official mustering into rebel service under the Confederate Partisan Rangers Act. Quantrill's third in line, George W. Todd, felt overlooked by Haller's selection. Eventually, Todd made his resentment known, which culminated in an argument concerning the matter. Afterwards, Haller left the gang and did not rendezvous with Quantrill and the others on November 3, 1862 for their trek south, away from the Missouri-Kansas border region. He subsequently became attached to another guerrilla band under the command of Charley (Ki) Harrison.

QUANTRILL'S THIEVES By: Joseph K. Houts, Jr.

Portrayed as a "young and dauntless spirit," Haller was considered "one of those men, who are themselves ignorant of their own powers, until a crisis comes." He was quoted as saying "the faster the horses went—the better the shooting." Another characterization has stated "he rode through his fitful military life at a gallop and drank the wine of battle to its drags." Lastly, he was described as "handsome" and being "gentle as a woman, but terrible in battle." There has been some confusion as to his death. One account has set forth that he died in late 1862, whereas two others have reported January 15, 1863 and April 1863 respectively as his date of death. He was buried in the Woodlawn Cemetery at Independence, Missouri. With his passing, it was said Quantrill "lost an arm and his country lost a hero."

G W Todd 2nd Lieutenant
(George W. Todd)

George W. Todd was called "the incarnate devil of battle." He was born in Canada in 1839. Another account has placed his birth in Scotland, where as a boy he killed a man and then fled to Canada. He settled with his parents in Kansas City, Missouri and like his father was a stone mason building bridges. His parents were George A. and Margaret Todd, both of them had been born in Scotland. Sometime around the war's beginning, he got into trouble and was arrested in Independence, Missouri. Afterwards, he enlisted with General Sterling Price's Missouri State Guard (MSG).

In December 1861, Todd left the guard and joined Quantrill, as one of his initial fifteen riders. Upon the guerrilla company's commissioning into the Confederate army, he was named 2nd among the lieutenants, with William M. Haller receiving top position. Todd resented the lesser rank believing only he should have been next in line to Quantrill. This slight embittered him towards both Quantrill and Haller. Later in 1864, Todd would openly challenge Quantrill over the point of his revolver while arguing over a drunken card game. Quantrill stood down, which led to the disintegration of his command and its splintering into groups under William T. "Bloody Bill" Anderson and Todd.

He participated in most all of the major guerrilla engagements, notably: Aubrey, Kansas, March 7, 1862; Independence, Missouri, August 11, 1862; Olathe, Kansas, September 6, 1862; Shawnee, Kansas, October 17, 1862; Lawrence, Kansas, August 21, 1863; Baxter Springs, Kansas, October 6, 1863; and Centralia, Missouri, September 27, 1864.

On the approach to Lawrence, he crossed the farm of Joseph Stone, who happened to be the individual who was responsible for his arrest in Independence. Since the guerrillas were so close to the town, Quantrill did not want Todd to shoot Stone. The sound of gunfire would alert the inhabitants. Todd thereupon ordered a new recruit, Sam Clifton, to club Stone to death with the butt of an old musket taken from the farmhouse. Todd was suspicious of Clifton's loyalty and he figured this occasion would be a good test of the young recruit's fervor. In watching the execution, guerrilla Frank Smith almost fell from his horse, sickened by the measure.

On the retreat from Lawrence, Quantrill put Todd in charge of the rear guard comprising sixty-three men. They were able to stave off a far superior contingent of pursuers led by General James H. Lane, Kansas' first United States Senator. 1st Sergeant William M. Gregg disputes the circumstances of the action and claims that he was actually the one in command.

In the spring of 1864, Todd, along with Anderson, returned to Missouri from the guerrillas' winter quarters in Sherman, Texas. Throughout the summer months he and Anderson operated in and around the Missouri River in Central Missouri. He raided the towns of Arrow Rock on July 20, Keytesville on September 20, and Fayette on September 24.

Todd accompanied the group that carried out the Centralia massacre, however he did not participate in the morning slaughter. A total of 149 men were eventually murdered that day, and there were numerous random mutilations of the bodies.

Todd joined with General Price upon entering Lafayette County immediately before the Battle of Westport. While scouting on October 22, 1864, two and a half miles northeast of Independence, he was shot in the throat by either a sniper or a member of the 2nd Colorado. There are two versions of his death. The first asserts that he died instantly, lunging forward in his saddle and falling to the ground. Whereas, the second version is that he was taken to Independence upon being shot and lingered two hours before he died.

The body was buried in the Woodlawn Cemetery, at Independence, Missouri. He was described as strikingly handsome with "blond hair and blue eyes, hot-tempered, callously brutal, absolutely fearless." He was also illiterate.

W H Gregg 1st Sergeant
(William H. Gregg)

William H. Gregg was born February 8, 1838 and lived with his parents Jacob and Nancy Lewis Gregg on their farm near Stony Point in Jackson County, Missouri. He joined the Missouri State Guard (MSG) early in the war. As a captain, he was attached to Colonel Rosser's Regiment, Rains Division. When his enlistment expired, he returned home because of an illness. Thereafter, at the age of 22 he joined Quantrill in December 1861 as one of his initial seven riders. Colonel Gideon W. Thompson elected Gregg 1st Sergeant upon the company's commissioning into Confederate service. He participated in the battles of Pleasant Hill, Missouri, July 11, 1862, where he was wounded; Independence, Missouri, August 11, 1862; Lawrence, Kansas, August 21, 1863; Baxter Springs, Kansas, October 6, 1863; and Centralia, Missouri, September 27, 1864. After the battle of Lone Jack, Missouri, Quantrill reorganized his command, making Gregg 1st Lieutenant.

William H. Gregg
Used by permission, State Historical Society of Missouri

He was described as a "grim soul among the guerrillas," and possessed "most of the constituent (sic) elements of military genius." (sic) When Quantrill went to Richmond, Virginia, seeking a colonel's commission, Gregg was put in charge of the command. The gang quartered in Northwest Arkansas and Southwest Missouri during the winter of 1862-63. On January 19, 1863, General John S. Marmaduke sent him to Jackson

QUANTRILL'S THIEVES By: Joseph K. Houts, Jr.

County, Missouri as a recruiter. He attended Quantrill's council of war concerning the Lawrence raid. Reportedly he stated, "Lawrence; it is the home of Jim Lane; the foster mother of the Red Legs; the nurse of the Jayhawkers." Years later, Gregg commented in his memoirs the real reason for supporting the venture was to recapture some of the Jayhawkers' plunder and distribute it among Missouri victims. After the attack, he rounded up stragglers for the return trip, many of whom were "roaring drunk." In his account of the affair, he stated Quantrill had placed him in charge of the rear guard. Although, other sources have established George W. Todd as being in charge. On maintaining the rear, Gregg reflected, "it really looked as though we were doomed" and that "the whole earth behind us was blue," referring to the onslaught of pursuing Federal troops.

While in Sherman, Texas during the winter of 1863-84, he had a falling out with two of Todd's men, Jim Little and Fletch Taylor. Consequently, he became the first to leave Quantrill. Gregg had called them thieves for not properly sharing with him the spoils of a previous raid. Sensing trouble, but not wanting to desert, he sought Quantrill's permission for a leave of absence. At the meeting, Quantrill told him to leave because he had enemies in the camp. Quantrill coyly praised Gregg stating he , "...had been a good officer and an honest man." However, Quantrill did not want to provoke the disfavor of Todd, so he encouraged Gregg's parting.

The following day, while Gregg was leaving, he passed Todd, Little, Taylor, and John Barker on the street. Todd told the others "there goes that damned son of a bitch—now kill him." Taylor responded that he would not, noting that Gregg had been a good Southerner and officer defending the cause, therefore, Todd should kill him himself if he wanted the deed done. Todd refrained from any further confrontation.

On December 25, 1863, Gregg joined General Joseph O. Shelby's brigade and was made a 1st Lieutenant in command of Company I, Shank's regiment.

On November 3, 1864, a dozen "long-haired" guerrillas in their Sunday best with polished pistols and spurs witnessed William Gregg's marriage to Miss Elizabeth Eleanor "Lizzie"

Hook of Odessa, Missouri. For the occasion, he put on a new uniform with four navy revolvers strapped around his waist. His comrades guarded their quarters that night. On November 7, 1864, with his new bride, Dick Maddox and wife, James A. Hendrix and wife (being Gregg's sister and brother-in-law), and accompanied by George Shepard and fifty others, he went to Texas. Once settled in Texas he returned to Missouri to carry on the fight.

After the war, Greg brought his wife back to Missouri and the couple had ten children. Greg worked as a carpenter, handyman, and teamster to support them. Through political patronage, he became deputy sheriff of Jackson County, Missouri. At times he was employed as a jail turnkey.

When the Quantrill reunions convened in 1898, he was a regular attendee and was listed on Stephen Ragan's 1895 Jackson County U.C.V. roster. Gregg wrote several accounts about his wartime experiences, sometimes clarifying or embellishing upon the guerrillas' deeds. In particular, he refuted the myth that Quantrill carried a black flag with his name in red letters printed upon it. He suffered from rheumatism, and on April 22, 1916, he died of cancer at the age of 78. His wife Lizzie died ten days later of the same disease.

QUANTRILL'S THIEVES By: Joseph K. Houts, Jr.

John Jarrette 2nd Sergeant
(Jarrette)

John Jarrette was employed as a carpenter at the war's beginning, residing in Big Cedar, Jackson County, Missouri. He was born in Kentucky and in 1860 took a bride named Josephine, who was only nineteen years old. At the age of twenty-five he and his brother-in-law, Thomas Coleman Younger, joined Quantrill's outfit. Reports vary concerning the time of Jarrette's initial association with Quantrill, with one stating October 1861 and another placing the date in January 1862. Upon the company's commissioning into Confederate service he was elected 2nd Sergeant. He was at the Tate house skirmish on March 22, 1862, where he was wounded; Independence, Missouri, August 11, 1862; Lawrence, Kansas, August 21, 1863; Baxter Springs, Kansas, October 6, 1863; and Centralia, Missouri, September 27, 1864.

Apparently, Jarrette had his own gang, which was merged into Quantrill's. During the winter of 1862-63, while Quantrill was in Richmond, Virginia, he served under General John S. Marmaduke in charge of a cavalry unit attached to General Joseph O. Shelby. He participated in the Lawrence war council, where he was quoted as saying "Lawrence by all means...the head devil of all this killing...I vote to fight it with fire – to burn it before we leave it."

Purportedly, he held strong Masonic convictions and on two occasions spared captives because of the bonds of Freemasonry. The first incident occurred while with General Shelby. His troops had seized Union officer Colonel King, the ex-governor's son. Jarrette noticed his Masonic ring and promptly intervened, making King promise to stop the burning of Southern sympathizer's property in Lafayette County, Missouri. King gave his word and for two to three months the burnings ceased. The other reprieve was during the Lawrence raid. He spared five prisoners who gave the Masonic sign of recognition.

At the battle of Baxter Springs, accompanied by Dick Yeager and Francis Smith, he chased Brigadier General James G. Blunt in hopes of running him down, however Blunt's horse outran them. After William H. Gregg, Quantrill's 1st Sergeant, left Quantrill, Jarrette and Cole Younger also separated from the group and served with the regular Confederate army. Thereafter, he and Younger were placed in Louisiana, Texas, Mexico, and Los Angeles, California at war's end.

Described as "the man who never knew fear" Jarrette's band stood next "in ferocity to only William T. "Bloody Bill" Anderson's and George W. Todd's. He was chosen by Jesse James to participate in the James-Younger gang's first bank robbery at Liberty, Missouri, on February 13, 1866. At the gang's bank holdup in Russellville, Kentucky, on March 21, 1868 Jarrette shot the bank's president as the man was opening the back door of the bank.

A great granddaughter claimed Jarrette and his wife, Josephine Younger Jarrette, were shot upon answering the front door of their house, which was possibly located in the proximity of Monagaw Springs in St. Clair County, Missouri. The house was set on fire, but Cole and Jim Younger arrived in time to save their two children. This incident apparently happened in the late 1860's. Another source has documented Jarrette owning a sheep ranch in Arizona, after the war. At some point, while a guerrilla, it is claimed that he said "we were wild beasts, yes, but we war on wild beasts."

QUANTRILL'S THIEVES   By: Joseph K. Houts, Jr.

J L Tucker 3rd Sergeant
(James L., James S. Tucker)

     James L. Tucker was one of Quantrill's early recruits. He was commissioned a 3rd Sergeant, upon the company's mustering into Confederate service. In early July 1862, accompanied by Cole Younger and James Vaughn, he helped lead a diversion during an encounter with Federal troops at Pink Hill, Missouri. Tucker, along with Dick Burns, John Jarrett, Henry Ogden, Dick Maddox, James Morris, George Shepard, and Toler, escaped on foot at the concluding moments of the battle of Pleasant Hill, Missouri, on July 11, 1862. A month later, on August 11, 1862, he fought at the battle of Independence, Missouri. Quantrill made him 1st Duty Sergeant on reorganizing his command after the battle of Lone Jack, Missouri.

     At some point, he left Quantrill and joined the 12th Missouri Cavalry, Company D, which was known as the Jackson County Cavalry because many of its enlistees were from that county. It was initially commanded by Colonel Upton Hays and later was called Shank's Regiment, after David Shanks. Hays, along with Tucker, was also on the original Roster of Quantrill's guerrillas. Tucker operated in Louisiana with Shelby, serving with distinction at a skirmish known as the Horse Shoe on the Mississippi River. On September 15, 1864 he served under the charge of Captain Joseph C. Lea in a campaign to stop the illicit export of cotton on the Mississippi. While participating in the exercise, he shot the Negro leader of a band of deserters six times. The Negro fired back three times, hitting Tucker once. It has been documented that he survived the war.

Andrew Blunt 4th Sergeant
(Andy Blunt, Blount)

Andrew Blunt's enlistment with Quantrill is shrouded in mystery. It was said of him "no one knew his history. He asked no questions and he answered none." There was an account of his being in the 2nd United States Cavalry where he killed a sergeant. Later, Blunt supposedly shot a lieutenant in New Mexico and then fled to Missouri. Upon the company's commissioning into Confederate service, he was elected 4th Sergeant. He participated in the skirmishes at the Jordan Lowe house, April 16, 1862; and Pink Hill, Missouri, in early July 1862; followed by the battles of Pleasant Hill, Missouri, July 11, 1862; Independence, Missouri, August 11, 1862; and Lawrence, Kansas, August 21, 1863. When Quantrill reorganized his command after the battle of Lone Jack, Missouri, he was made 3rd Lieutenant.

He and Joe Gilchrist were trapped at the Lowe house. Gilcrist was killed and Blunt was wounded. The Federals left him to die, but he managed to find save harbor in a farmhouse, where he was attended to by friends. Upon regaining his health, he shortly rejoined the outfit.

When Quantrill's learned of the execution of one of his men, Perry Hoy, by Federals in Leavenworth, Kansas, he immediately dispatched an order to William H. Gregg. The directive commanded Blunt to shoot a Union prisoner, Lieutenant Levi Copeland. Confederate Colonel Upton Hays had recently left the prisoner in Quantrill's custody. Gregg recalled, in his memoirs, that Blunt followed the order without haste.

In mid-December 1862, he and a man named Charley Higbee accompanied Quantrill to Richmond, Virginia, where Quantrill hoped to secure a colonel's commission.

He attended the war council on Lawrence, where he said, "count me in wherever there's killing." On the guerrilla's sweep into town, Blunt covered the west section. He, along with many of the older guard were reported to have done most of the killings. These seasoned veterans wanted revenge against the

Kansans, the Jayhawkers, and the Union army. As pointed out by several sources, some men went to plunder, but others like Blunt, went to kill, burning all.

On the return from Lawrence, he and several of his men found the mutilated bodies of fellow raider, Jim Bledsoe and two others. After viewing the scene, Blunt was quoted as saying "we have something to learn yet, boys, and we have learned it. Scalp for scalp hereafter." The next day he and William T. "Bloody Bill" Anderson, Peyton Long, Arch Clements, and William McGuire were said to have killed four Federal militia. He scalped each of them leaving the ears, remarking that he did not have any use for ears. The Bledsoe affair marked the beginning of guerrilla mutilations.

During the winter of 1863-64, Blunt remained in Missouri. He did not go south to Sherman, Texas with Quantrill and the rest of the gang. In the spring of 1864, he and twenty men commenced skirmishing again with Union troops.

On one occasion the band kidnapped the Reverend Moses B. Arnold of Lafayette County, Missouri and forced him to perform a marriage ceremony joining Miss Barbary Jane Gray in Holy Matrimony with Blunt's second in command, Mr. James W. Wilkinson. Because of this and other incidents, Union General Brown sent out numerous patrols in search of Blunt and his gang. On March 7, 1864, Blunt and ten of his men were killed three miles south of Oak Grove, Missouri, at the house of Steve Austin. He was left to "rot," because General Brown believed he was unworthy of burial. Purportedly, Brown also wanted the decaying body to stand, as a reminder to other would-be guerrillas.

Andrew Blunt was eventually buried in the Concord graveyard five miles south of Bates City, Missouri. In 1908 several former Quantrill men started a fund for the purpose of buying a tombstone for his grave. By the end of September 1908, L. John Brown reported $8.35 had been raised. Blunt was described as "a brooding and mysterious man." Of special note was his handling of a horse and prowess with a gun. He "died as a wild boar," plugged with eleven bullets from fifty foes, taking ten with him.

F M Scott Commissary
(Fernando M. Scott)

Fernando M. Scott was originally from Ohio. In 1858 he moved to Liberty, Missouri and was employed as a saddle maker. Upon Quantrill's company being commissioned into the Confederate army as partisans, he was elected commissary. Scott fought at the battles of Pleasant Hill, Missouri, July 11, 1862, and Independence, Missouri, August 11, 1862. When the command was reorganized following the battle of Long Jack, Missouri, he was made a 3rd lieutenant. While Quantrill was in Richmond, Virginia, he took charge of the outfit after William H. Gregg, 1st Sergeant, left to recruit for General John S. Marmaduke in Missouri.

Frank James was associated with Scott's band after James had been arrested for the second time, and following his escape from the Liberty, Missouri jail. In May 1863, Scott took James across the Missouri River, where they joined Quantrill. Scott's band traveled a wide region from Kansas City, Missouri to the Nebraska border. On May 19, 1863, accompanied by William H. Gregg, Joe Hart, Fletch Taylor, James Little, Frank James, and several others, Scott's gang laid a trap outside Richfield (Missouri City), Missouri. Two Federals were killed, their bodies stripped and plundered. On June 16, 1863, they raided Plattsburg, Missouri stealing $50,000.00 and leaving the courthouse burning in their wake.

It has been said, "Fernando Scott was one of those men whom revolutions cast up sometimes to be titans and sometimes monsters." Depicted as "no man better fitted for the life of a guerrilla," he was also described as "gentle, tender-hearted and true." Other characterizations noted he was a nervous and sensitive type, sleeping little, but the coolest among all the guerrillas, while under fire. He was killed on June 19, 1863 in Quantrill's failed attempt to attack Kansas City on Brush Creek in the Westport area. Purportedly, the fatal bullet was from an Enfield rifle nearly a mile away. Scott was buried at the Smith Cemetery in Jackson County, Missouri.

This was the only man for whom George W. Todd would openly weep among all of his fallen riders. At his interment, an observer remarked, "as his brief lifetime (sic) had been stormy, so was his burial. The night was tempestuous (sic). The wrathful wind smote (sic) the trees with the wings of a great darkness."

QUANTRILL'S THIEVES   By: Joseph K. Houts, Jr.

Richard Madox Quartermaster
(Dick Maddox)

Richard Maddox was called "the best rider among the bushwhackers." Upon the company's induction into Confederate service, he was made quartermaster. Maddox rounded out Quantrill's original officer staff. Born in 1834, his parents were Larkin and Jane Estill Power Maddox, who were married in 1825, Scott County, Kentucky. His brother George M. Maddox was also on Quantrill's muster roll. Accounts have recorded his presence at the battles of Independence, Missouri, August 11, 1862; Lawrence, Kansas, August 21, 1863; Baxter Springs, Kansas, October 6, 1863; and Centralia, Missouri, September 27, 1864. In addition, Maddox was at the failed attempt to attack Kansas City, Missouri, on June 16, 1863 where fellow officer Fernando M. Scott, Quantrill's commissary, was killed.

At the war council discussing the Lawrence raid, Maddox was quoted saying, "Lawrence an eye for an eye and a tooth for a tooth; God understands better than we do the equilibrium of civil war." It was reported that he did more killing at Lawrence than any of the other guerrillas, with the exception of William T. "Bloody Bill" Anderson, Peyton Long, Bill Gower and Allen Parmer.

He went with Quantrill to Sherman, Texas staying there during the winter of 1862-63. On Christmas Eve 1863, Maddox and several other comrades partook in the holiday festivities by drinking all of a friend's eggnog. This was followed by the consumption of a barrel of whiskey. Later the merry makers rode their horses into the town's hotel lobby, firing their guns at doorknobs and gaslights. The next day, adhering to Quantrill's insistence, the celebrants returned to the hotel to apologize and make restitution for the damages.

Besides being an excellent horseman, he was equally gifted at rope tricks. As to these talents, it was said "liquor did not diminish his skills: he got drunk every time he had the chance," which purportedly was quite often.

In November 1864, accompanied by his wife, James A. Hendrix and his wife, William H. Gregg and his wife, George Shepard and fifty others, he returned to Texas. One account has claimed that while enroute to Texas a Cherokee Indian killed Maddox in Oklahoma, whereas another source states that a Cherokee Indian killed him after the war. A third source has documented that he survived his run in with the Cherokee.

QUANTRILL'S THIEVES By: Joseph K. Houts, Jr.

Henry Acres
(Henry H. Akers)

Henry H. Akers was born in Lexington, Kentucky around 1838. His parents were Solomon and Matilda Mead Akers. The family moved to Missouri in 1840, settling in Cass or Jackson counties. Solomon died in 1876.

In 1860 Akers was a farmer. He was married to Eliza J. Akers. Two of Henry Aker's brothers also rode with Quantrill, Sylvester, or "Ves", and Mark. After the war, Ves stated the reason Quantrill went to Kentucky in 1865 was to join General Lee's Army of Northern Virginia in order to secure a pardon for himself and his men. This rendition has been pointed out to be contrary to some of the myths that he was going to Washington, D.C. to assassinate President Lincoln.

Later in the war, Akers served as a captain under guerrilla chieftain George W. Todd. Little else has been documented about his wartime experiences except that he set out with Quantrill for Tennessee, in November 1864. Upon reaching Pochantes, Arkansas, however, Akers, Ol Shepard, Rufus and Babe Hudspeth, John Koger, and Jesse James decided to leave the Quantrill's group and set off for Texas. While in Texas, Akers surrendered to Union forces in June 1865. Brother Ves was also part of Quantrill's exodus but Ves stayed with Quantrill and was captured outside Harrodsburg, Kentucky in 1865.

Akers eventually returned to Missouri and spent his remaining years living in a house north of Lee's Summit. On December 28, 1913, the Independence Chapter of the United Daughters of the Confederacy awarded him the Southern Cross of Honor. Akers and his brother Ves attended several of the Quantrell Reunions. Henry attended the 1890 and possibly the 1908 reunion. He died at 1:00 p.m. Tuesday, July 13, 1920, at the age of 82, and was laid to rest in the Lee's Summit Cemetery.

U L Anderson
(Hugh L. W., Hugh L.)

     Hugh L. W. Anderson was born in Tennessee around 1840. Little information has been found about his lineage, or as to when he moved to Johnson County, Missouri. In 1860, he was working as a store clerk for a merchant named Thomas Slack in Warrensburg, Missouri. He enlisted on August 1, 1862 into the Confederate Army in Johnson County, joining the 16th Missouri Infantry under General Sterling Price's Division, Parson's Brigade, serving under the combined commands of Colonels Jackman, Cummins, Vardaman Cockrell and Lewis. Anderson was assigned to Company D, with Captain David Raker as the ranking officer, where he would obtain the rank of 2nd lieutenant before war's end.

     Anderson's service included the battles of Lone Jack, Missouri, August 16, 1862; Prairie Grove, Arkansas, December 7, 1862; Helena, Arkansas, July 4, 1863; Little Rock, Arkansas, September 10, 1863; Mansfield, Louisiana, April 7, 1864; Jenkin's Ferry, Arkansas, April 30, 1864; and Springfield, Louisiana. Early on in the war and probably in between these conflicts, he also served with William Clarke Quantrill as a guerrilla. Records indicate that he was paroled at Shreveport, Louisiana on June 9, 1865, although we are unable to document where or when he was captured.

     After the war, his personal life has remained a mystery. It was reported, however, that he died in Pleasant Hill, Missouri sometime prior to 1923.

Sylvester Atchison
(Ves)

At the start of the Civil War Sylvester Atchison (Ves) and his brothers were the next-door neighbors of another guerrilla on the Roster, John H. Koger, and they remained neighbors after the war. Atchison was at the battle of Lone Jack, Missouri on August 16, 1862 and in all probability was at the battles of Pleasant Hill, Missouri, July 11, 1862 and Centralia, Missouri, September 27, 1864.

Although he initially rode with Quantrill, he eventually joined George M. Todd's gang, which accounts for his presence at Centralia. Shortly after the Centralia engagement he was wounded in another skirmish. After Todd was killed following the battle of Westport, Missouri in late October 1864, Atchison was under the command of David Pool.

On May 23, 1865 Atchison along with his brothers surrendered to Captain E. E. Rogers, the Provost Marshal at Lexington, Missouri. Between May 21-28, seven of the other original guerrillas turned themselves in at Lexington. They were David Pool, George McKinley Barnett, Samuel Clifton, R. (A.) Harris, John H. Teague, John H. Terry, and Robert Stephenson.

After the war, Sylvester returned home and commenced farming again. His mother was living with him in 1870. On December 10, 1871 he married Sarah J. Cupp. He and his brother's whereabouts after this period have remained a mystery. Apparently, they left Jackson County, possibly moving to another state or territory.

Wiley Atchison
(Willis G., W. G.)

Wiley Atchison was born in Tennessee in 1836. His mother's name was Milly or Mellie and his father was apparently deceased by 1860. Sometime in the 1850's the family moved to Jackson County, Missouri, settling outside the town of Stony Point. Two of his brothers, Sylvester and John, also rode with guerrilla chieftain William Clarke Quantrill and were on the Roster of original guerrillas. He and Sylvester were the same age and absent the possibility of being cousins were probably twins. In the 1860 and 1870 Jackson County Census, Wiley was listed as a farmer. On June 25, 1857 he married Barbara Ann Barnette.
At the start of the Civil War he and his brothers were the next-door neighbors of another guerrilla on the Roster, John H. Koger, and remained such after the war.

During the Civil War, Atchison was in all probability at the battle of Pleasant Hill, Missouri on July 11, 1862. Thereafter, he may have joined the 1st Missouri Cavalry, assigned to Company A formed on December 30, 1861 commanded by Colonel Elijah Gates and possibly Woodson's Cavalry formed in early 1864 from former Confederate prisoners of war. On the other hand he may not have been part of either unit. The individual listed in each was named either Willis or Willis G. Atchison. In fact there may have been such a person, but Wiley's formal name could have been Willis or Willis G. Towards the end of the war he may have ridden with George M. Todd, followed by David Pool after Todd's death following the battle of Westport, Missouri in late October 1864.

On May 23, 1865, Atchison along with his brothers surrendered to Captain E. E. Rogers, the provost marshal at Lexington, Missouri. Between May 21-28, seven other original guerrillas would turn themselves in at Lexington. They were David Pool, George McKinley Barnett, Samuel Clifton, R. (A.) Harris, John H. Teague, John H. Terry, and Robert Stephenson.

After the war, Wiley returned home and commenced farming again. In the 1870 census he and his wife were shown to have one child, a son named Jefferson age 13. He and his brother's whereabouts after this period have remained a mystery. Apparently, they left Jackson County, possibly moving to another state or territory.

QUANTRILL'S THIEVES By: Joseph K. Houts, Jr.

John Atchison

John Atchison was born in Tennessee in 1838. His mother's name was Milly or Mellie and his father was apparently deceased by 1860. Sometime in the 1850's the family moved to Jackson County, Missouri, settling outside the town of Stony Point. Two of his brothers Sylvester and Wiley also rode with guerrilla chieftain William Clarke Quantrill and were on the Roster of original guerrillas. John Atchison was the youngest of the three brothers. On August 13, 1857 he married Seletha A. Bernard. John was listed as a farmer in both the 1860 and 1870 Jackson County Census.

At the start of the Civil War he and his brothers were the next-door neighbors of another guerrilla on the Roster, John H. Koger, and remained such after the war. Atchison was in all probability at the battle of Pleasant Hill, Missouri on July 11, 1862. Towards the end of the war he may have ridden with George M. Todd, followed by David Pool after Todd's death following the battle of Westport, Missouri in late October 1864. On May 23, 1865, Atchison along with his brothers surrendered to Captain E. E. Rogers, the Provost Marshall at Lexington, Missouri. Between May 21-28, seven other original guerrillas would turn themselves in at Lexington. They were David Pool, George McKinley Barnett, Samuel Clifton, R. (A.) Harris, John H. Teague, John H. Terry and Robert Stephenson.

After the war, John returned home and commenced farming again. In the 1870 census he and his wife were shown to have four children. Their names were Sylvester age 13, Elizabeth age 9, James and Emily ages 5. Sylvester was in all likelihood named after his brother. Children James and Emily were probably twins, just like his older brothers, a common occurrence in subsequent generations of the same family. He and his brother's whereabouts after this period have remained a mystery. Apparently, they left Jackson County, possibly moving to another state or territory.

H Austin
(Henry)

H. Austin was born in 1834 with his place of birth being Tennessee. In the 1860 Lafayette County, Missouri Federal Census, he was shown to be residing with a Rufus and M. McCormack. However, in the 1860 Clay County, Missouri Federal Census, there was a Henry Austin, listed as a black laborer, age 30, with Missouri as his place of birth.

It should be pointed out that several African-Americans rode with or assisted William Clarke Quantrill and his guerrillas. In particular, there was John Noland and John Lobb. Noland even attended the Quantrill Reunions after the Civil War. Lobb was sent to Lawrence, Kansas prior to the raid on August 21, 1863 to scout for Union troops.

In all probability though the Austin whose name appears on the Roster was H. and not Henry. His war record has remained an unknown, but most likely he was at the battle of Pleasant Hill, Missouri on July 11, 1862.

QUANTRILL'S THIEVES By: Joseph K. Houts, Jr.

J D Brinker
(John D.)

John D. Brinker was a Missourian by birth, being born in 1841. His parents were John B. and Sarah B. Brinker. He was the eldest of seven siblings consisting of Martha G., Abraham, Robert, William Hugh, Fannie J. and Jessie B. Indians in Jackson County, Missouri killed Brinker's grandfather in 1830. John's father was in the dry goods business and died of cholera in 1855, while returning home from a buying trip to St. Louis. His mother, Sarah, took over the family store and John assisted her.

The Brinker family were slaveholders and, as a consequence, their home and business were plundered and burned by pro-Northern elements. On March 19, 1862 soldiers under the command of Captain Thomas W. Houts of the Missouri State Militia (MSM) visited Mrs. Brinker. Reportedly, the captain had received a tip suggesting gunpowder was hidden on her plantation. In searching the premises, 125 kegs of the powder were uncovered in various sites. In all likelihood this incident, together with the plunder and arson committed by the pro-Northern elements, motivated John to join Quantrill.

Mrs. Brinker, fearing for the family's safety, moved to St. Francis County in order to be out of harms way. Sons John and Abraham did not accompany her because they were fighting for the South. She remained in St. Francis County until 1869, then returned to Johnson County.

John enlisted sometime in 1862, in the 10th Missouri Cavalry commanded by Colonel Lawther. He was promoted to captain and fought at the battles of Pleasant Hill, Missouri, July 11, 1862 and Baxter Springs, Kansas, October 6, 1863.

Brinker, along with a Snelling and a combined force of 85-90 men escorted Colonel Upton Hays in mid-June 1862 in his efforts to recruit volunteers for the trans-Mississippi Confederate Army. Hays and Brinker skirmished with Major Emory S. Foster of the Seventy Cavalry, Missouri State Militia, outside Warrensburg on June 17, 1862. Area residents fled to Warrensburg upon their appearance. During this exodus,

Brinker's sister, Matty, and a younger brother were apprehended by Foster's troops. She was placed at the head of the column, along with another woman. This tactic prevented Hays from attacking for fear of killing them, which was exactly Foster's plan. In later years, noted historian John N. Edwards described Matty as "one of the most beautiful and accomplished women of the West." She and her brother were jailed for several weeks on the suspicion of having passed information to the guerrillas.

John Brinker's brother Abraham was in Captain Raker's Company D of the 16th Missouri Infantry Regiment, commanded by Colonel Vard Cockrell and Colonel Jackman of Parson's Brigade, in General Sterling Price's division. On January 13, 1863 he left the company and joined the guerrillas. Brinker's other brother, William, enlisted in the Confederate Army in 1864 at the age of 13. It has been speculated that he was in John's Company I of the 10th Missouri Infantry. He did participate in Price's 1864 Missouri campaign. In later years William would become the Prosecuting Attorney and a judge in Johnson County, Missouri.

At one point in the war Major Emory S. Foster of the Missouri State Militia referred to Brinker as a "notorious guerrilla chief." Unfortunately John Brinker failed to survive the great conflict. He was killed by Federal militia while on a scouting patrol in a swamp next to the White River outside Monticello, Arkansas. His men had been cut off from their company, leading to a surprise attack by Union troops. At his death, it was said "he died fighting rather than to be captured."

QUANTRILL'S THIEVES By: Joseph K. Houts, Jr.

Jas H Bowling:
(James H. Bowlin, Jas., Jim)

James H. Bowlin was born on July 30, 1838. His place of birth, parentage, and pre-Civil War experience has remained an unknown. He enlisted into regular Confederate service on October 20, 1862. However, there has been documentation supporting his enlistment in either May or August of that year. The place of recruitment was Keytesville, Missouri, where he joined a consolidation of the 8th Battalion Missouri Infantry and Colonel John B. Clark Jr.'s Regiment Missouri Infantry into the 9th Missouri Infantry. Bowlin was a private, assigned to Company I. His name is recorded on the company roll as of February 1864.

His service included the battles of Mansfield, Louisiana, April 8, 1864; Pleasant Hill, Louisiana, April 9, 1864; Saline River, Arkansas, and various operations along the Mississippi River. Prior to his enlistment, he probably served with William Clarke Quantrill. Records show that he surrendered on May 26, 1865 at either Baton Rouge or New Orleans, Louisiana and that he was paroled on June 7, 1865 at Alexandria, Louisiana.

His whereabouts immediately following the war have remained a mystery. He was married and had five children and his wife died around 1888. At some point he moved to Saline, Slater County, Missouri, where he worked as a laborer. Records show that he resided there for at least twenty years preceding 1913

On June 21, 1913 he made application for consideration for admission to the Confederate Memorial Home at Higginsville, Missouri. His application stated that he was not wounded during the war, and that he did not contract any disease while in the army. However, he claimed that he owned no property and that he was suffering from cancer. It seems that Bowlin's request to enter the Home was delayed for two reasons. First, he was receiving treatments from his local doctor for the aliment, and second, there was some concern as to the infectious nature, if any, of his disease. The cancer first presented itself as a small sore on his left ear. Within a year it had become cancerous.

Dr. W. M. Jarvis, his attending physician in Saline, wrote a letter to the Home detailing his condition and explaining it was not contagious. In another letter from Judge John A. Rich, Bowlin was described as poor, honest, and respected within the community and not one to partake excessively of alcohol. Judge Rich evidently entered an order granting Bowlin admission to the Home. The application stated he was approved on December 2, and notified on the 13th of his acceptance.

Even though a notation dated July 24, 1914 appears on his application indicating that he had been admitted to the Home confusion remains as to whether or not he actually was. It fact, it appears likely that he was turned away for some unknown reason. Apparently, there had been a change in the Home's administration and Colonel George P. Gross, the new superintendent, conducted a further review of Bowlin's application. On July 22 Judge Rich wrote a letter of introduction to the colonel for Bowlin, explaining that Bowlin had been delayed in entering the Home because his local doctor was attending him. Rich also wrote another letter to a Reverend Thomas M. Cobb at Lexington, Missouri asking him to intercede on behalf of Bowlin with the colonel. Cobb sent a plea to the colonel on July 28, requesting Bowlin be reconsidered for admission, pointing out, "The poor old fellow has nothing and no one to take care of him." Apparently, the request fell on deaf ears, because the Home's records have no record of his admittance.

Richard Burns
(Richard F., Dick, Burnes)

Richard F. "Dick" Burns was born in Kentucky around 1846. His parents were Wesley and Nancy F. Burns. In the 1860 Federal Census, eight siblings were listed, with Richard being the sixth. Their names were Felix J., Serilda, Dennis, William T., John T., Catherine H., Crittenden and William W. the youngest at age two. Mrs. Burns was manager of the family farm. The family owned seven slaves. Richard's father, Wesley Burns had died sometime prior to 1860.

Burns was one of William Clarke Qauntrill's earliest recruits, being part of the original 30 members. He was at the battles of Pleasant Hill, Missouri, July 11, 1862; Independence, Missouri, August 11, 1862; Lone Jack, Missouri, August 16, 1862; Lawrence, Kansas, August 21, 1863; and Centralia, Missouri, September 27, 1864.

It was said that, "Burns fought. Others might have ambition and seek to sport the official attributes of rank; he fought." There were few who could out gun him and Quantrill took pleasure in seeing Burns on the front line. When Quantrill reorganized his chain of command after the battle of Independence he was made a 2nd corporal,

In December 1864, Quantrill believed the war was played out in Missouri so he assembled thirty-three remaining men and headed for Kentucky by way of Arkansas and Tennessee. Burns was part of this contingent. He was captured in the vicinity of Harrodsburg in April of 1865 and sent to the prison at Louisville. After a short period of time he was released and returned to Missouri.

Commencing in 1866, Frank and Jesse James along with other ex-guerrillas started robbing banks. One source has stated that Burns was at the James gang's first robbery on February 13, 1866, at Liberty, Missouri. On May 22, 1867, at Richmond, Missouri, the Hughes and Wasson Bank was held up carried out by upwards of fourteen men. During the robbery Mayor John B. Shaw and three towns folks were killed in the hail of bullets associated with the robbery. Several former guerrillas were recognized among the bandits. They included Payne Jones, Andy McGuire, Ike Flannery, and Allen Parmer (Frank and Jesse James' brother-in-law), Tom Little, and Dick Burns. Little and McGuire would later be lynched by a mob for their participation, and Payne Jones would also be killed for his role.

Burns was found dead on November 29, 1867 at a farm owned by a Mr. Deering, located south of Independence, Missouri. One account stated he was found in an orchard, whereas a second account has claimed that the body was near a haystack. A witness described the scene saying, " . . . the next morning he was found with his head cleft in twain as though while he slept some powerful assassin had cloven it with an axe." His killer(s) were thought to be friends of Payne Jones. Supposedly, Burns had tipped ex-guerrilla Jim Chiles off about the possibility that Jones was planning to rob him. Burns and Chiles were close friends, with Chiles having once saved Burns' life. Burns' murder then was possibly Jone's retribution for spoiling the robbery plot.

QUANTRILL'S THIEVES By: Joseph K. Houts, Jr.

W M Burges
(William M., William McCown "Mack" Burgess)

William McCown "Mack" Burgess was born on January 6, 1838 in Kanawha County in what is now West Virginia. He was the second son of Reverend Garland A. and Henrietta H. McCown Burgess. Garland and Henrietta had five other children: Francis Marion, Mary Jane, Henrietta Elizabeth, Garland, and Julia A. Mack had been named after his mother's second cousin, William McCown. The family had extensive roots in America, commencing with William I. Burges, who arrived on the continent during colonial times prior to 1712. Originally, the Burgeses settled in Virginia 30 miles south of Washington, D.C. At some point, a second letter "s" was added to the end of their name, making it Burgess.

Garland Burgess, like his son William, was born in Kanawha County, Virginia on August 22, 1807. His father was Edward Burgess. He married Henrietta on August 30, 1831. In October 1837, he was ordained a minister of the Methodist Episcopal Church South. Prior to 1850, Garland moved to Post Oak Township and later to Centerview, Johnson County, Missouri, where he owned a farm in additon to being a preacher. The family entourage from Virginia also included a brother, Thomas N., and several of the McCowns from Henrietta's side.

On September 22, 1861, Garland died and was buried in the Old Smyrna Cemetery next to his church. In early 1862, the church was burned by Union militia under the command of Captain Thomas W. Houts. Henrietta along with Simon Taylor co-founded the Methodist Episcopal Church in 1867 to replace Garland's former sanctuary. On February 16, 1879, she died and was laid to rest beside him.

Little has been established concerning Mack's wartime experiences. In all probability he was at the battle of Pleasant Hill, Missouri on July 11, 1862 and other early skirmishes. Mack likely joined Quantrill after Union troops led a campaign against his family. On March 22, 1862 Captain Houts sent twenty men, led by Lieutenant J. M. Jewell, to a Mrs. Burgess' house located ten miles southeast of Warrensburg, Missouri. The lieutenant was to arrest several armed men hiding in her house. Once the house was surrounded, four men ran outside and commenced firing on Jewell's men. The Federals killed three of them, while losing one of their own, another Union soldier was wounded. Jewell and his men then proceeded to burn the house.

Several days later troops under Captain Houts burned Colonel McCown's house. In addition, they shot two brothers with the last name Burgess. The captain thereupon burned the Burgess house casting the family outdoors. It has remained unclear which Mrs. Burgess it was whose home was burned at the hands of Lieutenant Jewell, acting under the command of Houts. Likewise, it is unclear which Burgess brothers were the victims of Captain Houts' action. It has been speculated that Mrs. Burgess was the wife of one of Mack's brothers, either Garland or Francis Marion, or perhaps she was the wife of Mack's uncle Thomas. In any event, they were all family, including Colonel McCown.

Because of these atrocities, Mack either felt compelled to join Quantrill, either out of revenge or for his own protection. He was fortunate enough to survive the war. However, on October 2, 1865, he was shot and killed in an ambush after returning to Johnson County. Mack was buried in the Old Smyrna Cemetery with his father. Apparently, his murderers were never brought to justice. Reportedly, he had never married and therefore was childless.

W A Baker
(William H., Wm. H., W. H.)

William H. Baker was born in Tennessee in 1842. His parents were James C. and Maria L. Baker and he had one sister named Emma A. The family moved to Missouri prior to 1850 and settled in Johnson County, Jackson Township, located in the northwest quadrant of the county. In the 1850 census, James was listed as a farmer, but by 1860 he was a tailor by trade. Living in the same township at the time of the Civil War were eight other guerrillas on the Roster with him. They were Matthias Houx, Michael Moringstar Houx, Robert Washington Kavanaugh Houx, Robert Davenport, Charles A. Longacre, Otho Offutt, James R. Perdee, and Thomas D. Perdee. His regimental commander during the war, Jeremiah Vardaman Cockrell, also lived in Jackson Township.

Baker enlisted in the 16th Missouri Infantry in Johnson County. It was part of Major General Sterling Price's Division and in Parson's Brigade. Colonels Vardaman Cockrell and Jackman commanded the unit. Baker was a private in Company D that was under the command of Captain David M. Raker. Also serving in this company were nine other guerrillas set forth on the Roster, those being: Hugh L. W. Anderson; Obediah Strange Barnett; Lewis A. (Al) Cunningham; James Hamilton Cunningham; N. T. Doake; Charles A. Longacre; Henry Warren Ogden; and Henry C. Pemberton. In all probability he participated in the battle of Pleasant Hill, Missouri, July 11, 1862 and was at Lone Jack, Missouri, August 16, 1862; Prairie Grove, Arkansas, December 7, 1862; and Little Rock, Arkansas. Apparently, he was wounded and captured at the Little Rock engagement, where he was hospitalized and subsequently died on May 1, 1863.

Two factors of some bearing have been uncovered which have raised some question as to the actual William Baker whose name appears on the Roster. Most importantly, there were two other William H. Bakers from Johnson County. The first was William Baker, age 18, from Missouri, the fourth of seven children born of to Henry S. and Elizabeth Baker of Madison Township. The second was Wm. H. Baker, age 20, from Virginia, the first of eight children born of John and Myra Baker from the town of Rose Hill, also in Madison Township. Living in some proximity to him was David M. Raker, the future captain of Company D, 16th Missouri Infantry. However, Kansas Jayhawkers killed this William sometime during the war.

Among the three Johnson County William Bakers, it seems most likely that the William H. Baker who rode with the guerrilla chieftain William Clarke Quantrill was the one from Tennessee because the names of many of his neighbors appear on the Roster of original riders. In addition, Colonel Jeremiah Vardaman Cockrell lived close to this particular Baker.

The other factor that gives us a clue as to the true William Baker is found in his middle initial. On the Roster it was shown as "A", instead of "H". However, on a copy made of Captain Henry J. Stierlin's list, dated November 5, 1864, the name has William H. as opposed to A. as the initial. In examining the 1860 Johnson County Census, there is not a listing for a William A. Baker. Perhaps the "A" on the Roster may simply be attributed to poor penmanship. After all, an "H" could be mistaken for an "A" if the letters were slanted a certain way, or if one weren't too good at telling the difference between the two letters in the first place. By pinching the letter "H" at the top, it becomes an "A" in appearance. As with all facts obscured by the passage of time, those left to interpret the past must resort to speculation on occasion.

W H Butler
(William H., William)

William H. Butler was born around 1845. His place of birth was probably in Howard County, Missouri. The Adjutant General's office of the War Department in Washington D. C. has no record of him, however Union prisoner records have documentation of a Private William H. Butler in Company C of the 16th Missouri Infantry, Confederate States Army. In his application for a Confederate soldier's pension, dated June 13, 1913, he claimed to have been in Company A, commanded by Colonel Cummings, with Captain Smith as the company officer in charge. His application also stated he was not a member of a Confederate society and did not fight in any battles.

Union documents have Butler surrendering at New Orleans, Louisiana on May 26, 1865, as part of Major General E. Kirby Smith's army, followed by parole at Shreveport, Louisiana on June 8, 1865. Of some mystery, perhaps due to the passage of time and to Butler's advancing age, he wrote on his pension application that he was paroled at St. Louis, Missouri in June 1865. At the time of his pension request, he professed to be sixty-eight years old, living in Rocheport, Boone County, Missouri and having, "no property at all and no one to support me."

QUANTRILL'S THIEVES By: Joseph K. Houts, Jr.

G N Burnett
(George McKinley Barnett, George M, G. M.)

George McKinley Barnett was born on May 1, 1844 in Missouri. He was the third of eleven children born to George Harrison and Mary Frances Strange "Polly" Barnett. His father died in 1859, leaving his mother to run the family farm and raise the children. He enlisted in the Missouri State Militia on July 11, 1861 at the age of 17. Sometime in early 1862, he joined Quantrill's outfit. His older brother Obediah Strange also rode with Quantrill. In September 1862, he entered regular Confederate service assigned to William's 3rd Missouri Cavalry, Company A, commanded by Colonel Martin. At other times, he served under the commands of Mize and Cockrell.

Barnett was at the battles of Pleasant Hill, Missouri, July 11, 1862; Lawrence, Kansas, August 21, 1863; and Centralia, Missouri, September 27, 1864. He surrendered to Union military officials on either May 20 or 22, 1865 at Lexington, Missouri. George supported the South and probably joined Quantrill because Union troops had killed a brother, probably Columbus, burned his mother's house to the ground, stealing all her livestock and provisions, leaving her destitute.

Barnett believed in Quantrill's fabricated tale about why the guerrilla chieftain became a Confederate partisan. Quantrill had told many of his men that he was from Maryland, a fellow sister slave state. He and his brother first settled in Missouri, shortly before deciding to head for the California gold fields. While crossing Kansas, their camp was attacked by Jayhawkers, killing his brother and severely wounding him. He managed to survive and thereafter joined the same Jayhawker band, whereupon he systematically killed each of the attackers. In fact, Quantrill was from Canal Dover, Ohio, and simply ran amuck of the law in Kansas and turned on several of his compatriots during a raid on the Morgan Walker farm. Thenceforth, he became a transplanted Southern by necessity and, in time, assumed control of a home guard unit under the command of Morgan Walker's son, Andrew. This unit in time became the basis of his future guerrilla gang.

At the age of 87, Barnett vividly recounted many of his wartime experiences in the January 25, 1931 edition of the Topeka

<u>Daily</u>, imparting numerous particulars about the Lawrence Raid. Of note, he stated "They shot down men wherever we found them. We were accused of killing the women too, but we did not. I was sure of that – I was there." On being a guerrilla, Barnett explained "redlegs had come into Missouri ... and swept a wide swath for miles ... they took the small amount of federal money they found. We had been left only worthless Confederate notes."

    After the war, Barnett became a carpenter. On March 12, 1865, he married Missouri Emiline Barnett, who coincidentally had the same last name. The Barnetts eventually moved to Oklahoma. They became homesteaders in the land rush of 1889, living in Perry, Noble County, Oklahoma for twenty-one years. As a carpenter, he built houses in Perry. He was shot in a dispute over boundaries, however a pocket watch deflected the bullet preventing serious injury.

    In later years, the couple was admitted to the Confederate Home in Ardmore, Oklahoma. On May 17, 1932, Missouri Barnett died at the Home. George soon followed his wife of sixty-seven years, dying in a local hospital at 1:30 on Wednesday, September 25, 1932, as reported in the <u>Wichita Banner</u> of September 29, 1932. He had been ill for only a week before. Although he was a Baptist, the Reverend Fred Windsor of the Linwood Christian Church conducted the funeral. Services were on September 30 at 1:30 administered by the Byrd and Snodgrass Funeral Home. Interment was in the soldier's plot at the Rose Hill Cemetery Oklahoma Confederate Home at Ardmore under the supervision of the Harvey Douglass Funeral Home for the fee of $17.00. However, there has been one report that he was buried in Topeka, Kansas.

    George and Missouri had nine children; Mary Etna, Martha Elizabeth, Anna Lee, Georgia Alice, Minnie Myrtle, Dora Belle, Jennie Maud, Oscar Lee, and Ada Cleveland. There were only two surviving children at the time of his death, Mrs. Martha Elizabeth Bateman of Coyville, Kansas and Mrs. E. C. (Ada Cleveland) Davis of Portland, Oregon. Prior to his passing, Barnett stated the reason for his going to war, "It was certain, I thought, that I should go into battle and fight until I was killed. It all seemed hopeless – the odds were great; but there was no choice."

James Barnett
(James Monroe, Jim M. Barnett)

James Monroe Barnett was born in December 1843 in Lafayette County, Missouri. His father, Absolem Barnett, was born in Kentucky. It's been reported that as of 1860 Absolem was not a slave owner. Barnett married Esculania Evans and the union produced five children; Lee, Robert P., Samuel J., William Francis, and Dr. James J. They would also have two grandchildren, Lewis and Audra.

James enlisted in the 2nd Missouri Cavalry under General Joseph O. Shelby and fought in most of the battles that Shelby was engaged in. He was a private during the war and was paroled out of Confederate service at Shreveport, Louisiana, probably in 1865.

The reason for Barnett's early association with Quantrill has remained unknown. There were two other Barnetts on the muster roll, brothers Obediah Strange and George McKinley. Apparently the two brothers were no relation to James. In 1880, James Barnett's father passed away and was buried at Mt. Hope, Missouri. A year later in November 1881, James too died. Wife, Esculania, would live until 1908. Her parents were Levi and Narcissus Christian Evans, both from Bowling Green, Kentucky.

QUANTRILL'S THIEVES By: Joseph K. Houts, Jr.

O. S. Barnett
(Obediah Strange, Obediah S. Barnett)

    Obediah Strange Barnett was born on June 4, 1840 in Holden, Johnson County, Missouri to George Harrison and Mary Francis Strange "Polly" Barnett. He was the second of eleven children. Both of his parents had been born in Kentucky. Obediah received only a limited education as a youth. His brother George McKinley Barnett also rode with Quantrill.

    On August 14, 1862, Barnett enlisted as a private in Captain David Rakin's Company D, Parson's 16th Missouri Infantry Brigade, Price's Division under the command of Colonel Lewis. Barnett participated in battles of Prairie Grove, Arkansas, December 7, 1862; Helena, Arkansas, July 4, 1863; followed by Mansfield, Louisiana, April 8, 1864; then Pleasant Hill, Louisiana, April 9, 1864; and Willow Swamp, Arkansas. On May 25, 1865, he surrendered at Baton Rouge, Louisiana and was pardoned on June 8, 1865 at Shreveport, Louisiana. Upon returning to Missouri, he was administered the oath of allegiance at St. Louis, Missouri.

    Little has been documented concerning his association with Quantrill. He probably only rode with Quantrill briefly, prior to entering the regular Confederate Army. During the war his brother, George, purportedly had substituted for him. George had joined the Missouri State Militia (MSM) at age seventeen. Later, George entered regular Confederate service in September 1862 assigned to William's Company, a cavalry unit commanded by Colonel Martin.

    After the war, he became a farmer. His farm comprised 146 acres and was described as "pretty." On October 31, 1867, he married Martha Ann Key, the daughter of Gacy Key. She had been called "one of those rare human flowers." They had ten children and lived in the same area as Obediah's parents. His application to the Confederate Home in Higginsville, Missouri was approved on May 5, 1914. Apparently, he had fallen on bad financial times because the Home was for indigent Confederate veterans. His wife died July 16, 1925 and sometime afterwards he was expelled from the Home. He was found to have been a possible wartime deserter. Supposedly, he went to live with two of his children in Jackson County, Missouri. He died January 1, 1934 and was buried in the Confederate Cemetery at Higginsville next to his wife.

Obediah Strange and Martha Ann Key Barnett, 1913
Courtesy Marilyn Bailiff King and Kay Russell
Confederate Memorial State Historical Site, Higginsville, Missouri

Lee Ball
(Leander)

Leander Ball was born in Illinois in 1841. In the 1860 Jackson County, Missouri Federal Census he was listed as being employed as a laborer living in the vicinity of Lone Jack. In addition, the census showed that he had been married within the year. His wife's name was Nancy J, a fifteen year-old Missouri native. Living close by, with her seven children, was a Sarah Ball age thirty-nine. Sarah and four of the children had been born in Illinois also. The other three children were born in Missouri. She was possibly Leander's mother. Apparently, the family had moved to the state sometime prior to 1854, based on the ages of her children born in Missouri. Little has been found regarding Ball's war record. In all probability he was at the battle of Pleasant Hill, Missouri on July 11, 1862.

W M Bledsoe
(William M., Bill)

William M. Bledsoe was described as a "fat, jolly old guerrilla." Indeed, he was one of the more senior of his comrades, having been born in 1821. His father's name was Isaac with his mother's being unknown. Loving and Millicent Head Bledsoe were his paternal grandparents. Some might find a small bit of irony in a guerrilla's ancestor being named "Loving", since such a description would rarely be attributed to these irregular rebels.

George Bledsoe was the first of the line, journeying to America from England in 1652. As a result, there was a time when all of the Bledsoes in North America had the distinction of being related. In 1837 William married Mabel Melton. She was born in 1817, consequently she was four years his senior. They would have eight children named; Joel Joseph, John, Bi, Elizabeth, William Harvey, Charles Thomas, Mary Ann, and James Carrol.

Bledsoe was in the battles of Lone Jack, Missouri, August 16, 1862 and Baxter Springs, Kansas, October 6, 1863, where he was killed. In all probability, he was also at the battles of Pleasant Hill, Missouri, July 11, 1862; Independence, Missouri, August 11, 1862; and Lawrence, Kansas, August 21, 1863.

By May 1862, after having some near misses and several victories, the guerrillas were running short on munitions. Captain Quantrill accompanied by George Todd had been on a recent buying mission in Hannibal and St. Joseph, Missouri, where they procured 50,000 caps for their pistols. While riding in a carriage from St. Joseph to Kansas City, the coach was stopped by a Federal sentry. Seeing the problem before them, the two slipped out a side door and escaped to the Missouri River bank, which they followed in hopes of finding a safe place to cross and enter Jackson County. As if by pure coincidence, they stumbled onto Bledsoe and Andrew Blunt in a boat in the middle of the river fishing for catfish. They hailed them for assistance and safely made it to the other side, however without the caps which they had abandoned in their flight. The party then proceeded to Bledsoe's farm and hid out for a spell.

Bledsoe's death has been well documented, although one source has asserted that he may not have been killed at Baxter Springs, but instead he deserted and possibly went to Texas after the war. Most accounts have claimed otherwise, maintaining that he died while chasing Brigadier General James G. Blunt's bandwagon during the battle. He had pulled alongside and asked the solders, actually the musicians, inside to surrender. Their response was direct; they shot him off his saddle. Knowing he was mortally wounded, he beckoned Fletch Taylor to his side and said, "Fletch, that outfit have shot and killed me; take my two pistols and kill all of them." Following his dying friends instructions, Taylor pursued the wagon with several other guerrillas. In trying to flee, the wagon lost a wheel or broke an axle, which brought it to a stop, whereupon the musicians offered their surrender. However, it was too late for mercy and all were killed, including a 12-year old drummer boy. The guerrillas proceeded to set the wagon on fire and tossed the bodies into it. Sadly, the drummer boy was still alive, because afterwards he crawled on his belly thirty feet from the carnage, with his burning body leaving a trail of burnt grass.

Bledsoe's body was placed in a captured Union ambulance. In addition, John Koger was put in the back. Outside of Baxter Springs, the guerrillas stopped in order to bury thier fallen comrade. A Negro named Jack Mann had been captured as part of Blunt's entourage. He was ordered to dig two graves. Bledsoe was buried in the one and Mann was shot and thrown into the other, although, another source has claimed that Will Mcguire shot and killed Mann earlier. In March 1864, the guerrillas once again headed north to resume the war in Missouri. On passing through the Cherokee Nation, where Bledsoe had been buried the previous fall, they stopped by his grave to pay homage. Much to their disgust they found Bledsoe's and Mann's skeletons scattered about the ground, where they had been interned. The bodies had been dug up and eaten by "vultures and varmints."

In the fall of 1880 Bledsoe's widow Mabel moved to Texas. She settled near Van Alstyne on the Grayson-Collin County line. She died in 1892 of unknown causes. Prior to her passing it was said she had remarked that William had been a Northern sympathizer. However, the family thought that it was possible that his true loyalties had been misinterpreted. Given his association with the partisans, in all probability he was more of a Southerner than a Northerner.

W C Bell
(William C.)

William C. Bell became somewhat of an oddity after the Civil War. While many of Quantrill's former riders became outlaws and others quietly faded from view as simple law-abiding citizens, Bell established a reputation for himself as a pacifist. He was born in Missouri in 1840. His parent's names were Samuel R. and Sarah, both originally from Tennessee. The family moved to Missouri in the late 1830's. In the 1860 Jackson County, Missouri Federal Census both William and his father were listed as farmers. It can also be noted that he was the oldest of four siblings. The other children were named Tolmon, Keziah, and Susan C. Apparently at one time, he served in the 2nd Missouri Infantry, Company C, and the 6th Missouri Infantry, Company B. Most likely he was at the battle of Pleasant Hill, Missouri on July 11, 1862 and he was said to have participated in numerous engagements throughout Missouri and Arkansas. He was paroled in 1865.

After the war he returned to Jackson County, residing in the Sni-A-Bar Township. Although many former soldiers embraced ordinary lives from this point on, there were still rogue groups who at times spread terror about the land. In the autumn of 1871 a shooting occurred during a service at the Pink Hill M. E. Church. Three men died as a result of this incident. The residents of the area were outraged by this act and accordingly drafted a petition, which would be signed by ninety-nine men. As stated in the document, the undersigned opposed the "carrying of pistols and other deadly weapons in a peaceable community – believing as we do, that no necessity exists for any man so to arm himself, we regard the practice as destructive to the good morals of the young men and boys of our township, and productive only of evil, by setting bad examples as well as killing men." Both William and his father signed the appeal. It seems an extraordinary act for one of Quantrill's men to come out publicly against gunplay. What a difference a generation can have on society.

QUANTRILL'S THIEVES By: Joseph K. Houts, Jr.

J Bowers
(W. T., W. R., Joseph, Thomas B., Bower)

The true identity of the man named J. Bowers who rode with William Clarke Quantrill has remained something of a mystery. Records of several individuals named Bowers have been discovered. Which one of them was indeed the gang member is open to debate.

One of the suspects was a Joseph Bowers, age 34, who lived in Lexington, Missouri with his wife Caroline, age 30 and four children; Margaret, age 9; Mary A., age 7; Joseph H.; age 4; and William, age 1. He was born in Ireland, as was his spouse. His daughters were born in Pennsylvania, while his sons were born in Mississippi. The 1860 Lafayette County, Missouri Federal Census listed him as a laborer. Tracking the birth of his children one can assume that he first settled in Pennsylvania followed by Mississippi, arriving in Missouri prior to 1856. Bowers was in the 2nd Missouri Cavalry Regiment, assigned to Company G.

Another named that's surfaced in the search for the true identity of J. Bowers was that of a W T (sic) Bowers. There was not "J" Bowers on the original copy of Quantrill's muster roll but instead there was a W T Bowers. Since this was the actual roll, it can be argued there was not a "J" in the name. Adding credibility to the "W T" theory was the fact that there were two men with corresponding first names, a W. R. Bower and a Thomas B. Bowers, both serving in the Missouri Confederate Army. W. R. was in the 5th Missouri Cavalry Regiment, assigned to Company G and Thomas B. was in the 3rd Missouri Infantry Regiment, assigned to Company F. Possibly, W T was one of these individuals, or perhaps one and the same. The "T" in W T Bowers may have been Thomas. The "W" speaks for itself.

Unfortunately, none of the accompanying initials matched completely those of W T Bowers. The explanation for this variance could be traced to misspelling and the practice of phonetics in sounding out names. One other consideration has arisen which might have a bearing in that Otho Offutt, also on the Roster, was a corporeal in the same company as W. R. Bower and therefore may be the missing connection to Quantrill. There remains a final problem with this theory–"W. R. Bower" lacks the "s" as the final character. This could be reconciled though by simply attributing the discrepancy to misspelling.

    Whoever the real Bowers or Bower was may always remain unknown. Possibly those individuals who made the copies of the muster roll knew more about the Bowers' identity than the original writer since Union soldiers were transcribing it and may have had more precise information. A best guess, however, would be that W R Bower(s) is the true guerrilla. In reviewing the regimental movements of Joseph and Thomas B., most of their service was east of the Mississippi River. Accordingly, this fact would most likely remove these men from the guerrilla war in Missouri.

QUANTRILL'S THIEVES By: Joseph K. Houts, Jr.

James Cunningham
(James Hamilton, James L., J. L.)

     James Hamilton Cunningham was the first of eight children born to Henry Gibson and Mary Hammond Cunningham. He was born in Woodford County, Kentucky on May 5, 1839. Prior to the Civil War, probably in the early 1850's, the family moved to Johnson County, Missouri. The names of his siblings were John H., Lewis A., Nancy J., Henry G., Pelina, Julia A., and Elizabeth B. Through his father's ancestral lines he was related to Daniel Boone and had several relatives who fought in the Revolutionary War, as well as the War of 1812. Apparently, after the war, Cunningham married Susan Jeannette Carmichael who was from the Holden, Missouri area. Their marriage begot five children: Carrie, Stella Mary, Cornelia, James Hamilton and Henry Allen.

     Cunningham enlisted early in the war, sometime in 1861. On August 1, 1862, he joined General Sterling Price's division in the 16th Missouri Infantry, Parson's Brigade, assigned to Company D commanded by Captain David Raker, under Colonels Vardaman Cockrell, Lewis, Jackman and Cummins. He served as a private. At one point he also served under General Van Dorn.

     James was at the battles of Wilson's Creek, Missouri, August 10, 1861; Pea Ridge, Arkansas, March 6-8, 1862; Independence, Missouri, August 11, 1862; Lone Jack, Missouri, August 16, 1862, where wounded; Prairie Grove, Arkansas, December 7, 1862; Helena, Arkansas, July 4, 1863; Little Rock, Arkansas, September 10, 1863; Mansfield, Louisiana, April 8, 1864; Jenkin's Ferry, Arkansas, April 30, 1864; and Springfield, Louisiana. On June 8, 1865, he surrendered and was paroled out of the service at Shreveport, Louisiana.

     Little is known of Cunningham after the war. He returned to Missouri and lived the remainder of his life in Johnson County. On June 4, 1880, he died and was buried in the Carmichael Cemetery along side his daughter, Stella Mary, who died on February 8, 1878. His wife, Susan, outlived him by 40 years, dying on June 21, 1920 in DeSoto, Missouri.

His daughter, Carrie, recounted much of the family's history. She noted James' father had been a Democrat in 1860 and supposedly voted for Breckenridge for President. James was not a slave owner, although his father owned many. On a sad note, Carrie related how James' father-in-law, Pleasant Carmichael, had been killed in the war at the battle of Iuka, Mississippi while serving as a courier in the Confederate Army.

A L Cunningham
(Lewis A., Al, Albert, Abe, Ab)

Lewis A. "Al" Cunningham was described as "the man who fought as a lion…" It was claimed he died while raiding a German settlement in Lafayette County, Missouri with fellow guerrilla David Pool. Upon his death, it was noted "if he had a crime it was the pitiless patriotism of his conscience." Although his demise was well documented by John N. Edwards in his book <u>Noted Guerrilla</u>, such was not his true fate during the Civil War. In fact, he survived the conflict dying years later in Appleton City, Missouri. In several instances guerrillas were mistakenly identified as among the vanquished, only to actually survive the war and live out normal lives. Apparently, Al Cunningham was one of those confused casualties who in reality lived to see another day.

Cunningham was born in Kentucky in 1843. His parents were Henry Gibson and Mary Hammond Cunningham. He was the third of eight children, who were named: James Hamilton, John H., Nancy J., Henry G., Pelina, Julia A., and Elizabeth B. Cunningham's father was a slave owner at the start of the Civil War. The family moved to Johnson County, Missouri sometime in the early 1850's. Through his father's side of the family, he was related to Daniel Boone. In addition, various ancestors had served in the military during the Revolutionary War and the War of 1812. His older brother, James H. Hamilton, also rode with Quantrill and later enlisted in the regular Confederate Army.

On August 1, 1862 in Johnson County, Cunningham joined the 16th Infantry of General Sterling Price's Division. He was in Company D under Captain David Raker, Parson's Brigade, Commanded by Colonels Jackson, Lewis, Vardaman Cockrell and Cummins. Cunningham achieved the rank of corporal. Prior to and during his regular Confederate service, he rode at various times with Quantrill, where on one occasion he was wounded. Cunningham was at the battles of Lone Jack, Missouri, August 11, 1862; Prairie Grove, Arkansas, December 7, 1862; Helena, Arkansas, July 4, 1863; Little Rock, Arkansas,

QUANTRILL'S THIEVES By: Joseph K. Houts, Jr.

September 10, 1863; Mansfield, Louisiana, April 8, 1864; Jenkins Ferry, Arkansas, April 30, 1864; and Springfield, Louisiana. On June 9, 1865, he surrendered and was pardoned at Shreveport, Louisiana. He had never been captured during the war.

On Christmas day, 1862, Cunningham was part of a raiding party consisting of George Todd, Cole Younger, Fletch Taylor, George Clayton and Zach Traber. The plan was to seek out six soldiers in Kansas City, who had been responsible for the death of Cole's father, Colonel Henry Younger. The party dressed in Federal uniforms and wore large, loosely buttoned overcoats in which to conceal their weapons. The group entered the city around dusk and proceeded to hunt for their prey. They were confronted by numerous soldiers celebrating the day's merriment in the town's many saloons. Close to midnight the guerrillas found their men in a tavern. After scouting the premises they had a drink and then positioned themselves next to the soldiers who were sitting at two tables playing cards. Upon saying the signal-phrase "who said drink!" the guerrillas shot them through the side of their heads. All died instantly, with one of the victims tightly holding his unplayed cards. The gang escaped and hid at guerrilla Ruben Harris' farm.

After the war, little has been recorded as to Cunningham's life. Whether he married and had a family remains unknown. However, what was well known, was that he had "...carried the torch of the guerrilla name through all the border counties of Kansas and Missouri."

W Collesure
(W., William, Colclasier, Colelesure, Colglazier)

     W. Colclasier may have been the brother of Thomas Colclasier whose name appears next to his on Quantrill's Roster of original riders. Thomas was from Clay County, Missouri and had been born in Missouri. He was 16 years old in 1860. His mother's name was Lidia and he had a brother named Samuel, age eleven. Her place of birth was Kentucky and Samuel and his brother were both born in Missouri. Colclasier may not have been present when the enumerator came by collecting data for the Clay County Census of 1860, which may have explained why his name does not appear. He was in all probability at the battle of Pleasant Hill, Missouri on July 11, 1862.

Thomas Collesure
(T., Colclasier, Colelesure, Colglazier)

Thomas Colclasier was born in Missouri in 1844. His mother's name was Lidia and she was born in Kentucky. According to the Clay County, Missouri 1860 Federal Census, he also had a brother named Samuel, age eleven. Also, on the Roster was a W., or probably a William Colclasier. He was unaccounted for in the census, but could have been a brother or close of kin to Thomas. As with most all the other guerrillas on the Roster he most likely was at the battle of Pleasant Hill, Missouri on July 11, 1862.

QUANTRILL'S THIEVES By: Joseph K. Houts, Jr.

Kit Chiles
(Christopher Lillard Chiles)

Christopher Lillard "Kit" Chiles was the sixth of ten children. He was born in 1835 to Christopher Lillard and Rachael Davis Chiles. His place of birth was Jackson County, Missouri. The family had migrated to Missouri from Kentucky prior to 1830. At the start of the Civil War, he was living near Sibley, Missouri with his mother. Two of his brothers, Richard Ballinger "Dick" Chiles and William H. "Billy" Chiles, also rode with Quantrill.

Serving as a lieutenant under Colonel B. F. Parker, he and a gang of forty raided Liberty, Missouri on March 14, 1862. They captured several Federal troops attached to the recruiting office of Colonel W. R. Penick.

During the battle of Pleasant Hill, Missouri on July 11, 1862, his horse was shot out from under him while he was riding along side Cole Younger. Crying out, he was quoted saying, "I'm gone." However, Younger reassured him by saying, "No; courage Kit." Cole stopped and pulled Chiles from underneath the dead mount. The two then shared his horse in their flight from the scene amongst a rain of enemy bullets.

On August 11, 1862 at the outset of the fighting for Independence, Missouri, he was killed leading a charge into the town square. Chiles was shot by troops led by Captain W. H. Rodewald, who was guarding the command center of Lieutenant Colonel James T. Buel. Chiles' horse was again shot out from under him, only this time he met the same fate as his steed. He was the first fatality. The day's confrontation would end in a victory for Quantrill, with Federal casualties of twenty-six killed and seventy-four wounded. After being pardoned, Buel and his men had to walk back to the district's Federal military headquarters in Kansas City, Missouri.

On October 6, 1862 his brother Dick would be killed in a skirmish with Captain Daniel David outside Sibley. He was shot in both lungs. David had been on a campaign purging the area of guerrillas. Years later after the war Billy too would meet a violent death. Apparently, he had taken part in the 1867 attempted bank robbery at Savannah, Missouri led by Melvin Bond. Participating in the holdup were former bushwhackers Archie Clements, John Jarrette, Ol and George Shepard. For his part in the Savannah bank robbery Billy Chiles was hung in his mother's barn located on the Jackson and Lafayette county lines on January 28, 1870.

QUANTRILL'S THIEVES By: Joseph K. Houts, Jr.

Samuel Clifton
(Samuel L., Sam)

Samuel Clifton was born on January 4, 1833. He fought at the battles of Independence, Missouri, August 11, 1862 and Lawrence, Kansas, August 21, 1863. In May 1863, outside Blue Springs, Missouri his gang, along with those of Reid, Jarrette, Todd, and Younger were consolidated with Quantrill and his riders. These combined forces increased the outfit's size to between 125 and 150 men.

On the way to raid Lawrence, Clifton was given the gruesome task of killing Joseph Stone, who had been responsible for George W. Todd's, 2nd Lieutenant, earlier arrest in an affair at Independence. Stone's farm was located outside of Lawrence. The guerrillas had stumbled upon Stone's farm by accident on their approach to Lawrence. Todd wanted to shoot Stone, but Quantrill opposed the idea because the raiders were close to Lawrence and the discharge might alert the town's inhabitants to their presence. Upon Todd's order, Clifton clubbed the man to death with a Sharp's carbine. In watching the execution, guerrilla Frank Smith became so sickened by the sight that he nearly fell off his horse. By the time the events in Lawrence had fully transpired such an act of carnage would be considered common place. Clifton had been selected to kill Stone because he was relatively new to the gang and they were suspicious about his loyalty. Accordingly, his killing of Stone was meant as a test of his true colors. To say the least, he passed the test.

After the war, he resided in Kansas City, Missouri, where he eventually married and had a family. In 1880, he was a Kansas City policeman. He also worked as a bartender for Krist Koller. On August 27, 1894, Clifton died at his home located at 18th and Indiana streets in Kansas City of Bright's Disease. A disease affecting the kidneys characterized by albumin in the urine. Specifically, the kidney's filtering process has malfunctioned causing the body to retain water, which has the result of bringing on congestive heart failure. His funeral service was held at police headquarters on 12th and Grand, followed by burial in the Union Cemetery. Joe Clifton, his son, would follow in his father's footsteps as a lawman. In 1909 he was the inside jailer for the Jackson County jail at Independence, Missouri.

Wm Chamblin
(William)

William Chamblin has the dubious honor of being the only guerrilla on William Clarke Quantrill's Roster of original riders, where nothing can be found as to his existence. As with many of the other guerrillas, where little has been uncovered concerning their background, it can be assumed he was probably at the battle of Pleasant Hill, Missouri on July 11, 1862.

QUANTRILL'S THIEVES By: Joseph K. Houts, Jr.

Syrus Cockrell
(Synes, Silas, Simon N., Uncle Si)

Simon N. Cockrell was born in March 1801 at Petersburg, Tazewall County, Virginia. His father was Joseph Cockrell. His mother's name has remained unknown. She died early on in their marriage. In 1805, Joseph moved to Kentucky. He married a second time to Sally Hunt and out of this union one son, Alexander, was born in Breathitt County, Kentucky. Alexander would become a founding father of Dallas, Texas. His wife, Sarah Horton, would become one of the richest widows in the state.

During the war of 1812, Joseph served in the Kentucky company of Captain Samuel R. Combs and the regiment of Richard M. Johnson. The elder Cockrell would marry for a third wife, Nancy Ellis, on January 8, 1818 in Floyd, Kentucky. In 1831, he moved to Johnson County, Missouri and remained there until his death on November 3, 1837. His estate consisted of several chattels, including "a Negro blacksmith and Harry Man Jack". In probating his will, only the children of Nancy Ellis were mentioned as heirs, with some of his children claiming he had never been previously married. Joseph and Nancy Cockrell had eight children, most notably Francis Marion Cockrell, future Confederate General and United States Senator, and Jeremiah Vardaman Cockrell, future Confederate Colonel and a member of the United States House of Representative in the 52nd and 53rd congresses.

Simon Cockrell had a very adventurous life. In his early years he moved from Virginia to Kentucky and then to Johnson County, Missouri. At the age of thirty-two he moved to Texas, where he remained except for a few interludes. He served under Sam Houston during the Texas Revolution and fought at the deciding battle of San Jacinto. Afterwards, Cockrell became a homesteader, while at the same time fighting Indians and Mexican desperados. With the Mexican War, he again became a soldier, serving under Generals Scott and Taylor.

At the outbreak of the Civil War, and the age of sixty, Simon returned to Missouri and served the South in various capacities. In December 1861, he along with Matthias Houx, also on the List and apparently a friend, were responsible for saving the public records of Johnson County. Helping in the effort were Houx's wife and Deputy Recorder A. M. Perry (sic, N. W. or Nathan Washington). Fearing "marauding bands" would destroy these documents, Perry was sent from General Price's army to assist Circuit Clerk and County Recorder Colonel James McCown in securing them. Around midnight, thirty-five books and a sizable lot of loose court papers were put in a dry goods box and two empty barrels. Simon and Matthias hauled them away in a wagon. After driving around in order to disguise the wagon's trail, they hid them in the attic of Matthias' Aunt Polly. Reportedly, both men were at risk because they had been "dodging Federal men". Returning later, the two buried the records in a densely wooded thicket, believing it a better sanctuary.

Afterwards, Mrs. Houx would visit the location to make sure that everything was in good order. On one occasion, the wind had blown the cover off, followed by a rain that soaked the contents. She and Aunt Polly dried the records in the sun before depositing them back into the box. Another time she and her son were stopped by Federals while en route to a routine inspection of the site. The soldiers suspected her of knowing where the guerrillas had stashed gunpowder. Come to find out, she was apprised of the powder's whereabouts, but managed to throw them off track.

Outside of these occurrences and except for random inspections, the records lay undisturbed at this location until July 1865. By this year in the conflict, hostilities had begun to subside and most of the guerrillas were dead, or had surrendered, or had been granted amnesty. For all purposes, the war was over. Now satisfied that the documents would be safe, the parties who originally hid them took the records back to the courthouse.

Cockrell was at the Battle of Lone Jack, Missouri on August 16, 1862 and was credited with being instrumental in the victory. In addition, he operated as a recruiter in Missouri and was responsible for the enlistment of 400 men for Major General Sterling Price's army. His half brother, Colonel Jeremiah Vardaman Cockrell, was one of several Confederate officers placed in charge of recruiting for Missouri by Major General Thomas L. Hindman in the summer of 1862. Colonel Cockrell was also one of the commanding officers at the Battle of Lone Jack. In all probability, Simon returned to

Missouri in order to assist his two half brothers, Francis and Jeremiah. During the war he reportedly married, in July 1863, at Chapel Hill, Missouri.

It has been documented that a S. Cockrell, claiming to be a Confederate Colonel, wrote a letter of protest to Union Major General Samuel J. Curtis. The date of the letter was February 7, 1863. The letter protested the Union army's "scorched earth" policy and the "no quarter" given to unarmed men. Cockrell challenged Curtis to abate these actions by publishing an order to such effect in the newspaper Republication. Otherwise, he would direct his men to ride under "a black flag" and show "no quarter" themselves. He stressed that he and his men were regular army, not guerrillas. However, if the Union command persisted in the illegality of their conduct of the war, then they would become relentless in their actions.

After the war Cockrell returned to Texas and was said to have lived a quiet life. Although, he was married and had children, all were dead by 1899. He was a widower for almost fifty years. An article in the Weekly Standard newspaper of Warrensburg Missouri, reported that he was still alive at the age of 98. Cockrell was described as one of Texas' few remaining pioneers and despite his age "... he does not show its infirmities. His step is firm, and he reads and shoots without glasses...He lives in the present, believes in progress and thinks the latest improvements the best."

During the war, he became a close friend of Allen Parmer, also one of Quantrill's guerrillas. It was noted that at the age of 98 he would still travel alone great distances. He had no home and journeyed widely about the state visiting and residing with relatives. While passing through Coryrell County, Texas, on such a trip he was said to be on his way to Fisher County some 400 miles away, next to the New Mexico border. He was making the journey in a two-horse wagon in which he slept in at night. He lived off the land for his food. Cockrell spent two days in the county visiting his old friend Parmer. Accompanying him were a double-barreled shotgun and a Winchester rifle. As sport, he spent his spare time shooting plover and jackrabbits. Cockrell was called "Uncle Si" by his older friends and it was stated he would "...be among the very last of the Texas pioneers to pass away."

W F Cheatham (Dead)
(William F., William)

  William F. Cheatham was listed as deceased on William Clarke Quantrill' Roster of original riders. Since the Roster was made either before the battle of Pleasant Hill, Missouri on July 11, 1862, or on the very day of the battle, it can be assumed his death preceded this engagement. His fellow soldiers may have placed him on this list as a point of honor, beyond this theory little explanation can be given for his name appearing on the document.

  There was a William Cheatham listed in William's Regiment in Company F. The commander of the brigade was Lieutenant Colonel D. A. Jackman, serving in General Joseph O. Shelby's Division. Possibly, this individual was one and the same as William F. or W. F. Cheatham.

QUANTRILL'S THIEVES By: Joseph K. Houts, Jr.

W. H. Campbell
(William H.)

William H. Campbell was born in Missouri in 1842. His parents were Colin C. and Lucy Ann Campbell and he was the first of six children. The names of his siblings were Colin C., Alexander, George W., Emma, and John V. The entire Campbell household was from Missouri, except for Mr. Campbell who was from Pennsylvania. In the 1860 Johnson County Census, his father was listed as a physician.

At the start of the Civil War, Campbell enlisted under the command of Major General Sterling Price. In all likelihood, he was at the battle of Pleasant Hill, Missouri on July 11, 1862 and at this time was associated with guerrilla chieftain William Clarke Quantrill. Unfortunately, his wartime experiences have remained a blank. Apparently, in 1865 he went to Mexico with General Price and other former Confederate officers. Campbell was reported to have been associated with Generalissimo Maximillian, France's self-imposed dictator in its bid to re-colonize the New World. Afterwards in 1876, he participated in the Cuban revolution. Following his many years as a warrior or possibly a mercenary, he purportedly spent his retirement years as an artist of some notoriety.

It should be pointed out that there were two other W. Campbell's living in Johnson County, Missouri in 1860. Both men resided in Madison Township and were listed as farm hands in the 1860 census. The first one was named William H., age 21, with his place of birth being Kentucky. The second one was named Wilson A., age 29, wife's name Louisa Hodges, with his place of birth being Missouri. Wilson served with the 16th Missouri Infantry, which was formed in Johnson County on August 1, 1862.

Although either of these men could be a close match, the Campbell who rode with Quantrill was born in 1842, thereby eliminating the other contenders. Also, it seems unlikely that Wilson would have had the opportunity to participate in so many other wars and revolutions. Being a married man his family responsibilities probably would have required him to stay closer to home. Only an unmarried person, being free of attachments, would have been able to roam about the continent in support of various causes. The William H. Campbell who was born in 1842 remained unmarried.

J J R Dejarnatt
(James R., J. Q. R., I. J. K., J. K., Dejarnatte, Dejarnette, Dejarnett)

James R. Dejarnnett was listed as a member of the 10th Missouri Cavalry Regiment, assigned to Company D. John D. Brinker, William M. Haller, John Terry, Robert W. Houx, and William Doores were also both in this regiment and listed on the Roster of William Clarke Quantrill's original 93 riders. He was in all likelihood at the battle of Pleasant Hill, Missouri on July 11, 1862.

QUANTRILL'S THIEVES By: Joseph K. Houts, Jr.

Robert Davenport
(Bob)

Robert Davenport was born in 1838 outside Columbus, Johnson County, Missouri. His mother, Lucinda, was born in Kentucky and reported to be a farmer in 1860. In addition to Robert, there were three other children: Anne, Lawrence, and Rebecca F. Their farm was located next to guerrilla chieftain Matthias Houx. This in part may have explained Robert's early association with Quantrill.

On January 17, 1862, Kansas Jayhawkers and redlegs set Mrs. Davenport's home on fire and proceeded to plunder the Columbus community. Several other farms were burned, leaving the town devastated. As part of the pillage, slaves were stolen. Among the many tragedies, two small children were cast out into the snow. They stood by and watched their house burn to the ground. Later, on June 17, 1862, Mrs. Davenport was again visited by hostile elements. In a report filed by Major Emery S. Foster, it was stated that Lieutenant Sandy Lowe, Company G of the Seventh Missouri State Militia (MSM) advanced upon her home. A group of nine guerrillas were at her house. The militia attacked, killing two and departed with several horses and some arms. A fight ensued which resulted in the militia being surrounded by upwards of 150-200 bushwhackers. It was reported that two men were savagely mutilated, with one sustaining over a dozen shots and his head mangled. Returning to Mrs. Davenport's, the premises were empty, but a large table had been set with numerous provisions prepared and bundled together. Lowe then proceeded to burn the house.

As a result of these events, Davenport most likely joined the guerrillas seeking protection and retribution. On August 1, 1862, he enlisted into regular Confederate service by joining the 16th Missouri Infantry in Johnson County, Missouri. He was assigned to General Sterling Price's Division, Parson's Brigade, in Captain David Raker's Company D under the command of Colonel Vard Cockrell, Colonel Jackman, Colonel Lewis and Colonel Cummins. Davenport was made a 1st Sergeant and fought at the battle of Lone Jack, August 16, 1862; Prairie Grove, Arkansas, December 7, 1862; Helena, Arkansas, July 4, 1863; Little Rock, Arkansas, September 1863; Jackson's Ferry; Mansfield April 8, 1864; and Springfield, Louisiana. On June 9, 1865, he was paroled out of the army as a 3rd Lieutenant at Shreveport, Louisiana. His promotion came when 3rd Lieutenant Wm. W. Murrey died. After the war, Davenport moved to Texas where he died.

N F Doke
(William T., W. T., W.J. Doake, Doak)

William T. Doak lived in Rose Hill, Johnson County, Missouri, at the start of the Civil War. He was born in 1830 and was listed as a farmer in 1860. His place of birth was Missouri. His wife's name was Jane and in the 1860 Johnson County Census they were shown to have four children living at home: Josephine, Martha, Henry, and Francis. Reportedly his parents, Alexander A. and Mary A. Campbell, were not slaveholders, although a brother, John Alexander, owned one.

Early in the war, Doak served with Quantrill, but on August 1, 1862 enlisted into regular Confederate service. Doak joined the 16th Missouri infantry in Parson's Brigade under General Sterling Price's Division. As a private, he was in Captain David M. Raker's Company D. Doak fought at the battles of Lone Jack, Missouri, August 16, 1862, and at Prairie Grove, Arkansas, December 7, 1862. He had three brothers who joined Price and also served with him in Company D of the 16th Missouri Infantry. Joining him in this company were eight other guerrillas listed on Quantrill's Roll of original guerrillas: H. C. Pemberton, Harry Ogden, Hugh L. W. Anderson, William H. Baker, James Cunningham, Al Cunningham, Charles A. Longacre, and James Thompson. His other brother, Hall, was killed at the Battle of Wilson's Creek, Missouri on August 10, 1861. A sister named Sarah had assisted Captain Raker during the war and married him afterwards. The relationship between Sarah and Raker may account for why her four brothers enlisted simultaneously as a family.

Apparently, Doak and two of his brothers were either wounded at the battle of Prairie Grove or became sick shortly thereafter. All three were confined to a hospital in Little Rock, Arkansas. On March 9, 1863 he died while still a patient there. His brothers, N. F. and Samuel, died in the same hospital. N. F. died on February 14, 1863, followed by Samuel on March 1 of the same year. The last of the brothers, John, although wounded once during the war, was still alive in 1924 and was residing in Holden, Missouri. Commenting on the fate of his family during the war, he was quoted saying, "Five of us brothers went into service. One was killed at Wilson's Creek in battle, three died in Little Rock, Arkansas and I only, survived the war."

J N Dickers
(John B., W., M., Dickey)

John B. Dickey was born in 1840 with his place of birth being Kentucky. According to the 1860 Jackson County Census there were four other Dickey households in Independence, Missouri, in addition to the John B Dickey household. Another John Dickey headed one of them; he was listed as a wagon maker, age 49. There also was an Elizabeth Dickey from Kentucky, age 46, and she owned two slaves. She may have been John Dickey the wagon maker's estranged wife. It is possible that the two of them were John B. Dickey's parents. The senior Dickey could have been the real rider on Quantrill's Roster, although it would more likely be John B. because of his youth. The other Dickeys were from Kentucky, except for a Thomas Dickey who was from North Carolina, although his wife, Mary H., was from Kentucky. Therefore, it could be suggested that they were all part of one large transplanted family. The census listed John B. being employed as a clerk.

The record of Dickey's early years remains somewhat of a mystery. He was in all probability at the battle of Pleasant Hill, Missouri on July 11, 1862 and was said to have been part of Andy Blunt's gang.

In 1862 Dickey apparently moved to Miami, Missouri in Saline County. While in residence, he became a close friend of Judge Robert G. Smart, who had moved from Jackson County because of his Southern sympathies. The judge had owned ten slaves and was fearful of losing them to raiding Kansas Jayhawkers. Unfortunately for the judge, a company of Federal troops killed him. Two men named Walker and Ricehouse had at one time been in the Confederate Army, but after a short while they left and returned to Miami stating that they were now in support of the Northern cause. As proof of their newfound loyalty, they went to Bonneville and told a contingent of Union soldiers that Judge Smart was giving shelter to guerrillas. Without verifying the story, the soldiers rode to his house arriving at dawn on July 20, 1862. Seeing the approaching column, Smart ran out the back door of his house only to be swarmed upon and gunned down while attempting to surrender. Purportedly, he was struck by three bullets and died instantly. The soldiers on their return to Bonneville stopped at a farmer's house to have breakfast and in the process spoke of the incident. The farmer advised them that they had been duped, upon which they "expressed great regret that the mistake had been made, and that they had come at all."

Dickey vanished sometime in March of 1863, only to reappear as a lieutenant under the command of Blunt. The guerrillas rode into Miami and immediately sought out Walker and Ricehouse. Upon finding them the two were taken captive. The guerrillas then proceeded east a few miles from town and stopped at a farmer's house for dinner. Later the farmer noted he did not know that Walker and Ricehouse were prisoners because of their "good humor". After leaving, the band journeyed about two miles northwest of Edmonson Creek at which point they threw ropes around the prisoner's necks and then flung them over a tree limb. They begged for mercy but their pleas went unheeded. Blunt's men next engaged in target practice by filling the dangling corpses full of bullets. Eventually the bodies were unstrung and buried. Years after the war the skeletons were dug up and buried in the town cemetery. Dickey bore the large part of the responsibility for avenging his friend Judge Smart's death. Sad to say, several months later Dickey would meet the same fate as his friend in a skirmish on the boundary of Saline and Lafayette Counties. To his credit, he killed several of the attackers and severely wounded four others before falling victim to the enemy bullets.

M H Doors
(W. M., W. H., William E., Doores)

     W. M. Doores was supposedly a doctor at the time of his association with William Clarke Quantrill and his guerrilla band. His early life, and his life after the war, has remained a mystery. He was listed on Quantrill's Roster next to Jere F. Doores, who may have been a brother or some other relation. Jere was killed at the battle of Pleasant Hill, Missouri on July 11, 1862. In the Jackson County, Missouri 1860 Federal Census, there was a listing for a F. and Sarah O. Doores, age 54 and 59, respectively. W. M. Doors was not listed in the census, but he may have been away at medical school or simply absent for some other reason. Jere may have been F. and Sarah O.'s son, but he was not listed in the census as a member of their household. He may have already been living on his own at the time.

     There was a William E. Doores from Johnson County, Missouri in the 10th Missouri Cavalry Regiment assigned to Company E. In 1860, he was living with James, Amanda, and Emma Doors/Doores. A fact of some interest, and as a potential connection, is that six other guerrillas on the Roster were in his regiment. They were John D. Brinker, William M. Haller, John H. Terry, James R. Dejarrette, Robert Houx, and James Oliphant. Possibly, the initial "E" was listed incorrectly and should have been an "M". In all likelihood, Doores was at the battle of Pleasant Hill.

J F Doores
(Jeremiah F., Jerre T., Doors)

Jeremiah F. Doores was born in Kentucky in 1839. According to the 1860 Jackson County Census his parents in all likelihood were F. and Sarah O. Doores with his father's place of birth being Virginia and his mother's Kentucky. He was the second of four children. His siblings were named Elizabeth, James E., and Nancy B. Jeremiah's last name was spelled Doors, probably a misspelling by the census taker in the process of transcription. In 1860, he was listed as a laborer residing with the Patience Conn family in Lone Jack.

The date of Doores's association with William Clarke Quantrill was probably in the spring of 1862. He was at the battle of Pleasant Hill, Missouri on July 11, 1862. At the climax of the fight on the Sears farm, he received a mortal wound while trying to escape the onslaught of Union troops. A bullet went through his knee while he was in the process of mounting his horse and he bled to death. Two other Roster guerrillas, John Hampton and Ezra Moore, were also killed either during the conflict, or in the process of fleeing.

Noah Estes
(Estis)

    Noah Estes was born in either 1835 or 1836 with his place of birth being North Carolina. In 1860 there was a grouping of Estes families listed in the Federal census. Four of the five families were of North Carolina extraction. Estes was listed as one of them. Two sets lived in close proximity to each other. First, Noah age 25, and Richard age 30, resided within the same tract, followed by Micajah age 35 and Richard age 59, residing in close proximity to each other. In all probability, Richard was the father and the other three were brothers attending to their own farms, or in Noah's case working as a farm laborer. Richard was married to Delpha age 58 and in their household resided three children, Daniel, Mary, and Alvis. The other Estes was named Yelvington age 29 and she had been born in Kentucky as was the younger Richard's wife, Martha A., and the seven year old son of Micajah, named William. Possibly, Yelvington was a daughter, daughter-in-law, cousin, or niece to the other Estes families.

    Brothers Daniel and Alvis also fought for the South. Daniel enlisted in 1862 in Jackson County, serving in Clark's regiment, Ruffner's Battery, commanded by General Parsons. Alvis served with Quantrill, but was killed before July 11, 1862. Noah joined Colonel Upton Hays' command as a private and was at the battle of Lone Jack, Missouri, on August 16, 1862. He was captured at Linn Creek, Camden County, Missouri by Major O. Halleran, on January 6, 1863. Estes was incarcerated in the Gratiot Street Prison in St. Louis, Missouri.

    Noah's death has been recorded as February 18, 1863. The cause of death was listed as Rubella or "German Measles." The body was laid to rest in the Jefferson Barracks National Cemetery, St. Louis, Missouri and can be located in Section 20, grave 4759.

QUANTRILL'S THIEVES   By: Joseph K. Houts, Jr.

J G Freeman
(James G.)

James G. Freeman was born in 1834 with his place of birth being North Carolina. In the 1860 Johnson County Census, he was listed as a farmer living in Post Oak Township. His wife's name was Sarah C., who was born in Tennessee around 1837. They had four children named Wesly, age eight; George, age six; James C., age four; and Martha A., age two. Wesly and George were born in Illinois, with James and Martha being born in Missouri. The household moved to the state sometime before 1856 and was the only Freeman's living in the county in 1860. He probably participated in the battle of Pleasant Hill, Missouri on July 11, 1862. Living in the same township with Freeman were William Mc. Burgess and F. M. Robertson/Robinson, also on Quantrill's Roster of original guerrillas.

J H George
(John Hicks, Hix)

John Hicks George was born on March 24, 1838 outside Oak Grove, Jackson County, Missouri. His parents were David C. and Nancy E. Bates George. His father was born on July 8, 1798, a native of Kentucky. He was murdered on February 15, 1863 because of his sympathy with the South. His mother was from Tennessee and was born on January 10, 1808 and died on April 5, 1888. In 1860, he married Lavisa Adeline White, born June 18, 1841 in Jackson County. She died on April 22, 1920 in Oak Grove. Lavisa's father was John White of Tennessee, born in 1809, and her mother was Annie Burns, who died within the vicinity of Oak Grove in 1851. Six children would be born to John and Lavisa: John N., Dr. John H., Callie M. Middleton, Gilbert W., Arthur W., and Melvie C. Carrell. In 1860, he was a farmer and did not own any slaves, although his father owned one.

On June 14, 1862 in Jackson County, he enlisted in Company C of the Second Missouri Cavalry commanded by Colonel Upton Hays. Early in the war, George was hung by Federal troops searching for Quantrill. Miraculously though, he survived the experience and apparently it gave him good reason to join the guerrillas. He fought at the battles of Pleasant Hill, Missouri, July 11, 1862; Independence, Missouri, August 11, 1862; Cane Hill, Arkansas, November 28, 1862; Prairie Grove, Arkansas, December 7, 1862; Lawrence, Kansas, August 21, 1863; Baxter Springs, Kansas, October 6, 1863; Mark's Mills, Arkansas, April 25, 1864; and Jefferson City, Missouri, October 7, 1864. During these many engagements, he was wounded only once.

On several occasions, his father's farm served as a rendezvous place for the guerrillas. At Pleasant Hill, he and Bob Houx were the pickets who sounded the alarm at the onslaught of Union troops. A brother-in-law, Ezra Moore, also rode with Quantrill, but unfortunately was killed at Pleasant Hill. In

QUANTRILL'S THIEVES By: Joseph K. Houts, Jr.

October 1864, George was taken prisoner and sent to Fort Scott, Kansas. He was then transferred to several prisons including St. Louis, Missouri, Alton, and Rock Island, Illinois. Eventually, he ended up at Richmond, Virginia, where he was paroled on March 23, 1865. After being paroled, he sought to rejoin the war effort and went first to North and South Carolina and then to Shreveport, Louisiana, where in May 1865, he surrendered to Union officials.

    The war had been hard on the George family. Their house had been burned three times, the father and also a son, Gabriel W., were killed. John returned home in 1878 and reportedly worked as a carpenter. He remained in this occupation until 1897, thereafter he pursued farming. George attended the reunion of Confederate Veterans, Shelby's Camp on August 29, 1885 at Higginsville, Missouri. He and several other former guerrillas met his former guerrilla chieftain's mother, Caroline Clarke Quantrill, on May 11, 1888 at the City Hotel in Blue Springs, Missouri. He attended the first Quantrill reunion on September 7, 1898 and also those in 1906 and 1908. His brother, Hiram James, accompanied him on several occasions. Besides attending reunions, he was a member of the United Confederate Veterans Camp, Upton Hays, B. F. Harding commander. On January 26, 1926, he died and was buried in the George Cemetery, south of Oak Grove. As a testament to his stamina and bearing, George was described as "... an iron man, who could sleep in his saddle, and eat as he ran...."

Mike Houx
(Michael Morningstar, M. M. Houx)

Michael Morningstar Houx was born in Cooper County, Missouri in 1821. He was the eighth of eleven children born to John Jacob and Dorothy "Dolly" Simmons Houx. In 1816, his family migrated from Kentucky to Missouri, bringing some of the first slaves into the territory. Originally, the Houx clan had settled in Maryland, transplanted from the province of Lorraine, a crossroads between Germany and France. The name Houx was of French origin initially pronounced "Holly," but eventually was given a German pronunciation and called "Howx." Prior to 1860, Michael moved to Johnson County and was a farmer. On July 27, 1847 he married Harriet McFarland. They would have six children.

Michael Morningstar Houx
Courtesy A. Pauline Hall

Houx's Civil War experiences have remained somewhat of a mystery. It has been established that he rode with Quantrill early on, along with his older brother Matthias and a nephew, Robert Washington Kavanaugh Houx. Another brother, Robert Sloan Houx, was neutral in his sympathies, but fearful that he may be pressed into service on the Union side. He consequently left the state and went to Palo Pinto County, Texas at the war's onset in order to avoid the possibility of fighting against his brothers.

Matthias and Robert were documented at the Battle of Pleasant Hill, Missouri on July 11, 1862. In all probability,

QUANTRILL'S THIEVES By: Joseph K. Houts, Jr.

Michael was also at this engagement, due to his close association with Matthias and Robert during this period. Although undocumented, evidence suggests his presence at the raid on Lawrence, Kansas on August 21, 1863 and at the massacre at Baxter Springs, Kansas on October 6, 1863.

His wife died unexpectedly on May 2, 1863. She was buried in the Houx family cemetery outside Centerview, Missouri. Following this loss, he went to Texas sometime later in the year and was reported to be staying with his brother Robert.

Of coincidence, Houx's farm was in the same general proximity as Captain James Perdee's on the Blackwater River, outside Columbus, Johnson County, Missouri. The Perdee farm had been the staging place for Quantrill's Lawrence Raid. Several months later it was the rendezvous site for the guerrilla's trek south to Sherman, Texas for winter quarters between 1863-1864. In addition, two of Perdee's sons, James R. and Thomas D., were on the list with Michael. Palo Pinto County, Texas was located roughly 100 miles southwest of Sherman, only a few days ride away. All of these time and place relationships open the question of his involvement at Lawrence and Baxter Springs.

After the war, Houx remained in Texas. He briefly returned to Missouri in order to marry Martha Jane McFarland Gillet on May 1, 1867. They would have three children, a daughter named Armelda, another daughter who died in infancy, and a son named Robert Haden. Both Michael and Martha Jane had been previously married. Although both Michael's first wife, Harriet and his second wife, Martha had the same last name (McFarland) they were not sisters. Houx died in 1877 and was buried at the foot of a mountain outside McSpadden, Texas. On January 1, 1883, his brother Robert passed away and was interred at the base of the same mountain.

Houx, Mat
(Matthias, Uncle Mat, Houk, Hauck)

Matthias Houx, the sixth of eleven children, was the elder of brother of fellow guerrilla Mike and nephew Robert. Born February 28, 1814 in Russellville, Logan County, Kentucky, his parents, Jacob and Dorothy Simons Houx, migrated to Centerview, Missouri in 1816, bringing some of the first slaves into the territory.

In younger days, Houx had joined a company organized and commanded by his future father-in-law during the Mormon uprising. He was present at the capture of Mormon founder Joseph Smith. Following service in the Mexican War, he journeyed to California as a "49er" caught up in the country's gold fever. In California he made the acquaintance of Kit Carson. He returned home in 1851 with $2,000.00 in his pocket and purchased a tract of land outside Warrensburg, Missouri. He married and settled down as a farmer.

Matthias Houx

At the outbreak of the Civil War he was a slave owner and acknowledged as "a Confederate in sentiment, but not in activities." Arrested at the war's outset, Houx was charged and convicted of murder by a court martial in Lexington, Missouri. Colonel James D. Eads, a Federal officer, having contrary information of his guilt, intervened two days before the execution, convincing the court of his innocence.

Thereafter, he joined General Sterling Price's Missouri State Guard (MSG) as a private in Colonel Hurst's division, assigned to Company G, under the command of Francis M. Cockrell. The company was attached to General John S. Marmaduke's Cavalry unit. Private Houx fought at the battles of Wilson's Creek, Missouri, August 10, 1861; Lexington, Missouri, September 18-20, 1861; and Pea Ridge, Arkansas, March 7-8, 1862; where he joined with Quantrill after Price's defeat.

In December 1861, he along with Syrus Cockrell, N. W. Perry, and Colonel James McCown stole the public records of Johnson County, Missouri and hid them in a densely wooded thicket in order to safeguard the records from marauding bands. Thereafter, Mrs. Houx and others would regularly inspect the hiding place, making sure the papers were safe. With the war's end, the records were returned to the courthouse in July 1868.

Reports have established his guerrilla band approached upwards of 300 men. During the war, Union troops ransacked his house in search of munitions. Many of the family's personal effects were stolen or destroyed. Surprisingly, the house was spared the torch. Local folklore said the Federals did not burn the house because they were scared of retribution from him and his close friend, Quantrill. Fearing for his safety, he would frequently hide in a cave located on the far side of his farm. At night the family slave would bring him supper in an old pail.

In early March 1862, Union Commander Henry W. Halleck issued his infamous "no quarter" decree—General Order No. 2. Confronted with the consequences of this measure, Houx sought an honorable surrender for himself and his men. In his overture though, he stated "in case they are to be treated as outlaws, they will ruin the countryside, burning houses and murdering loyal men." An agreement could not be arranged, and a skirmish followed shortly at Post Oak Creek, Missouri on March 26, 1862 near the Blackwater River. Inaccurate Union reports circulated of his death. Later in the year, he was at the Battle of Pleasant Hill, Missouri on July 11 where Union officials found Quantrill's muster roll on one of the dead guerrillas.

Union troops had ransacked Mat's house every so often, a common occurance in the war. Purportedly, the trespassers had been in search of munitions. Sadly, the motive was probably more vindictive, not an uncommon practice either. In the process, the troops destroyed and carried away many of the family's personal items. Of special loss was a cut out overcoat purchased by Mrs. Houx in Lexington, and six deer skins dressed and prized by Mat. Most likely the skins would have become new guerrilla garb. Surprisingly, the house was spared the torch.

Houx's farm was located near the staging point for the Lawrence Raid on August 21, 1863, that being Captain James Perdee's farm. The captain's sons, T. D. Perdee or Thomas and J. R. Perdee or James, were also on the List. Afterwards, it served as the rendezvous for the guerrillas' trek south to Sherman, Texas, where they wintered from 1863-1864.

Several accounts have placed he, his brother, and nephew in Texas during this period. Although undocumented, evidence supports possiblity that he was present at Lawrence and the Baxter Springs' massacre on October 6, 1863.

Upon returning to Missouri at the war's conclusion in 1865, he was captured and then paroled. On May 30, 1866, the United States government brought a suit against him for his wartime activities. This was the 159th proceeding brought against former partisans. Houx's daughter, Mary, raised $4,000.00 for his bond. In 1871, he professed religion and became a member of the Cumberland Presbyterian Church. Residing in Warrensburg the rest of his life, he became a respected member of the community. He was often referred to as Uncle Mat. At the age of eighty-two he still enjoyed a good fox chase and could jump his horse over a six rail fence. On July 21, 1900, Mat Houx died and was buried in the family cemetery outside Centerview, Missouri. His obituary eulogized him as a "sterling pioneer."

QUANTRILL'S THIEVES   By: Joseph K. Houts, Jr.

STAR-JOURNAL, WARRENSBURG, MO.

Walnut Box Holds Memories, Reminiscenses of Days Past

(J. L. Ferguson)

It is a pleasure to consider the possessions of this age and it is also a pleasure to let our mind wander back to frontier days in Johnson County and to recount traditions of families and peoples who builded this county's civilization from its very beginnings.

Man's ingenuity has blessed us with marvelous things. We push a button and have dazzling light, turn a knob and have the temperature as we desire, finger a dialand hear voices or music from the air, but man has not yet found a way to get from inanimate things the story of the parts they have played in men's experiences. Think of the long list of sacrifices a crucifix might give or the story, far more thrilling than the one printed on its pages, that a book might tell. A small wooden box in the possession of a descendant of Orlando Bradley could give an interesting account of itself, had it such power.

Came West in 1830

Orlando Bradley brought his family and his slaves from his native Virginia to Lafayette County about 1830 and settled near the Missouri river. He lived for a number of years in the home he first built. Then in 1854 he decided it was no longer adequate and built the fine large house which still stands, in an excellent state of repair, on Highway No. 13, beyond Higginsville.

The builder of Mr. Bradley's house was George Garr, an expert in his trade. While the house was in process of construction, Mr. Bradley's small granddaughter, Susan, and her mother, Elizabeth (Bradley) Houx visited him and Mr. Garr became so attached to the little girl that he made her a box in which to keep her own, or her doll clothes. The box was made of nicely planed walnut, the kind of lumber of which the house was largely constructed, and now after over 80 years of continual and varied use, it wears a soft rich polish and is seemingly in as perfect condition as at the time it was made.

—Star-Journal Engraving

Matthias Houx, 1816-1900, farmer, stockman, hunter, soldier of Mormon, Mexican and Civil Wars, prominent pioneer of Johnson County. He is shown above in his buckskin coat with cougar trimmings and epaulets, the animals having been killed by him in Texas during the Civil War.

Matthias Houx Courtesy Houx Geneological Papers, Alice Kinyoun Houts.
Used with permission of The Warrensburg Star-Journal

QUANTRILL'S THIEVES By: Joseph K. Houts, Jr.

Federals Searched House

Little Susan took her box with her when she returned to her home about eight miles west of Warrensburg and northwest of Centerview where it continued to be for her personal use until the Civil War. At one time during that war Federal soldiers searched the premises of her home, the home of her father, Matthias Houx, as they did those of all others suspected of being southern sympathizers, ostensibly hunting for hidden gunpowder.

In their zeal and ill will much property was taken or destroyed. When Mrs. Houx heard that the Federals were near she began a hurried hiding of everything of value. Of course the children helped and in the haste and excitement, much to their dismay, they had trouble later in remembering just where they had put some of the things, among those things being a heavy overcoat for Mr. Houx that Mrs. Houx had had cut out at Lexington but had not yet made.

Hid Deer Skins In It

Among Mr. Houx's prize possessions were six beautifully dressed deer skins, the deer had been killed and the skins dressed by him. These skins must be put where they would not be injured by water, should it rain before they could be returned to the house. Mrs. Houx thought of Susan's little walnut box so she hastily packed in it the six deer skins, the family silver and daguerreotypes, two delaine dress patterns and some gray jeans for pants. The box was then taken to the timber north of the house and buried under leaves and brush. By this time the Federals had arrived, so to keep them from suspecting anything was hidden in the timber, Mrs. Houx and her sister-in-law, Mrs. Peggy Houx, innocently returned by separate and roundabout ways.

Later, however, when they went to recover the little box, it had been found and forced open and the contents taken. The hinges and lock were broken but otherwise the little box was not injured. The "Feds" had the deer skins but what use they made of them was not known.

Joined Cockrell's Group

Mr. Houx had passed the age for war service but he volunteered and went south with Cockrell's men and for awhile was near Palo Pinto, Tex. where relatives lived. While there he killed more deer, dressed their hides and his sister and niece made him deer skin suits. He had also killed a cougar and from its skin were taken strips of fur with which to trim the suit. On the shoulders epaulets were made from the claws of the cougar and from the skin of its head was made a cap.

He had overshoes made from buffalo skin, the upper part had the fur turned to the inside. The soles were made from cowhide—sole leather. The deer skins were also made into the famous buckskin gloves which were in common use. Mr. Houx wore his suit for many years after the war. The coat was finally worn out but one pair of the deer skin pants were given to George Cranmer, now one of Denver's most prominent citizens. Mr. Cranmer who was a great nephew of Mr. Houx, spent many happy boyhood days with his Missouri Houx relatives.

Box Now In Use

The walnut box was repaired with hinges and lock and Susan grew to womanhood but all the time revered the box more and more. She married George Anderson, moved to Barton County and later to the Indian Territory where she and Mr. Anderson made their home until his death some years later. She then returned to Missouri and her girlhood home where she spent the rest of her life, but as long as she lived the little wooden box went with her wherever she made her home.

This box is still in use and one of the deer skins and many other mementoes of those early days are in the possession of Mrs. Susan (Houx) Anderson's sister, Miss Mary Houx of Warrensburg. And thus this small walnut box, because of its sturdy character, the quality of its material, the fine workmanship used in its making and the love of its first little owner, continues to give pleasure and service through the passing years.

Matthias Houx Courtesy Houx Geneological Papers, Alice Kinyoun Houts. Used with permission of The Warrensburg Star-Journal

QUANTRILL'S THIEVES By: Joseph K. Houts, Jr.

Robert Houx
(Robert W. K., Bob Houk)

     Robert Washington Kavanaugh Houx was born on May 19, 1836 in Lafayette County, Missouri. He was the fifth of eight children born to Philip Simons and Margaret Hutchinson Morrow Houx. The Houxes moved to Johnson County, Missouri in 1837. His father was a man of numerous interests and pursuits. He was a shoemaker, farmer, raiser of livestock, and the county's sixth sheriff. Kansas red legs burnt the family's house during the war. At the age of sixteen young Robert became a Christian and joined the Cumberlin Presbyterian Church, later serving as a deacon. His brother, James Henry, also known as the "Reverend Jim Henry," was the preacher.

     At the war's outset, he followed his uncles Matthias and Michael Morningstar Houx as a guerrilla with Quantrill. He was junior to them by 21 and 12 years. Houx was at the Battle of Pleasant Hill, Missouri on July 11, 1862. In his memoirs, William H. Gregg, 1st Sergeant later recalled that Bob Houx along with Hicks George were posted as rear guard pickets during the night preceding the battle. The next day, Union forward advance troops under the command of Captain Martin Kehoe fired upon them when attacking Quantrill's encampment. There has been

Robert W. Houx
Photo Album of Rev. James H. Houx Family

138

some evidence suggesting that he participated in the Lawrence, Kansas raid on August 21, 1863. Other sources have also possibly placed him with Quantrill in the guerrilla's trek south to Sherman, Texas for winter quarters during 1863-64. In which event, he would have been at the massacre of Baxter Springs, Kansas on October 6, 1863. A cousin, Robert Sloan Houx and the brother of his guerrilla uncles, lived in Palo Pinto, Texas, a relatively short distance from Sherman. All of them were reported to have been in Palo Pinto during this period. From this point on, his guerrilla activity has remained unknown. However, fellow comrades described him as a "good soldier," and stated there was none braver. Because of his courage and cool headedness, he was frequently positioned in potentially tight situations.

After the war, he settled on his father's homestead north of Centerview. In 1884, he went to the Indian Territory, a land where strangers were looked upon with suspicion. Within a brief period, Houx secured the Indians' trust and respect, receiving the name, "Big Fish in Shallow Water." He was also called "Lagany", meaning "good." An Indian named Little Coon at first would not let him use his spring water. In time the two became close friends, with the Indian later sharing his resources. When Little Coon became fatally ill he requested Houx's attendance. Houx kept vigil over him until his death.

A man of "good mental endowment," he spoke little. However once his mind was set "he was firm as a rock." He died unmarried at the age of 59 years, 9 months and 20 days, in the Osage Nation, Indian Territory. His brothers, Reverend Jim Henry and George Washington Houx brought the remains back to Missouri for burial. The body was laid to rest in the Houx family cemetery outside Centerview. The last line on his tombstone reads, "Gone But Not Forgotten," a fitting tribute to a former guerrilla.

QUANTRILL'S THIEVES   By: Joseph K. Houts, Jr.

W Hally
(William, Wilse, Wils, Bill, Halley)

William Halley was probably the only former guerrilla to be confined to a state hospital for the mentally ill. He died on December 18, 1900 at St. Joseph, Missouri in State Hospital Insane Asylum No. 2. Halley was admitted on December 1 because of "a general breakdown of his mental powers." He had been exhibiting violent tendency. Upon examination he was diagnosed as suffering from melancholia, a mental illness characterized by feelings of withdrawal and rejection, often associated with manic-depressive psychosis or a phase thereof. It was reported he was "morbidly suspicious" of people around him. On December 14, he had a cerebral hemorrhage, which left him unconscious and paralyzed on one side. He died four days later.

William Halley tombstone
Mount Mora Cemetery, St. Joseph, MO

His funeral services were conducted by the Heaton-Begole Funeral Home contracted by his brother, Samuel Halley. This funeral home has the dual distinction of burying fellow guerrilla Jesse Woodson James in April 1882 and being the oldest business still operating in St. Joseph. It now has the name of Heaton, Bowman, Smith and Sidenfaden Chapel, representing a merger of several funeral parlors over the years. O. F. Sidenfaden handled Mr. James' services. Halley's service was conducted by clergyman M. W. Goode at 10:00 a.m. on December 20, 1900, with George Begole officiating on behalf of the funeral home at 637 Charles Street, the residence of Halley's brother Samuel. C.

A. Woodson of the St. Joseph State Hospital signed the death certificate. The pallbearers were John Banny, J. D. Davis, Frank Watson, C. H. Kelley, Edward Sieffart and Roger Martin. The body was interred at the Mount Mora Cemetery in St. Joseph. The total cost of the service was $88.75, broken down as follows: $40.00 for the casket; $10.00 washing, shaving, and embalming; $12.00 burial suit; $5.00 first hearse; $12.00 three carriages; $6.00 funeral coach hearse; $.75 newspaper notice; and $3.00 ambulance.

Halley was the son of William R. and Lucinda Halley. He was born in Frankfort, Kentucky sometime between 1841-1842. His father was a carpenter and he had four brothers and sisters: Emily, Elizabeth, Samuel, and Marie. Prior to 1860 the family moved from Kentucky to Johnson County, Missouri, settling outside Independence. At the start of the war Halley, being a Southern sympathizer, had been arrested and placed in jail for some minor offense. Purportedly, Quantrill arranged for his release, after which he joined the guerrilla chieftain. In all probability, he was at the battle of Pleasant Hill, Missouri, July 11, 1862. Accounts have shown that he was also at the battles of Lone Jack, Missouri, August 16, 1862 and Lawrence, Kansas, August 21, 1863.

Following the massacre at Lawrence, he returned to Independence where he was arrested based on his name appearing on Quantrill's Roster. He was tried and sentenced to be shot three days hence. Through the efforts of a Southern maiden who brought him food while incarcerated he managed to escape and rejoin Quantrill's gang outside of town. The jail was subsequently burned. Supposedly, Halley had fallen in love with his female rescuer and consequently never married. He carried a picture of her to his dying days. A close acquaintance reported he spoke of her just a few days prior to his passing.

At war's end, Halley was purportedly serving with Major General Joseph O. Shelby in Texas. Thereafter he moved to St. Joseph and became a freighter, escorting wagon trains for local businesses across the Great Plains. Eventually, Salt Lake City, Utah became his home where he was the chief herder on a ranch. From there, Halley began to wander about the West until tiring of his travels. He moved back to St. Joseph in 1875. He resided with two sisters, Dee and Fannie, at 909 Charles Street. His brother Sam also lived in town and served the fire department as a driver, hauling the chemical engine. Working at various jobs, Halley occasionally would journey west. Eventually, his wanderings stopped and he was employed by C. A. Perry. In June of 1887, he joined the St. Joseph Police Department. On his application he was described as a former teamster, unmarried, with a height of 5'9¼."

His service with the police department bordered on the extreme. He was described as not being an energetic officer, but was very reliable once called upon for duty. Other characterizations noted that he was excellent at shooting a pistol and a rifle. It was pointed out his Quantrill association had refined these proficiencies. He became famous for his role in stopping Roy's Branch holdup, where he killed two of the robbers with his bare hands. Unfortunately, his career with the force ended under somewhat tarnished circumstances. In 1898, Halley was dismissed for being intoxicated while in uniform.

In spite of his claims to have ridden with Quantrill, other former gang members had faint recollection of him. Hi George remembered a man named Wils Halley, but believed his association with the guerrillas was brief. Time has a way of fogging the memory, especially after many years. In all likelihood, he was a guerrilla and may have been lost in the countless number of men who at one time or another rode with the famous bushwhacker. Regardless of how his life began and ended, during his period as a guerrilla, it was said, "...he was as brave as a lion."

John Hampton
(Jno., J.)

John Hampton was born around 1836, with his place of birth being Virginia. In the 1860 Jackson County Census he was listed as a farmer having a wife named Mary C. and a one-year-old child named Martha. The census also revealed a cluster of Hampton homesteads located roughly within the same general area. Based on their age and place of birth, many of them were probably siblings. In particular, there was Jemima, age 46; Nancy, age 35; and Valentine, age 31, all of whom were born in Virginia.

According to historian John N. Edwards, in his book <u>Noted Guerrillas</u>, Hampton was part of William Clarke Quantrill's original band of bushwhackers. Others included James and John Little, William Haller, Andrew Walker (Morgan Walker's son), Edward Koger (John Koger's brother), Solomon Basham and James Kelly. Unfortunately, his guerrilla days were short lived. He was killed at the battle of Pleasant Hill, Missouri on July 11, 1862 when Union Captain Martin Kehoe opened fire at long range on Quantrill's line. Guerrillas Jeremiah F. "Jere" Doors (Doores) and Ezra (Ezry) Moore were also killed in the fighting. George Maddox and William Tucker were wounded. The battle has also been referred to as the Sears Farm. After the war Hampton was praised for his many deeds in returning stolen property to women who had been victimized by either Missouri Unionists or Kansas Jayhawkers.

QUANTRILL'S THIEVES   By: Joseph K. Houts, Jr.

O Hampton
(Oscar L.)

Oscar L. Hampton at middle age was described as "a well respected citizen." He was the fourth of six children born to David and Susan Gaines Hampton. His date of birth was March 22, 1843. Both of his parents had been raised in Kentucky, although he and his siblings were all born in Missouri. His siblings' names were Catherine, Margaret, John, Congrove, and James. David Hampton was one of the first settlers to arrive in Triplett Township, Chariton County, Missouri in 1836. The region was described as "...a shipless (sic) sea-an almost trackless wild, the white inhabitants of which could be numbered on one's fingers." The town of Keytesville was the principal trading center. The elder Hampton had opened this virgin land to many others and was a farmer until his later years.

Following in his father's footsteps, Oscar was also a farmer. He had attended the local schools. During the war, he was in the 12th Missouri Cavalry Regiment assigned to Company E. Also serving in the regiment were nine other guerrillas set forth on Quantrill's Roster of original riders: Richard Maddox, William H. Vaughan, James Vaughan, John Jarrette, A. Harris, Fernando F. Scott, William Campbell, James A. Hendrix, and Boone T. Muir. Most likely, he was at the battle of Pleasant Hill, Missouri on July 11, 1862. Thereafter, his service record has remained blank, except that he joined Major General Sterling Price's army in 1864 in the South's last failed bid to seize Missouri.

After the war, Hampton returned home and commenced farming again. He married Dorcas Ballew from the county, and they had six offspring named Oliver, Kinla, Mable, Susan, Nannie, and Wade. His farm contained 110 acres and he was one of the founders of Friendship Lodge No. 2094 organized on March 12, 1880.

G N Horn
(Given N., Givens, Horne)

Given N. Horn was born in Kentucky in 1843. His parents were Richard and Mattie F. Horn with his father's place of birth being North Carolina and his mother's Virginia. There has been documentation though that his mother's maiden name was Irene Lucille "Michelle" Lumford, whose parents were Bennie Lee and Irene Lucille Lumford. In the 1860 Cass County, Missouri 1860 Federal Census, Given was shown to have had three younger siblings named Sarah F., Thomas M., and Richard C. Horn.

In all probability he was at the battle of Pleasant Hill, Missouri on July 11, 1862. Horn was at the Lawrence, Kansas raid on August 21, 1863. On November 18 of the same year he was indicted, along with 35 other guerrillas, by the Douglas County, Kansas's grand jury for their role in the death of George Burt during the raid. Towards the end of the war he and Doc Campbell, George Maddox, Al Scott, and James Stewart were attacked by Union troops while forging the Osage River. During the encounter he was wounded in the left arm, but it was of only minor consequence. His whereabouts after the war, or whether he even survived, has remained an unknown to this date.

QUANTRILL'S THIEVES   By: Joseph K. Houts, Jr.

J J Hall
(Thomas J, Tom, J J)

Thomas J. Hall was in all probability related to the Hall brothers from Cass County, Missouri: Robert H., John "Lit", Joseph, and Isaac "Ike". Robert H. Hall was also on the Roster of William Clarke Qauntrill's original guerrillas. However, aside from the common surname, nothing has been found establishing Thomas J. Hall's connection, or his lineage and whereabouts prior to the Civil War.

He did have a sister who was among the group of seventeen women arrested in 1863 by General Thomas B. Ewing, Jr. The ladies were held in a dilapidated hotel in Kansas City, Missouri. John McCorkle's sister was arrested along with Thomas J. Hall's sister. Eventually, the building would collapse and kill five of the women who were kin to many of the guerrillas. McCorkle's sister died as a result of the tragedy.

If Hall was related to the Hall brothers, he may have shared their motivation for joining Quantrill. Apparently, the Hall family had heard of the Morgan Walker incident in Blue Springs, Missouri in 1860 which set Quantrill on the path towards becoming the noted guerrilla chieftain.. Sometime later they saw Quantrill passing through the area and this must have inspired them to become guerrillas. Joe Hall joined Quantrill in late 1861, with Ike soon following in either April or May 1862. Later in the year, Robert too would put in his lot with them and the guerrillas. However, the date of John's association has remained a mystery. In the winter of 1862, Kansas Jayhawker Dr. Charles R. "Doc" Jennison and his men burned the Hall family house. Mrs. Hall was forced to set the fire herself. When she cried and tried to wipe the tears from her eyes, the raiders pulled her hands away and then cursed the woman. Jennison and his gang also torched the homes of four neighbors.

Hall was likely at the battle of Pleasant Hill, Missouri on July 11, 1862 and may have been with Quantrill in the raid on Lawrence, Kansas, August 21, 1863. During the latter part of the war, he may have ridden with William T. "Bloody Bill" Anderson, and have fought at Centralia, Missouri, September 27, 1864 and Westport, Missouri, October 23, 1864. By November of 1864 the war was played out in Missouri and Quantrill assembled thirty-three of his remaining riders, including Thomas and the Hall brothers, and headed for Kentucky. After the war Thomas settled in Samuel's Depot, Kentucky, along with Robert and Ike Hall.

M Houston
(Magnus, Marion, M. F., M. M., Nathan)

M. Houston could be any one of five Missourians, all named Houston, who served in the Confederate Army. There is little information to be found about any of them.

The first candidate is Magnus Houston a schoolteacher born in Missouri in 1838. In 1860 he was living in Lafayette County, Missouri in the household of Evans and Sally Dillingham. The second individual was named Marion and he was in the 1st Northeast Missouri Cavalry Regiment, assigned to Company H. The third Houston prospect is named M. F. and he was in Clark's Regiment Missouri Infantry, assigned to Company B. The next Houston had the initials of M. M. and was in the 4th Missouri Cavalry Regiment assigned to Company I.

The last potential contender was named Nathan, a farmer from Johnson County, Missouri, living in Madison Township. The name of his wife was Isabel and they had four children: Napoleon, age ten; Mary B., age eight; Thalena, three; and Alexander, age one. Nathan, his wife, and their two oldest children had been born in Kentucky, while the two youngest were born in Missouri. The family had moved to the state sometime before 1857. Although his name started with the letter "N" and not "M" it could have been misspelled on Quantrill's Roster and the mistake carried forward until the present. Of some interest, Nathan lived in close proximity to Obediah Strange Barnett, George Barnett, John Oliphant, James H. Cunningham, and Al Cunningham, all listed on the Roster.

An argument could be made as to any of these men being the one who rode with the guerrilla chieftain. The most logical guess would be Nathan, since he resided closest to the other guerrillas on the Roster. Also, Johnson County was a hot bed of rebel and in particular guerrilla activity during the war. Marion should be ruled out because his regiment consisted of recruits from northeast Missouri, which would geographically distance him from the partisans. There was not enough information to draw a conclusion concerning Magnus, M. F. and M. M.

A Harris
(Rueben Alexander Harris)

Reuben Alexander Harris was born on October 14, 1829 in Jackson County, Missouri. His parents were Samuel and Jane Hall Harris. His father was born on May 16, 1807 in Patrick County, Virginia and his mother was born on June 12, 1814, also in Patrick County. Reuben's father died on November 6, 1854, leaving his mother to manage the family farm.

Samuel's parents, Reuben and Margaret Ann Alexander Harris, had moved to Jackson County, Missouri in the 1830's, being some of the first settlers in the Blue Township located in the area of Independence. The senior Reuben established a horse-drawn mill on the Little Blue River in 1840. Although it was conveniently located from a commercial standpoint it did not produce much income. The family had many children.

In 1860 young Reuben married Mary Elizabeth Dillingham, daughter of Joshua and Susan Walker Dillingham. Both of her parents were born in Kentucky. Her father was born on May 29, 1816 and her mother was born on September 26, 1826. The Dillingham household was located next to the farms of Morgan Walker, George Rider, and George Rider's son John W. Rider. The Walker homestead was the scene of William Clarke Quantrill's famous raid, wherein Quantrill betrayed his Jayhawk companions, foiled their plan to steal Walker's slaves, and declared his sympathies as a Southern partisan. The events at Walker's farm set Quantrill on the path towards becoming the noted guerrilla chieftain. Both George Rider and his son John were on the Roster along with Harris.

In all likelihood, Harris was at the battle of Pleasant Hill, Missouri on July 11, 1862. During this period he played several different roles. It has been documented that he rode with Quantrill, but more importantly his farm was used as a sanctuary for the guerrillas throughout most of the war. In particular, Quantrill and his men rendezvoused at this place prior to the skirmish at the Jordan Lowe house on April 15, 1862, and also prior to the battle at Pleasant Hill. The farm was used countless other times as a staging point or rest area, even as late in the war as early July 1864, prior to Quantrill's seeking to hide in Howard County.

It should be noted that there was another Reuben Harris, age fifty-six, living in Jackson County at this time. He probably was an uncle who may have been the real Reuben lodging the guerrillas. In addition, young Reuben possibly had another uncle named Alexander. Either of these men might have been the "A." Harris on the roster. However, several sources have indicated it was their nephew, especially in light of his close proximity to Morgan Walker and the Riders.

All the while being a guerrilla or harboring them, Harris was also a member of Shank's Regiment assigned to Company C. On June 16, 1865 he surrendered in either Shreveport or New Orleans, Louisiana and was subsequently paroled for his service to the South. Apparently, he returned home and had two children, named Hester Hollowly and Neeley or Nealy A. Harris. In 1920, Neeley was the chief of police in Independence, Missouri. Harris died at Independence on May 19, 1906 and his wife died at Blue Springs on June 26, 1911. It was said of him and a few others who offered a hideaway for the guerrillas, that their "...patriotic devotion and unremitting care, none surpassed...."

QUANTRILL'S THIEVES   By: Joseph K. Houts, Jr.

U Hays
(Upton, Hayes)

      Upton Hays was born in Callaway County, Missouri on March 29, 1832. He was one of thirteen children fathered by Boone Hays, a grandson of Daniel Boone. In 1837 the family moved to Jackson County, outside of Westport. In 1849, at the age of seventeen, Upton went to California with his father and older brother, Amanzon, as part of the Gold Rush. His father died in California in 1850. The two boys returned to Missouri where Upton was to attend school. After a week, he left and joined a wagon train headed for Santa Fe, New Mexico. On returning, he along with Amazon, Henry Clay Chiles, and Mr. Hunter pooled $2,500 apiece and started a freighting company. They were successful in securing government contracts and one train alone consisted of 101 wagons. Besides starting his own business at age nineteen, he married fourteen year old Margaret J. Watts, the daughter of John S. Watts of North Carolina. Watts first migrated to Kentucky in 1794, where he fought in the War of 1812 in the battle of the Thames on October 5, 1813, where Indian leader Tecumseh was killed. Watts moved to Missouri sometime in 1844 and died prior to the Civil War.

      Although the 1860 Jackson County Census shows that he owned seven slaves, Upton Hays had remained neutral up to this point in time. He voted for Breckenridge for president and Jackson for governor in the 1860 presidential election. As one of his first Jayhawking exploits, Dr. Charles R. "Doc" Jennison pillaged one of Hays' wagon trains. Jennison next attacked Upton's house, burning it and stealing the livestock. His wife Margaret was astonished by the glee displayed on the faces of her slaves as they loaded up and rode off in her stolen carriage during the raid. After this second encroachment, Hays organized a local militia unit to defend against further trespasses. In another encounter Jennison advanced on Upton's brother Sam's homestead. Upton arrived upon the scene and several of his men fired at the Jayhawkers, accidentally wounding Sam. On one occasion sixteen burning farms were visible from the Hays' house.

At the Little Blue River, he and 150 "irregulars" made a stand against an attachment of the Seventh Kansas Cavalry, which was actually Jennison's Jayhawker outfit cloaked as a formal military unit. Leading the Seventh at this engagement was Daniel R. Anthony, second in command to Jennison and the brother of the famous woman suffragette Susan B. Anthony. Hays eventually had to retreat in the skirmish and was reported to have lost nine men.

As a result of these jayhawker transgressions, Hays enlisted in the Second Missouri Cavalry in 1861. He rose to the rank of colonel by June 1862. He fought in the early battles of Carthage, Missouri, July 5, 1861; Wilson's Creek, Missouri, August 10, 1861; and Pea Ridge, Arkansas, March 9, 1862. On July 8, 1862 he returned to Missouri under the orders of Major General Thomas C. Hindman, Confederate commander of Arkansas. In addition, Colonels Gideon W. Thompson, J. Vard Cockrell, John T. Coffee, Warren Lewis, and Joseph O. Shelby were sent into the state to recruit new troops for Hindman's planned invasion of Missouri. Hays was to set up a recruiting base in Jackson County. Because of Quantrill's activities in the county, he asked the guerrilla chieftain to leave the area, so as to draw off local Federal troops. Quantrill obliged, and left George Todd, 2nd lieutenant, with thirty men to act as Hays' escort.

Hays established two recruiting camps, one at Independence and the other at Blue Springs. Within a short period, he had enlisted 300 men. The success of his efforts stemmed in part from several directives issued by Union Brigadier General John M. Schofield. As a follow-up to Major General Henry W. Halleck's "no quarter" order of March 13, 1862 Schofield reinforced the measure by declaring all captured partisans were to be "shot down on the spot." Prior to this measure Union officials had some case by case discretion in dealing with suspected partisans. Now summary execution had become the law. The general also issued his mandatory enlistment order on July 22, 1862, whereby all able-bodied men in Missouri were required to join the Union army. The

QUANTRILL'S THIEVES   By: Joseph K. Houts, Jr.

combined effect of these decrees left few choices for those men with Southern sympathies.

On July 11, 1862 Hays and some of this new enlistees participated with Quantrill at the battle of Pleasant Hill, Missouri. After this near disaster for the guerrillas, Quantrill, Hays, Hughes, and Thompson regrouped in Jackson County. Forces under the command of Hays and Quantrill attacked Independence, Missouri on August 11, 1862 resulting in the surrender of Lieutenant Colonel James T. Buel. Hughes was killed in the attack. Hays was wounded in the foot, however he assumed command of Hughes' troops and also those belonging to Colonel Thompson.

Following this battle, Thompson officially mustered Quantrill and his men into regular service under the Confederate Partisan Rangers Act of April 21, 1862. Quantrill remained in the vicinity of Independence, but Hays and Thompson joined up with Colonels Cockrell and Coffee at the battle of Lone Jack, Missouri on August 16, 1862. Cockrell and Coffee had been sent from Springfield, Missouri by General Hindman. Schofield sent Brigadier General James G. Blunt to intercept Cockrell and Coffee, but they were unable to close ranks on them. On the day of the battle the Confederates had amassed over 1,000 troops, opposing 800 Union soldiers under the command of Major Emory S. Foster. Before the day was over the Southern forces had won the contest, but not without costs. Upton was again wounded, however, apparently only slightly. As a result of Quantrill, Hays, Porter, and Poindexter's summer activities, Schofield extracted $300,000 in Assessment Bonds from North Missouri counties, as retribution.

Within a week, Hays decided to leave the area and return to Arkansas. One unfinished matter was the fate of a prisoner in his custody, Lieutenant Levi Copeland. Quantrill agreed to take charge of the captive in hopes of exchanging him for guerrilla Perry Hoy, who was being held by Union officials at Fort Leavenworth, Kansas. Unexpectedly, his incarcerators hanged Hoy. Quantrill learned of Perry's demise while he was sitting with William Gregg reading a local paper. Without hesitation, he scribbled an order, gave it to Gregg and instructed him to deliver same to Andy Blunt. Several minutes later shots rang out as Blunt executed Copeland. In further retaliation for Hoy's death, Quantrill and his gang raided Olathe, Kansas on September 6, 1862, killing twenty-four men.

    Upton was killed by Wisconsin troops at the battle of Newtonia, Missouri on September 30, 1862. He was leading a contingent to dislodge the Federals. However, upon his approach a Union soldier unloaded his carbine into Hays' head. The ladies of Westport had made him a flag, which he had sewed into his overcoat. At his burial in Newtonia, it was used as a shroud. In 1898, the United Daughters of the Confederacy exhumed his body and reburied it in the Confederate Cemetery at Westport, now known as the Forest Hills Cemetery. He was described as "...a military Moses who, raised up for a certain glorious work, died before reaching the promised land."

    His widow later moved to California and would remarry becoming Margaret Overstreet. Hays fathered six surviving daughters: Mrs. Elfreda Hays Apperson, Mrs. Pauline Hays Ersey, Mrs. Floy Hays Forbes, Mrs. Alice Hays McAdam, Mrs. Elizabeth Hays Montrey, and Mrs. Jennie Upton Hays Whitesides, all of California.

QUANTRILL'S THIEVES   By: Joseph K. Houts, Jr.

Robert Hall
(Robert H., Bob)

Robert H. Hall was born in 1842 with his place of birth being Kentucky. His parents were Joseph and E. B. Hall. He was the third of five children and the names of his siblings were John "Lit", Joseph, Isaac "Ike" and Margaret. Thomas J. Hall, who was also on the Roster, may have been kin. The family resided in Cass County, Missouri at the start of the Civil War. Their homestead was approximately fifteen miles south of Kansas City, Missouri.

Hall and his brothers rode with guerrilla chieftain William Clarke Quantrill during the war. Apparently, the family had heard of the Morgan Walker incident involving Quantrill at Blue Springs, Missouri in 1860 wherein Quantrill betrayed his Jayhawk companions, foiled their plan to steal Walker's slaves, and declared his true sympathies as a Southern partisan. The events at Walker's farm set Quantrill on the path towards becoming the noted guerrilla chieftain. Sometime later they saw the guerrilla leader passing through the area. Older brother Joe was the first to join in 1861, followed by Ike in April or May 1862, and Robert in that same year. The date of John's association is unknown.

In the winter of 1862, Kansas Jayhawker Dr. Charles R. "Doc" Jennison burned the Hall family house. Mrs. Hall was forced to set the fire herself. When she tried to wipe the tears from her sobbing eyes, the raiders pulled her hands away and then cursed the woman. Jennison and his gang torched the homes of four of their neighbors that day.

In all probability, Hall was at the battle of Pleasant Hill, Missouri on July 11, 1862. He was at the battle of Lone Jack, Missouri on August 16, 1862, and most likely fought at Centralia, Missouri, September 27, 1864 and Westport, Missouri, October 23, 1864, after aligning himself with William T. "Bloody Bill" Anderson's outfit.

Hall witnessed the confrontation between Quantrill and chief lieutenant George M. Todd in the spring of 1864, when the guerrillas were returning from winter quarters at Sherman,

Texas. The two had been at odds for some time, but during a card game Todd pulled his gun on Quantrill after being accused of cheating him. Todd forced Quantrill to back down and even to state that he was afraid of him. Consequently, the gang broke up into three groups, with Todd and Anderson each splitting into separate factions, leaving Quantrill on his own for the most part with only a few followers.

Following the battle of Westport, Quantrill realized the war was essentially over in Missouri and assembled thirty-three of his remaining riders, including the Hall brothers, and headed for Kentucky. On reaching Pocahontas, Arkansas, several members of the group left and set out for Texas, riding under "Ol" Shepard. Shortly before this event, Joe contracted smallpox, necessitating that he be left behind. One of his brothers, either John or Ike, stayed with him in order to give care. Robert continued on with Quantrill to Kentucky.

Hall was the company's blacksmith and upon reaching Kentucky, Quantrill decided to have his faithful stead, "Old Charlie" reshod. In the process of refitting the horse, Hall accidentally severed the animal's main tendon on his right hoof, which ruined the animal. The horse had been with Quantrill since the war's beginning. It was said this occurrence spooked the guerrilla leader and instilled in him a premonition of impending doom. Within a few short months he would realize this fear and die.

After Quantrill's death, Hall and the remnants of the gang finally surrendered to Union officials on July 26, 1865 at Samuel's Depot, Kentucky. Those accompanying him were his brother Ike, Jim Lilly, Bud Pence, Frank James, Lee McMurty, Dave Hilton, John Ross, John Harris, Andy McGuire, Payne Jones, Ran Venable, Bill Hulse, and Allen Parmer.

Robert and his brother Ike would settle in Samuel's Depot, Kentucky, as would Thomas. Joseph either died of smallpox or was killed in early 1865. John returned home and attended the Quantrill Reunions in his later years. However on one particular day John's wife, tiring of his many times being drunk, killed him with a rolling pin while she was in the process of making biscuit dough.

J A Hendricks
(James A., Hendrix)

James A. Hendricks was born in Kentucky in 1833. He was the youngest of six children born to James and Sarah Land Hendricks. His father had been born in the Carolina's around 1799. A grandfather, Peter Hendricks, migrated from Germany and was a farmer. When James was eight years old, his family moved to Missouri. At the age of eighteen, he went to California with an ox team, reaching the state on October 14, 1852. Hendricks prospected for gold on the South Yuba River and the Washington Creek. On average, he usually made $50.00 a day. He expended a portion of his savings while working less productive mining regions. After four years as a prospector he became a butcher in Washington and Nevada counties.

Three years later, Hendricks returned to Missouri, settling at Stony Point in Jackson County where he opened a general store. In the 1860 county census, he was listed as a merchant living in the J. Patterson family. His mother was also listed as being sixty years old, owning one slave, and residing with the family of J. G. Hendrickson. Apparently her husband was deceased.

As the Civil War engulfed the western regions of the state, Hendricks became an early victim, loosing his store and all of its wares. He joined Quantrill's outfit sometime in December 1861, Other early members of the group included William Haller, George Todd, Joseph Gilchrist, Perry Hoy, Joseph H. Vaughan, John Little, James Little, John Koger, and Hendricks future brother-in-law, William H. Gregg.

He fought in many battles during the war and was wounded three times, the most notable being at the battle of Prairie Grove, Arkansas on December 7, 1862. He was shot in the leg at this engagement and his horse was shot out from under him. As some point Hendricks enlisted as a private in General Joseph O. Shelby's brigade. He rose to the rank of lieutenant by war's end.

QUANTRILL'S THIEVES By: Joseph K. Houts, Jr.

On October 11, 1864, he married Miss Ellen Gregg, William's sister. A month later, on November 7 or 13, 1864, he and his wife accompanied by William Gregg and Dick Maddox, and their wives, headed for Texas along with fifty other men. After entering the Cherokee Nation, the group skirmished with black militia, Indians, and Federal Cavalry. Upon reaching the Red River, most of the others split off.

After the war, Hendricks and his wife returned to Missouri, where he began farming and raising mules. In 1870, he went to Golden City, Colorado as part of a cattle drive. In 1883 or 1884, he and his family moved to Marysville, Montana and built a residence. Until the railrode arrived, he operated a freighting service between Marysville and Helena, Montana. The advent of this new form of transportation caused him to change his route, running it between Helena and Empire. For six years Hendricks was the constable of Marysville, and he served four years as deputy sheriff of Lewis and Clark County under Sheriff T. J. Davidson. In the 1900 Helena City Directory he was listed as residing at 316 Pine Street. He suffered from a kidney mality or disease during the last eight years of his life. Hendricks died in early April 1904 at St. John's Hospital. He was survived by his wife and by their eight children: Lydia G. Halterman, Riley E., Clarence E., Charles J., Arthur J., Henry C., Carrie E., and Bessie Hendricks. The N. B. Forest Camp of Confederate Veterans, of which he was a member, conducted his funeral service. At the August 26, 1904 Quantrill reunion he was remembered as one of those who had fallen within the year. Hendricks was considered "...one of the honored and respected early settlers..." of this part of the state.

W F Judd
(William F., William, Willis)

William F. Judd was a private in Company B of the 2nd Missouri Cavalry, Confederate States of America. During his association with guerrilla chieftain William Clarke Quantrill, he in all likelihood participated in the battles of Independence, Missouri, August 11, 1862; Lone Jack, Missouri, August 16, 1862; and Pleasant Hill, Missouri, July 11, 1862. He was captured on October 8, 1863 in Benton County, Missouri. While in Gratiot Street prison Judd contracted the measles and subsequently died. His date of death has been established as either January 17 or February 17, 1864. Final internment of his remains was at Jefferson Barracks National Cemetery, St. Louis, Missouri, in Section 19, Grave 9775.

QUANTRILL'S THIEVES   By: Joseph K. Houts, Jr.

J W Koger
(John William, James William Kogar, Coger)

John William Koger was described as "one of the most fearless men," to have served under Quantrill. He was born on March 23, 1834 in Jackson County, Missouri. He joined Quantrill's gang in December 1861, along with his brother Ed. The Koger brothers were among the original ten members. In the spring of 1862, John Little and Ed Koger were killed in an ambush, while crossing a stream with George M. Todd. Koger served in the war without interruption from 1861 through 1865. He was captured near the end of the conflict and sentenced to be shot, but he managed to escape and avoided execution.

Koger was at the Clark house skirmish on March 30, 1862; and the battles of Pleasant Hill, Missouri, July 11, 1862; Independence, Missouri, August 11, 1862; Lone Jack, Missouri, August 16, 1862; Cane Hill, Arkansas, November 28, 1862; Prairie Grove, Arkansas, December 7, 1862; Springfield, Missouri, January 8, 1862; Hartville, Missouri, January 9-11, 1863; Lawrence, Kansas, August 21, 1863; Baxter Springs, Kansas, October 6, 1863 and Centralia, Missouri, September 27, 1864.

At Centralia, he was quoted saying; "The fools are going to fight us on foot. God help 'em." This statement had been made in response to Major A.V.E. Johnson's decision to dismount his troops and attack the guerrillas on the ground. Johnson and his men were annihilated as a result of this strategy, except for a few who manage to flee the scene.

In December 1864, Koger left Missouri for Kentucky with Quantrill and other veteran gang members. On reaching Pocahontas, Arkansas, Koger split off from the group and went to Texas with Ol Shepard, Babe and Rufus Hudspeth, Ben Morrow, and Jesse James. He later reported that Quantrill went to Kentucky either because he planned to join up with General Robert E. Lee's Army of Northern Virginia and thus secure a pardon at the close of the war, or because he planned to return home to Ohio. Contrary to some speculation, Quantrill's journey east did not have the objective of assassinating President Abraham Lincoln.

Wounded twelve times during the war, Koger was known as "the man who carried more lead than any other member of Quantrill's gang." On one occassion, he was shot in the back with three buckshot and an ounce ball. Guerrilla comrade, John McCorkle said, "It seemed that it was impossible to kill him." At one time there were eight bullets in his body. He extracted three of them himself in a single sitting, using a knife. When questioned about his loyalty after the war he stated that the only thing Union about him was "several pounds of lead and he carried a good deal." During the battle of Pleasant Hill, he was again wounded. In addition, his horse was shot while he and Quantrill were fleeing from the fight.

Probably his most severe wound occurred at Baxter Springs where a Federal soldier ran out of the fort and shot him in the shoulder. Koger was placed in an ambulance wagon that had been abandoned during the fight by Major General Major James G. Blunt's men. While lying in the wagon after the engagement, when all the guerrillas were resting near the Canadian River, he heard the approach of oncoming horses. It was said that he yelled out, "Des b (sic) d____d (damned) if you hadn't better stop. This is Quantrill." Approaching the encampment was Colonel McIntosh with a contingent of Confederate cavalry. They had mistaken the guerrillas for Union troops and were readying to attack, but for Koger's loud bellow.

He established himself early on as a true and loyal guerrilla. It was noted that he would always obey an order to the letter, although not necessarily in its "spirit." After a run in and escape from Federal cavalry, Quantrill had given the command not to fire any weapons. The reason was so as not to alert the enemy of their changed position. Koger had the uncanny ability of determining either the approach or withdrawal of horses by listening to the ground. On this occasion, the Federals had momentarily fled the scene, but Quantrill was not sure whether they would regroup and return. Because of this uncertainty, he had issued the no-gunfire order and had also instructed Koger to put his ear to the ground and make an analysis. Unfortunately, a

Union soldier had been left behind due to a severe gunshot wound to the head. His brains were oozing out and at the same time he was moaning loudly, preventing Koger from detecting the cavalry's movements. Finally, exasperated with the situation and realizing the man was going to die, but not wanting to countermand Quantrill, he devised a solution. Scouring for a club, he found a sturdy hickory limb, which he used to strike and kill the man. Thereafter, he promptly placed his ear to the ground and immediately informed Quantrill the Federal cavalry was not in retreat, but rapidly approaching.

After the war Koger settled down as a farmer. He married Elizabeth Bowman the daughter of Reverend Bowman. They would have eight children. His son Frank became a Kansas City, Missouri policeman and was killed in the line of duty while making an arrest. On May 11, 1888, Koger was part of the old gang welcoming Quantrill's mother, Caroline Clarke Quantrill, to Blue Springs, Missouri. He met Mrs. Quantrill at a reception in the City Hotel. He was listed on Captain Ragan's 1895 Jackson County United Confederate Veteran's Roster and reportedly attended the first Quantrill Reunion in 1898, in addition to the one held in 1908.

Although he was a prosperous farmer at one time, he eventually fell upon bad times and lost his farm. On August 11, 1909, he applied to the Confederate Home in Higginsville, Missouri for residency. Attached to his application was an affidavit signed by M. L. Belt in which he stated "the war never produced a better soldier." His request for admission to the Home was approved on September 2, 1909. Koger's wife died in 1912, and on July 8, 1917 he too passed away. He was buried alone in the Confederate Cemetery at Higginsville. Concerning his ability as a soldier, it was said, "He who had Coger (sic) at his back had a mountain." Probably the most fitting statement made about this guerrilla was by historian John N. Edwards when he said, "John Koger never missed a bullet." In testimony to this fact, he still carried five bullets in his body upon his death.

QUANTRILL'S THIEVES By: Joseph K. Houts, Jr.

C A Longacre
(Charles A)

Charles A. Longacre, next to Cole Younger, probably had the most interesting family lineage of all of Quantrill's guerrillas. Ironically, he has a faint connection to Cole through the marriage of his brother Richard Ireson Longacre to Martha Jane Oldham. His parents were John and Phoebe B. Thurlton Longacre and he was born in 1838 in Roane County, Tennessee. He was the ninth of eleven children. The names of his siblings were: Ruth Isabella, Adelaide Ann, Sarah Eveline, Richard Ireson, Benjamin W., James Henry, John Keil, Robert T., William Nelson, and Susan Catherine.

Longacre was the seventh American generation of his family. His great great great great grandfather arrived in Chester County, Pennsylvania, known as "New Sweden" aboard the ship Kalmer Nyckel in 1640 from Sweden. From Pennsylvania, the clan moved to Frederick County, Virginia in the late 1700's, followed by Jefferson and Roane Counties, Tennessee in the early 1800's, and finally to Johnson County, Missouri by the 1840's. Charles' first marriage was to a woman named Eliza who died without giving birth to any children.

At the start of the Civil War, Longacre was living in Kingsville, Missouri. On August 1, 1862, in Johnson County, Missouri, he enlisted in the Missouri 16th Infantry, General Parson's brigade, and was assigned to Company D of Captains D. M. Raker and Lewis under the command of Colonels Jackman and Jeremiah Vardaman Cockrell. Longacre's brother James Henry was married to Mary H. Cockrell the sister of Brigadier General Francis Marion Cockrell, a brother of Colonel Cockrell. Apparently, an unknown brother, Joseph D. Longacre, had earlier enlisted in 1861 with Major General Joseph O. Shelby and was paroled in 1865 and had previously served in the Mexican War.

Charles was at the Battle of Lone Jack, Missouri, August 16, 1862. On November 29, 1862 he was transferred to Company C of Pindalls, Sharp Shooters, Missouri Volunteers by order of General Parsons. However, on January 17, 1863, he deserted from the Confederate Army at the Arkansas River.

After the war, Longacre became a doctor and moved to Westphalia, Anderson County, Kansas. On May 1, 1877, he married for a second time to a widow named Missouri Ann Burris Bouse. They would have four daughters named Nancy, Josephine, Ida, and Susan E. On December 30, 1905, Missouri died in Westphalia. Longacre went to Freeman, Missouri in April of 1905 and was in hopes of reaching an agreement with a Drs. Roger and Huff to open a sanitarium in Westphalia. However in May, Dr. Roger sold out to Longacre, and in September 1906, Longacre and a Dr. Harris established a partnership practicing medicine. The doctor bought a Ford automobile in April 1909 in order to better serve his patients. Sometime in September 1910 Longacre moved to Siloam, Arkansas where he probably retired and eventually died.

Although listed as a deserter, Longacre was a member of the "ex-Confederate Missourian Association" and attended its 8th annual meeting in 1890 at Nevada, Missouri. He was also a member of the Jasper County United Confederate Veterans Camp #52 in Carthage, Missouri and attended the 1902 reunion.

As mentioned earlier, Charles had a distinguished lineage. His family constituted some of the country's first settlers. Other descendents gained notoriety in their own right. James Barton Longacre, a second cousin once removed, was head of the Philadelphia Mint and designed the Indian head penny. John Morton, a second cousin twice removed, was a signer of the Declaration of Independence and was a fourth cousin to Rebecca Bryan the wife of Daniel Boone. In addition, Charles was a fourth cousin twice removed to Harris Flanagan, Arkansas governor from 1862-1864, who also served with the 2nd Arkansas Mounted Rifles as a colonel. Lastly, it has been noted that Longacre was a distant relative of Kate King, the wife of William Clarke Quantrill.

QUANTRILL'S THIEVES By: Joseph K. Houts, Jr.

B L Long:
(Benjamin F., S.)

Benjamin F. Long was from Vernon County, Missouri. He served in the 5th Missouri Cavalry Regiment during the Civil War, assigned to Company B. He was listed as a sergeant. William Tucker and Otho Offut were both also in this regiment and on Quantrill's Roster of original riders. Long, along with other citizens, helped to reestablish local government and law and order in the county after the war. A petition was filed with Governor Fletcher seeking the creation of a county court. The first court was convened on October 17, 1865 and the second on November 13 in Nevada City. He was appointed Justice of the Peace at the third court session which was held on November 14 at Little Ozark, along with F. P. Anderson and Hiram Johnson for Center Township. Later in the year, Long and E. I. Fishpool were officially elected to the position with each receiving sixty votes. The election was the first since the conclusion of the war.

James Lyon
(Lyons)

James Lyons was born in Missouri 1843. His parents were Daniel and Martha J. Lyons who were both born in Kentucky. According to the 1860 Cass County Census, James had four siblings: William, Laura A., John, and Peter. Living next to the family was another Lyons household. The head of this family was a woman named Cynthia A Lyons. She had three children, who were named William S., Josephene, and Taylor. Cynthia was from Kentucky and her offspring had been born in Missouri. Both clans had moved to the state around 1840. It is possible that she was married to a brother of Daniel, and that she was widowed after the family arrived in Missouri.

In all probability, James was at the battle of Pleasant Hill, Missouri on July 11, 1862. At the beginning of the war, James, his brother William, and his cousin William S., enlisted in the 12th Missouri Cavalry, which was originally formed under the command of Colonel Upton Hays. The colonel was also on the Roster of William Clarke Quantrill's original riders, as was James. All of them were in Company A. This particular regiment was formed predominantly of Western Jackson County men and was referred to as the "Jackson County Cavalry." It would also be called Shank's Regiment, after being reorganized later in the war. Of some coincidence, ten other men on the Roster were in this regiment. They were William Tucker, John Hicks George, William H. Gregg, James A. Hendricks, John Jarrette, Richard Maddox, Boone Traveler Muir, William Vaughan, James Vaughan, and Charles T. Williamson. Most likely the early association of these individuals explains in part how they became a large core of Quantrill's gang. In particular, how Lyons came to be associated with Quantrill, since he was from Cass County as opposed to Jackson and Johnson Counties, where the bulk of the guerrillas were from.

Other than his ties to the 12th Missouri Cavalry, little else has been uncovered concerning his wartime service. There was mention of a Lyons deserting in August 1864 from William T.

QUANTRILL'S THIEVES By: Joseph K. Houts, Jr.

"Bloody Bill" Anderson's outfit after a raid on the riverboat *War Eagle*. Possibly, this man was one and the same individual. However, it does appear that he surrendered at Shreveport or New Orleans, Louisiana in May 1865. It should be mentioned that there was another James Lyon/Lyons from Cass County. In all likelihood, he was not the Lyons on the Roster because he was younger and did not have the close association to William and William S. Lyons, who were living next to the other James Lyons.

B. T. Muir
(Boone Traveler, Boon T., B.)

Boone Traveler Muir was born in Missouri on October 15 1836. His middle name is derived from the fact that he was born while the family was "travelling" to Missouri from Kentucky. He was the son of William and Matilda Muir of Independence, Missouri. Siblings included Martha J., Louisa, Maria, Mary E., Lucinda, James F., Sally A., and Samuel D. In 1860, there were four other Muir homesteads located in Jackson County within the same general area. All of them were related as either in-laws or cousins, with James F. Muir living on his own. The entire clan was from Kentucky. During the war, William's farm would on occasion operate as a sanctuary for guerrillas passing through the region.

Muir first enlisted into the Missouri Sate Guard at Hickman Mills, Missouri in 1861. Thereafter, he rode with William Clarke Quantrill, and later joined Colonel Upton Hays' regiment under the command of Mayor General Joseph O. Shelby in the summer of 1862. While attached to Hays' outfit, he was a sergeant assigned to the 12th Missouri Cavalry, Company E. Other guerrillas on Quantrill's Roster serving in the regiment were Oscar Hampton, Richard Maddox, William H. Vaughn, James Vaughn, John Jarrette, A. Harris, Fernando F. Scott, William Campbell, and James A Hendricks.

During the war, he fought at the battles of Independence, Missouri, August 11, 1862; Lone Jack, Missouri, August 16, 1862; Prairie Grove, Arkansas, December 7, 1862; Springfield, Missouri, January 8, 1863; Hartsville, Missouri, January 9-11, 1863; and Cape Girardeau, Missouri, April 26, 1863.

Prior to the battle of Independence, he participated in a reconnaissance of the area, led by Colonel Hays along with Cole Younger, Dick Yeager, Virgil Miller, and William Young. In the process, they entered the town of Westport dressed as Union troops and stole a newly unfurled flag belonging to the fifty garrisoned troops of Kansas Jayhawker Dr. Charles R. "Doc" Jennison. A brief fight and a chase ensued, but the scouting party was able to escape safely back into the bush. In the spring of 1865, he was paroled at Corsicana, Texas.

Muir was purportedly killed in 1863 and buried in the Smith Cemetery located in Jackson County. The circumstances of his reported death have remained unknown. The graveyard was also the last resting-place for Fernando Scott, one of Quantrill's chief officers. In addition, Susan Crawford Vandever, Armenia Crawford Selvey, and Charity McCorkle Kerr were buried in the cemetery. They were three of the five women killed in the Kansas City building collapse on August 13, 1863, which sparked the raid on Lawrence, Kansas eight days later on August 21. Of special note, they were related to guerrillas Cole Younger, and John and Jabez McCorkle.

In a letter to his family dated March 17, 1864 (the year after Muir had supposedly been killed), guerrilla Richard F. Yeager made mention of Muir. Apparently, the two were close friends having grown up together in the same area of Jackson County. More important though, they were brother-in-laws, for Yeager had married Boone's sister, Martha.

Like Mark Twain, the report of Muir's death appears to have been grossly exaggerated, for he was very much alive even up to 1910. On May 10 of that year, he submitted his "Application for Admission to the Confederate Home of Missouri at Higginsville, Missouri." He was living in Belton, Cass County, Missouri at the time, having recently returned to the state after residing in Texas the previous fifty years. In 1910, he was suffering from a debilitating illness, most likely a stroke, which left him paralyzed and unable to support himself. Unfortunately, on June 7, Muir was notified that his application was rejected because he did not meet the state's residency requirement. It set forth that all individuals seeking admittance must have lived in the state one-year preceding acceptance. In his case, he had only been in the state for eleven months.

On May 7, 1916, Muir died while a resident of the Masonic Home in St. Louis, Missouri. He was buried in the Belton Cemetery, Cass County, Missouri under the direction of Belton Masonic Lodge No. 450. Boone had been a charter member. His burial took place at 6:00 p.m. on May 8. In his obituary, he was described as "...a good, law abiding citizen after the war."

James L. Morris
(James S., James)

James L. Morris was born in Missouri in 1843. His parents were Thomas W. and Burilda L. Morris. In the 1850 Carroll County Census, James was shown to have one younger sibling named Thomas A. The census also listed his father as a farmer. The entire Morris household had been born in Missouri, meaning that they were some of the state's first settlers, arriving when the area was still a territory.

Morris enlisted as a private in the Missouri 1st Infantry unit at Carrollton, Missouri in 1861, assigned to Company D, under the command of Captain C. M. Morrison in Slack's Brigade. He fought in the battles of Cartage, Missouri, July 5, 1861; Wilson's Creek, Missouri, August 10, 1861; and Lexington, Missouri, September 18-20, 1861.

In the spring or summer of 1862, he joined guerrilla chieftain William Clarke Quantrill and his partisan rangers. As a guerrilla, Morris was at the battles of Pleasant Hill, Missouri, July 11, 1862, where he was wounded and his horse killed, followed by Independence, Missouri, August 11, 1862; and Lone Jack, Missouri, August 16, 1862. During the early part of February 1863, while riding with Cole Younger, John Koger, and Jabez (Job) McCorkle, he and the others were betrayed by John McDowell resulting in all of them being wounded and the death of another associate named Thomas Talley.

Morris came to an untimely end on August 11, 1863. While wrapped in a blanket catching some rest, members of the Missouri State Militia attacked and shot him. Although mortally wounded, he rolled over on his left elbow and killed three of his assailants. Two other attackers were wounded in the assault. At the time of his death, Morris was riding with William T. "Bloody Bill" Anderson. The place of his last fight and demise was Georgetown, Missouri.

QUANTRILL'S THIEVES By: Joseph K. Houts, Jr.

George Madox
(George W., George William, George Webster, Maddox)

George W. Maddox was born in 1831, a native of Missouri. On December 1, 1859, he married Mary Boswell in Cass County. In 1860, Maddox was listed as a farmer residing in Big Cedar, Jackson County, Missouri. He was known to have at least nine children: Anna E., John, Richard, George Webster, Leonard, Earnest, Raymond, Dora Maddox Varner, and Hallie Maddox Meyers.

His parents were Larkin and Jane Estill Power Maddox of Kentucky. They were married in 1825 and moved to Callaway County, Missouri with "a team of oxen and a blind horse." After settling in the county, they would ride 15 to 20 miles to church on either the horse or an ox, all within "the same day." Mrs. Maddox died and Larkin married Emeline Belcher. She was from Cass County, Missouri. Between both wives, Larkin would sire 12 children. Larkin was "outspoken" in his support of the South. Fearing possible repercussions from Union authorities because of his sentiments, he deeded his land in Johnson County, Missouri to a friend. The individual decided to keep the land after Larkin was killed in 1865. Eventually, the family regained title to the property after pursuing the matter for four years in the courts.

In January 1862, Maddox along with Ol Shepard and Fletch Taylor joined Quantrill's gang as some of the guerrilla chieftain's earliest recruits. He was at the battles of Pleasant Hill, Missouri, July 11, 1862; Lawrence, Kansas, August 21, 1862; Baxter Springs, Kansas, October 6, 1863; and Centralia, Missouri, September 27, 1864. At Pleasant Hill, he was wounded and his horse was killed, thereby requiring escape by foot. Maddox was also with Quantrill in the attempted attack on Kansas City, Missouri, planned for June 16, 1863. During the journey to Lawrence, he served as Quantrill's main scout. His brother, Richard, was credited with being one of the top killers at Lawrence, next to Peyton Long, Bill Gower, and Allen Parmer.

After the battle at Baxter Springs the guerrillas captured two Negro civilians. One of the two, a fellow named Rube, was driving General James G. Blunt's carriage. Maddoxx was readying to shoot him when the prisoner asked if George Todd was present. Todd recognized Rube immediately and stated that he would kill anyone who might harm his old friend.

One time Rube had saved Todd's life. Rube was a freed black man who operated a barbershop in Kansas City. While cutting a Union officer's hair, he overheard the outline of a plan to capture Todd. He shared this information with Todd's father, and Todd stayed with Rube for ten days, hiding until he could safely leave the area. Todd took him to Texas with the gang where he took up cutting hair again, this time for the guerrillas.

Unlike Rube, the second captive, Jack Mann, was a runaway slave from Missouri. He had served as a scout for the Jayhawkers. During a raid on Maddox's house, Mann had put on George's wedding suit, undressing in the presence of Mrs. Maddox. Maddox was eager to kill Mann for this outrageous transgression, but Quantrill intervened because the gang needed to finish some looting. Mann was placed under the guard of Will McGuire. Apparently realizing that he was doomed, Mann began to taunt McGuire, who, after he had suffered enough insults, shot him. Being denied his right of personal revenge; Maddox was outraged and turned his gun on McGuire. Fortunately for McGuire, several guerrillas intervened and separated the two.

On November 18, 1863, a Douglas County, Kansas grand jury issued indictments against Maddox and other participants in the Lawrence raid. After the war, he was apprehended and transferred to Lawrence authorities on February 8, 1866. He was placed in jail and the militia was summoned to guard him, fearing friends might attempt a rescue. There has been some controversy as to how he came to be incarcerated. The *Missouri Republic* claimed he had been kidnapped, whereas, the *Kansas Tribune* wrote that he had been arrested and charged with the murder of a Union supporter outside Pleasant Hill, Missouri. Through the request of the Douglas County sheriff by way of Kansas's governor, he had been extradited to Lawrence. A change of venue was granted, whereby the trial was moved to Ottawa, Kansas. Obviously, he would have been hard pressed to secure a fair trial in Lawrence. Nevertheless, many Lawrence citizens attended the proceedings confidant of Maddox's conviction. The trial involved more than the purported killing of a Missouri Union citizen, it was also an attempt to prosecute a guerrilla for the Lawrence massacre. In either case, the jury acquitted Maddox. Quickly, he sneaked out to the alley behind the courthouse, where his wife was waiting with a getaway horse. Before anyone knew what was happening, Mr. and Mrs. Maddox were well on their way back to Missouri. George would be the only guerrilla to stand trial for the Lawrence raid.

Sometime after the war, Maddox moved to Nevada, Missouri and worked for the railroad. In 1897, he became a guard at the Missouri State Penitentiary at Jefferson City, Missouri. He belonged to the United Confederate Veterans Camp of General M. M. Parsons, Commander James B. Gault. In addition, he was listed on the muster roll of the United Confederate Veteran's Camp at Jefferson City. Maddox attended the second Quantrill Reunion held at a fair in 1899. Purportedly, on January 4, 1901, he died in Arkansas and was buried by ex-Confederates. However, another account claimed that he was still alive and in Jefferson City as of April 5, 1901. This was according to George H. Noel, who visited with him on the street.

Sons of George and Nancy Boswell Maddox: Seated John (on the left) and Richard (Dick). Standing, believed to be George Webster on the left, either Lenard or Earnest in the middle, and Raymond. Courtesy Amos Vannarsall.

Ezry Moore
(Ezra)

Ezra Moore was born on April 4, 1836 in Ohio. He lived in Oak Grove, Missouri. On March 21, 1860, he married 19 year old Frances Fitzhugh George. Her brothers, Gabriel W., Hiram James, and John Hicks George, were all members of Quantrill's gang. She was the daughter of David C. George, a slave owner, who was born on July 8, 1798 in Kentucky and was murdered on February 15, 1863 because of his Southern sympathies. Frances' mother, Nancy E. Bass George, was born on January 10, 1808 in Tennessee, and died on April 5, 1888. Both of her parents were residents of Oak Grove at the time of their death. Ezra and Frances Moore had one daughter, Mary E., born on February 22, 1861.

In the middle of September 1861, Moore enlisted in the Confederate Army. He was wounded the same month at the battle of Lexington, Missouri by a stray shot to his leg. Contracting typhoid fever, he left the army and returned home to recuperate. On January 23, 1862, accompanied by N. B. George, Addison Philpott and J. M. Harding, he went to Texas with some stock. In February 1862, he again enlisted in the Confederate Army for a three-month stint. At the end of his enlistment, he returned home with B. F. Harding, arriving May 22, 1862. Ezra took up farming, planting corn on a 40-acre tract that was given to him by his father-in-law. On June 11, 1862, Union troops from Lexington advanced on Moore's farm in search of him, but he was not to be found. The next day they went to his father-in-law's house and burned it to the ground. Because of this action, Moore, along with several associates, joined Quantrill's partisan band.

Soon after joining Quantrill, Moore went into combat at the battle of Pleasant Hill, Missouri on July 11, 1862 at the Sears farm. Unfortunately, it would be his last fight. There were two reports of his death. The first account said that he was shot several inches above the heart while climbing out of a ravine. The other report stated that he was shot off his saddle. Other guerrilla fatalities included Jerre Doores and John Hampton. Fellow Bushwhacker, William Tucker was wounded. Moore's body was buried in the George family cemetery outside Oak Grove. His wife would later remarry, known as Francis Fitzhugh (George) Moore Kabrick. She died on February 22, 1922.

QUANTRILL'S THIEVES By: Joseph K. Houts, Jr.

J N Olliphant
(John Newton, John N., John W., J. S., Newton, Olifant, Oliphant)

John Newton Oliphant was born in Tennessee in 1836. At the beginning of the Civil War, he was a farmer living in Madison Township, Johnson County, Missouri. His wife's name was Margaret M., Tennessee was also her place of birth. The 1860 Johnson County Census listed numerous other Oliphant's from Tennessee and Missouri. Probably, the couple had ventured west in order to settle among their kinfolk within the state. They apparently did not have any children.

John Newton's parents may have been John and M. J. C. Oliphant. This couple was listed in the 1860 census which indicates that they were from Tennessee and that Mr. Olipant was age 56, and his wife's age 46. The 1860 census listed him as a merchant and having two children living with him, named James S. and M. D. Oliphant. Neighbors of the Oliphants were William M. Burgess and his parents. William Burgess was also on the Roster with John.

In all probability, Oliphant was at the battle of Pleasant Hill, Missouri on July 11, 1862. He also participated in the fight at Lone Jack, Missouri on August 16, 1862. Thereafter, his service record remains something of a mystery, except that he rode off and on with guerrilla chieftain William Clarke Quantrill, and at other times with fellow partisans Fletcher "Fletch" Taylor and William T. "Bloody Bill" Anderson. After the battle at Centralia, Missouri on September 27, 1864, he was killed while riding with Anderson during Major General Sterling Price's last campaign in Missouri. The details and circumstances of his death are unknown.

J Owings
(Joshua, J., Owens)

Joshua Owings was born on July 8, 1821, with his place of birth being Kentucky. His parents were Richard and Winifred Owings. Neither he, nor his father, owned any slaves in 1860. The senior Owings voted for Breckenridge in the presidential election that same year. At the start of the Civil War, Joshua Owings lived in Oak Grove, Jackson County, Missouri. He was a farmer.

Before the war Joshua had been married first to Mary J. Ricketts, and subsequently to a second cousin named Martha E. George. Martha was born on September 13, 1829 in Tennessee. Her parents were David C. and Nancy E. Bass George and her brothers, Hiram J. "Hi," and John H. "Hicks," or "Hix," George were guerrillas with William Clarke Quantrill. Both brothers were also on the Roll with her husband. The Owings and George clans all lived in Oak Grove and their residences were in close proximity to each other. Joshua and Martha had ten children: Andrew P., David R., Francis M., Nathan B., John H., Levi, Dudley J., Melissa, Nancy, and Amanda. From this stock, there would be 43 grandchildren, and several great grandchildren, and great, great grandchildren. Descendants, Henry K., Walter and Ernest Owings would serve in World War I.

On August 1, 1862, Owings enlisted in the Confederate Army at Jackson County into the 2nd Missouri Cavalry, Company C, Shank's Regiment, under the command of Major General Joseph O. Shelby. He was a private and was paroled out of the army at war's end. Owings had not been wounded or taken prisoner during his service. Prior to joining the army, he rode with Quantrill, attributed in large part to his brother-in-laws' association with the guerrilla chieftain. In all probability, he was at the battle of Pleasant Hill, Missouri on July 11, 1862. After the war he returned to Oak Grove and most likely took up farming again. He died at the age of 59 and was laid to rest in the George Family Cemetery located in Jackson County, Missouri. His wife Martha would out live him by 46 years, dying at the age of 96 on January 27, 1926. She was buried next to her husband.

Harry Odgen
(Henry Warren, Henry)

     Henry Warren Ogden was born on October 21, 1842 in Abingdon, Virginia. In 1851, he and his family moved to Warrensburg, Missouri. His parents were Elias and Mariah L. Ogden. There were six children in the family with Henry being the third. The names of his siblings were Mary S., Frank, Beverly J., Louisa, and Newton. He received his education by attending the common schools.

     Ogden was at the Battle of Pleasant Hill, Missouri on July 11, 1862, where he escaped on foot because his horse had been shot. His brother, Frank or F. M. Ogden, also one of Quantrill's original 93 riders, was at the battle and aided John Jarrett, 2nd Sergeant, in escaping. Eventually, Henry left the guerrillas and joined the regular Confederate Army. He was a 1st Lieutenant in Company D, 16th Regiment, Missouri Infantry. Later, he served on the staff of Brigadier General Lewis, Second Brigade, Parson's Division. On June 8, 1865, he was paroled at Shreveport, Louisiana.

     Following the war, he remained in Louisiana and pursued agriculture as a livelihood. Ogden entered politics by way of an appointment from Governor Nickolls as a tax collector. In 1879, he was a member of the state constitutional convention. From 1880-1888, he served in the Louisiana House of Representatives and was Speaker of the House between 1884-1888. One account has also held that he served as Lieutenant Governor. Thereafter, he was elected to the 53rd United States Congress as a Democrat. He had been chosen to fill the vacated seat of Newton C. Blachand, upon his ascent to the United States Senate. Twice re-elected, his term in Congress was from May 12, 1894 to March 5, 1899. Upon retiring from politics, he returned to his previous career in agriculture as a planter. Being a Mason, he twice served as the Worshipful Master of Cypress Lodge No. 89 F. and A.M. In addition, he was the district's Deputy Grand Master. On July 23, 1905, he died at his home on Cat Island Plantation three miles south of Benton, Bossier Parish, Louisiana and was buried in the Cottage Grove Cemetery. The Reverend W. H. Zeiger conducted the funeral service, followed by a Masonic burial ceremony over Ogden's open grave performed by Worshipful Master E. M. Laughlin. His wife had preceded him in death. Four children and a sister, Louie Ogden, survived. The names of his children were: Mrs. J. C. Dickson, Mary Scott Ogden, Louie Ogden, and Frank Ogden. Daughter, Louie, had obviously been named after his sister, as was son Frank for his guerrilla brother. It was said upon his passing "great is the loss to our community, and there is no one to take his place."

QUANTRILL'S THIEVES By: Joseph K. Houts, Jr.

F M Ogden
(Frank M., F. V.)

Frank M. Ogden was born in 1840 with his place of birth being Virginia. In 1851, he and his family moved to Warrensburg, Missouri. His parents were Elias and Mariah L. Ogden. The 1860 Johnson County Census, listed his father as a farmer. He was the second of six children. Their names were Mary S., Henry Warren, Beverly J., Louisa, and Newton. Except for Elias, who was from New Jersey, the entire Ogden household had been born in Virginia. Along with his brother Henry, he received his education by attending the common schools.

He was at the battle of Pleasant Hill, Missouri on July 11, 1862. In the retreat from the engagement he assisted John Jarrette in escaping. His brother Henry participated in the fight and was also one of the original guerrillas set forth on the Roster, as was Jarrette.

Ogden's whereabouts for the rest of the war and thereafter remains a mystery. One source has indicated that he possibly died during the conflict. The Ogden family as a whole left Missouri after the war and moved to Louisiana. This was attributed in large part to son Henry settling there upon his surrender in June 1865. Although undocumented, Frank may have also joined the family. Henry would become a prominent politician in the state, eventually being elected to the United States House of Representatives, serving from May 12, 1894 to March 5, 1899. On July 23, 1905, Henry died and in his obituary it stated that a sister and four children survived him. From this announcement, it can be established that Frank had predeceased him. However, in a lasting statement of affection to his older brother, Henry's youngest child was named Frank.

Otho Offutt
(Oath, O., Offit)

Otho Offutt was born in 1840. He lived in the northern part of Johnson County, Missouri prior to the Civil War. Early in the war, he served in the 5th Missouri Cavalry Regiment as a corporal assigned to Company G, the 9th Missouri Battalion Sharp Shooters, as a sergeant assigned to Company B, and the 11th Missouri Infantry assigned to Company H. Offutt was at the Tate house skirmish on March 22, 1862 and the battles of Lawrence, Kansas, August 21, 1863; Baxter Springs, Kansas, October 6, 1863; and Centralia, Missouri, September 27, 1864.

At 6 feet 3 inches in height and weighing 210 pounds, Offutt was described as the tallest and most powerful man riding with Quantrill. There was one exception, guerrilla Ol Johnson was said to be taller. However, he was killed at Fayette, Missouri in 1864, thereby giving Offutt the height honor.

At the battle of Pleasant Hill, he probably saved fellow bushwhacker Al Cunningham's life. In fleeing the fight, he noticed Cunningham did not have a horse. Offutt also noticed Al had been wounded in the arm, which was bound up by a handkerchief. Accordingly, he stopped and had him jump on the back. They then proceeded to jump over a three-rail fence. Both men were rather large and knew the horse would not be able to carry them for very long. Cunningham slipped off and they parted ways. Cunningham left on foot, with Offutt on his horse going to a prearranged rendezvous place that the guerrillas had established in case there turned out to be trouble at Pleasant Hill. The next morning, much to Offutt's surprise, Cunningham arrived at the regrouping point, having walked all of the way. He had never expected to see him again.

Besides those major conflicts that he fought in, Offutt also experienced several wartime scrapes. In the fall of 1863, he and five other comrades were holed up at the house of Mrs. Helms, a widow. Captain Jehu Smith of the 1st Regiment, Missouri State Militia (MSM) attached to the Union post at Warrensburg, Missouri was patrolling around Odessa, Missouri

QUANTRILL'S THIEVES   By: Joseph K. Houts, Jr.

looking for William T. "Bloody Bill" Anderson, who was supposed to be in the area near relatives. In the process, Smith stumbled upon the guerrillas at daybreak. Immediately, the six bushwhackers ran to the brush for their horses. Four of them were promptly cut down by the Federals. Offutt and another guerrilla were wearing blue overcoats, which they had probably procured off a dead Yankee. The coats may have helped to disguise them in the confusion of combat. He had a revolver in each hand as he made his way for his horse. Both men escaped through an orchard on the west side of the house. Riding a powerful animal he collided with a Union officer and his mount, knocking both rider and animal to the ground. Although having been shot through a lung, he managed to escape, thereafter recuperating and hiding at a friend's house until fully recovered.

In another incident, during the fall of 1864, he and Bill Stewart left General Sterling Price's army and decided to head for the north side of the Missouri River. Due to the war, there were no skiffs to be used in the crosing. They could not swim it either, because of the weight of their supplies and revolvers. The best place to cross was at Brunswick, Missouri, where there was a ferry of sorts. First though, they needed to change out of their guerrilla garb because the area contained numerous Union troops. At a friend's place they found new attire, with Offutt donning a "long white linen duster and an old stovepipe hat." The outfit made him appear seven feet tall, but the duster served the purpose of hiding his guns, although it hung to the heels of his boots. After landing on the other side of the river, they casually strode through the town, until they heard two drunken Union soldiers yell out to them "Halt!" Immediately, they pulled their guns and shot one of the soldiers off his horse. Next, they started shooting randomly to the left and right scattering the townfolks, while galloping down the street. Looking back on their exit, Offutt noticed the duster trailing six yards behind his horse. He observed you "could play a game of cards on it," because it was so long and level. Both he and Stewart had a good laugh over the spectacle. Once safely far enough away from the town, they left their clothing on a fence. Three weeks later, they returned to Brunswick in order to buy a horse. While conducting their business, they heard a tale about a preacher and an associate recently shooting their way out of town. Offutt and Stewart thereupon told the horse seller the real story.

In February 1865, he and six others were hiding out in Howard County, Missouri. Their camp was on Peach Creek, roughly seven miles from Columbia. They had plenty of supplies, which had been given to them by friends. One night after a heavy snowfall, they were sleeping under a moonlit sky. At 1:00 a.m. someone shouted, "Get up!" Offutt was instantly on his feet with pistol in hand, but fell over a log. Upon standing up, he was hit on the head and fell down again. He next heard someone say "Shoot him again, he is not dead." Looking up he saw a man standing overhead readying to shoot him. Quickly, Offutt fired his gun with the bullet passing through the man's chin and head, killing him instantly. Four of his companions were killed, while arising from their blankets. Once again, Offutt had been wounded. A bullet had grazed him after striking a compass that he carried inside a breast pocket. Miraculously, he escaped.

After the war he returned to Johnson County and was in the livery and stock business. In 1887, it was reported that he built a large stone livery stable in Holden. Offutt ran for sheriff of Johnson County as announced in the Johnson County Star on October 30, 1893. There was a field of eight candidates. The newspaper commented, "the Star takes pleasure in submitting his name to its readers, to a large portion of whom he is well known." Offutt was married three times. He married his first wife, Eleanor Coffman, on February 25, 1876. On January 19, 1900, she filed for divorce, somewhat of an uncommon practice at this time in America. Shortly thereafter, he married again. Unfortunately, his second wife, Mary M. Offutt died on December 8, 1903. It has been documented that he attended the 1890 Shelby Veterans Reunion at Nevada, Missouri followed by the 1899, and 1904 Quantrill Reunion. In 1934, he packed up and left for Grand Junction, Colorado, with his third wife.

T D Perdee
(Thomas B., T. B., Tom, Purdee, Pardee, Pardue)

Thomas B. Perdee was the fourth of sixth children born to James and Mary Perdee of Johnson County, Columbus Township, Missouri. He was born in Johnson County in 1842. The names of his sibling were George W. and Andrew J. (twins), James, Franklin, and Jefferson. His father and mother were born in Virginia and Tennessee, respectively. The Perdee's had been some of the original settlers to arrive in Columbus Township, setting down stakes sometime prior to 1840.

James Perdee was a farmer owning a tract of land lying in a hollow adjacent to the Blackwater River. On many occasions his farm served as the rendezvous place for Quantrill and the guerrillas. In particular, it was their staging point for the raid on Lawrence, Kansas on August 21, 1863 and two months later for the guerrillas trek south to winter quarters at Sherman, Texas, where in route they surprised the Union fort at Baxter Springs, Kansas on October 6, 1863. The farm was an ideal cover for these partisans. There were sharp cliffs, a source of water for man and beast, plus dense foliage in which they could be made invisible against patrolling Union cavalry. Kansas Jayhawkers had decimated the town of Columbus early in the war, forever instilling an appetite for revenge among the inhabitants. This factor alone was probably why Thomas and his brother James joined Quantrill.

Perdee served in the 10th Missouri Cavalry Regiment, assigned to Company G. Six other guerrillas on Quantrill's Roster were also in this regiment. They were John D. Brinker, William M. Haller, John H. Terry, James R. Dejarnett, Robert W. Houx, and William Doores. Thomas was in all likelihood at the battle of Pleasant Hill, Missouri on July 11, 1862, and probably many others. His whereabouts after the war have remained a mystery.

J R Perdee
(James P., J. P., Jim, Purdee, Pardee, Pardue)

    James P. Perdee was the third of six children born to James and Mary Perdee of Johnson County, Columbus Township, Missouri. He was born in Missouri in 1838. The names of his siblings George W., and Andrew J. (twins), Thomas B., Franklin, and Jefferson. His father and mother were born in Virginia and Tennessee, respectively. The Perdee's were some of the original settlers to arrive in Columbus Township, setting down stakes sometime prior to 1840.

    James Perdee was a farmer owning a tract of land lying in a hollow adjacent to the Blackwater River. On many occasions his farm served as the rendezvous place for Quantrill and the guerrillas. In particular, it was their staging point for the raid on Lawrence, Kansas on August 21, 1863 and two months later for the guerrillas trek south to winter quarters at Sherman, Texas, where en route they surprised the Union fort at Baxter Springs, Kansas on October 6, 1863. The farm was an ideal cover for these partisans. There were sharp cliffs, a source of water for man and beast, plus dense foliage in which they could be made invisible against patrolling Union cavalry. Kansas Jayhawkers had decimated the town of Columbus early in the war, forever instilling an appetite for revenge among the inhabitants. This factor alone was probably why James and his brother Thomas joined Quantrill.

    Perdee was in all likelihood at the battle of Pleasant Hill, Missouri on July 11, 1862. The 1870 Johnson County Census listed him as residing with his parents.

QUANTRILL'S THIEVES By: Joseph K. Houts, Jr.

Captain Perdee's farm on Blackwater River, Columbis, Missouri. Point of Quantrill's rendezvous for the raid on Lawrence, and for the trek south to Sherman, Texas. Courtesy Homer Jarmen.

Captain Perdee's homestead. Home of sons T. D. and J. R. Perdee
Courtesy Homer Jarmen

QUANTRILL'S THIEVES By: Joseph K. Houts, Jr.

D M Pool
(Francis Marion, David M., Dave, Davey, Poole)

Francis Marion "David" Pool was an actor of sorts and...could imitate any character or dialect. He was also very proficient with the six-shooter." It was said "he laughed loudest when he was deadliest, and treated fortune with no more dignity in one extreme than another." David was the second of six children born to James Monroe and Jane Thompson Pool, who were married in 1835. The names of their children were Christopher Columbus, Francis Marion, John Adams, Amanda/Armilda, Martin M., and Thomas B. Jane Pool died sometime prior to 1848. On October 19, 1848, James married Elizabeth Ann Harkins. They would have two daughters, named Amanda Powell and Catherine.

David M. Pool, middle, and two cohorts
Used by permission, State Historical Society of Missouri

James was born in 1805, Wyeth County, Virginia. The family eventually moved to Elk Creek, Virginia and then to Lafayette County, Missouri, where David was born in 1837. In the 1850 Lafayette County Census, James' occupation was listed as a "gold hunter". He was described as a wanderer traveling the

QUANTRILL'S THIEVES By: Joseph K. Houts, Jr.

states of Tennessee, Kentucky, Missouri, and Texas. When James' first wife died, the family was broken up. Sons Christopher, David, and John would be raised by three uncles, Stephen, Pleasant, and Ephraim. The fate of the other children has not been documented. Apparently, James left his children in the custody of relatives so he could continue wandering about the Midwest. In 1880, the year of his death, he was reported residing with his daughter, Catherine "Kitty" and her husband, James S. Johnson, in Parker County, Texas.

    Purportedly, Pool joined Quantrill's outfit out of revenge for the shooting of a family member in his uncle Archibald's household. In addition, Archibald's home had been sacked by Kansans. In time, Pool became the leader of those guerrillas associated with Quantrill who were from Lafayette County. He participated in the battles of Independence, Missouri, August 11, 1862; Pleasant Hill, Missouri, July 11, 1862; Prairie Grove, Arkansas, December 7, 1862; Baxter Springs, Kansas, October 6, 1863; Fayette, Missouri, September 20, 1864; and Centralia, Missouri, September 27, 1864.

    Pool was considered a captain under Quantrill along with guerrilla chieftains, William H. Gregg, George M. Todd, and William T. "Bloody Bill" Anderson. At first, he tried to conduct war as a regular, giving amnesty to those captured, but after the Federals denied equal treatment, he forever fought and rode under the "Black Flag." As to his fighting ability, he was described as "a dashing daredevil, by the way, but pitiless as a famished Bengal tiger. A terror to the Federals." For some unknown reason, he had a passion for killing "Dutchmen" or Germans. On at least three occasions, he raided various German settlements in Lafayette County, in particular the town of Concordia. On one occasion, Anderson accompanied him. Many an unarmed farmer was gunned down in his tracks at the hand of Pool and his cohorts.

    In the fall of 1863, Quantrill's forces headed south to Texas for winter quarters. Pool served as lead scout, and he captured two Union wagons. Upon questioning the teamsters, he learned of a new fort being constructed at Baxter Springs, Kansas. After killing the drivers, Pool reported the discovery to

Quantrill. In short order, the guerrillas attacked the fortification. They lost several men, but in the process they nearly captured Union Brigadier General James G. Blunt. In leading a charge against the fort, Pool unfurled a Federal flag, initially tricking and forestalling a Union response to his assault. The battle was a victory for Quantrill and his men. Afterwards, many of the victims were mutilated.

While camping at Sherman, Texas in the winter of 1863-64, Quantrill's gang began to unravel among his leaders. The first to leave was William H. Gregg. He had a falling out with George Todd due to an argument over the spoils of a raid. Pool and John Jarrette warned Gregg about Todd's intent to kill him. After meeting with Quantrill about his departure, Gregg left, but not before starring down Todd. With this event, Pool and Jarrette also left and joined Major General Joseph O. Shelby's command in the fall of 1863, which was camped on the Red River. They served under Captain Lea, hunting cotton smugglers in Louisiana along the Mississippi River. When the guerrillas returned to Missouri from Texas in the spring of 1864, Pool again put in with them, this time riding with Todd's gang. At the battle of Centralia, he distinguished himself by walking on the dead, in order to properly count the bodies, with a cigar neatly tucked in his mouth. On October 26, 1864 at the battle of Westport he assumed command, after Todd fell dead to a sniper's bullet.

On May 21, 1865, Pool and anywhere from 48 to 129 men surrendered to Colonel Chester Harding at the provost marshal's office in Lexington, Missouri. He and his men were given the oath of loyalty and thereupon paroled. By month's end, 200 additional guerrillas had surrendered and been granted amnesty at Lexington. Upon hearing of Pool's surrender, Major General Grenviille M. Dodge responded by saying "Bushwhacking is stopped." After being paroled, Pool became a scout for the Union military, seeking out guerrillas still in hiding and convincing them to also give up. It was said he "became a celebrity with Union officials."

On October 30, 1866, the Lexington bank was robbed, purportedly by Frank and Jesse James along with several former guerrillas. Pool was in charge of the posse pursuing the bandits. However, they managed to escape apprehension. The town newspaper was suspicious of his efforts and "commented only that the pursuit was not especially vigorous." Shortly thereafter, Pool, accompanied by George Shepard, moved to Texas and settled in Sherman. He was reported to have visited Lexington on or about February 15, 1878, where it was claimed that he was returning to his ranch in Texas with a wife. Within a few years, he supposedly moved to New Mexico, followed by Arizona. The <u>Kansas City Star & Times</u> ran a story on June 5, 1899 reporting his death. As a fitting tribute to this once hardened guerrilla veteran, it was said, "Poole, an unschooled Aristophanes of the Civil War laughed at calamity and mocked when any man's fear came. But for its less picturesqueness, his speech would have been comedy personified."

H C Pemberton
(Henry C., Henry, D. C.)

Henry C. Pemberton was born in Missouri in 1841. His mother, Louisa, was born in Kentucky. Apparently, his father had died because there was not a listing for him in the 1860 Johnson County Census. The census showed Louisa was engaged in farming and had two other children; William age 22, and Elizabeth age 12. The family resided in Madison Township, which in time would be realigned and the southwest portion renamed Rose Hill Township.

On August 1, 1862, Pemberton enlisted in the 16th Missouri Infantry, a part of Major General Sterling Price's Division in Parson's Brigade. He was assigned to Captain David M. Raker's Company D, under the command of Colonels Vardaman Cockrell, Jackman and Lewis. During his service he was a private and fought at the battles of Lone Jack, Missouri, August 16, 1862 and Prairie Grove, Arkansas, December 7, 1862. In all likelihood, he was at the battle of Pleasant Hill, Missouri on July 11, 1862. Records have established that he was never wounded or taken prisoner. His company surrendered on May 26, 1865 as part of Major General E. Kirby Smith's forces. However, Pemberton was reported missing and apparently had died on May 14. One report has asserted that he was killed by Jayhawkers from Kansas. His place of death has remained unknow, as has his burial spot.

Of all the original guerrillas set forth on the Roll, there has existed some confusion as to the real Pemberton. Captain Raker's roster and the Record of Missouri Confederate Veterans compiled for The United Daughters of the Confederacy Missouri Division (hereinafter UDC) have listed a D. C. Pemberton within their ranks. Whereas, the 1860 Johnson County Census has the name Henry. Yet another source, of Quantrill's men at the battle of Lone Jack, have a H. C. Pemberton participating in the engagement. The UDC lists D. C. Pemberton as fighting at the same battle. In all likelihood, both D. C. and H. C. Pemberton have been misconstrued as two separate individuals.

QUANTRILL'S THIEVES By: Joseph K. Houts, Jr.

There are several reasons for this conclusion. First, D. C. Pemberton was listed being from Rose Hill Township in Johnson County. In 1860 only Madison Township existed, Rose Hill would be created out of the other in 1869. Second, someone other than Pemberton filled out the UDC form posthumously, thereby continuing the error originating from Raker's roster. In other words, the form was not a true statement by the veteran himself because he was no longer living, leading to the conclusion that the writer was merely perpetuating the mistake. Also, the mistake can be more clearly seen by comparing the letters D. and H. written in a formal, embellished, capital style. In reality, the truth may never be known, but the circumstances behind this case make it almost conclusive.

F M Robinson
(Frank, L. W., F. W., Robertson, Roberson)

F. M. Robertson was born in 1839. His place of birth was Kentucky. In 1860 he was employed as a farm laborer working on the farm of Mary McCown and Margaret Burk. The name of Robertson's wife was Wealthy J., age 23, and his daughter's name was Mary M., age 10. Wealthy had been born in Tennessee, and Mary in Missouri.

Some confusion has surrounded Robertson, if in fact that was his name. Quantrill's Roster showed it as Robinson, but a search for a Robinson with the initials F. M. reveals no such person.

There was a Frank Robinson who was from Saline County, Missouri with the rank of colonel. He was in charge of 600 men from the county who were on their way to join Major General Sterling Price in December 1861, but he was forced to surrender his command near the Blackwater River when confronted by a superior Union force. He was imprisoned for some time along with his troops, which would logically remove him from consideration as one of Quantrill likely early gang members.

However, there was a F. M. Robertson living in Johnson County, Missouri in 1860 in close proximity to William McCown Burgess and James G. Freeman, individuals who were on the Roster of original guerrillas. Residing in the Burgess household was William McCown, age 13, who may have been a relative of Mary McCown, Robertson's employer. It can be assumed by Burgess' middle name of McCown, that he was also kin to Mary McCown.

Through phonetics the name Robertson could have been mistaken for Robinson, resulting in it's misspelling. If Robertson was actually the Robinson on Quantrill's roster, then it was likely that he participated in the battle of Pleasant Hill, Missouri on July 11, 1862, with most of the other initial guerrillas who joined Quantrill's ranks.

J W Rider
(John Winiard, John W.)

John Winiard Rider was born on March 11, 1837 in Jackson County, Missouri. In 1860 he was married to Malinda "Linda" Harrison Ligett. He was a farmer and owned one slave. His farm was located next to his father's, George Rider, who was also on William Clarke Quantrill's Roster of original guerrillas. Both father and son lived in close proximity to Morgan Walker and his son Andy. The Walker household was the scene of Quantrill's defection to the South. George's slave found two of Quantrill's cohorts whom Quantrill had betrayed. Their names were Ball and Lipsey. These two had escaped initially. The slave tipped off the Walkers and Quantrill to their whereabouts. Upon finding them, Quantrill and Morgan Walker killed the men.

Rider and his wife had seven children named: Walter, Mary Eliza, Charles Quantrell (sic), Nellie, Alfred Tralle, Elizabeth, and Winiard Martin. Quite obviously, their third child, Charles Quantell (sic), had been named in honor of the guerrilla chieftain.

John and his father served in the 8th Missouri Infantry Battalion, assigned to Company D. In their company were John, Ab, and Thomas Teague, who were also on Quantrill's Roster. In all probability, John was at the battle of Pleasant Hill, Missouri on July 11, 1862. He survived the war and died on February 12, 1907 in Independence, Missouri.

George Rider
(George W.)

George W. Rider was born on May 16, 1807 with his place of birth being Kentucky. His parents were John and Mary Ann "Polly" Rider. He married Alisa Bush on July 3, 1824 and they would have eight children named, William E., Eliza Jane, Miley "Milly", Samuel B., John Winiard, Oliver J., and Elizabeth. In 1860 he was a farmer and owned three slaves. Son John lived close to his father.

At the war's outset, he was a neighbor to Morgan and Andy Walker, outside Blue Springs, Missouri. The Walker household would be the scene of William Clarke Quantrill's defection to the South and his betrayal of several comrades. Quantrill had devised a scheme to steal Walker's slaves, twenty of them or more, and then sell them back into slavery. However, upon reaching the ranch, he approached the Walkers and informed them about the plan, blaming his cohorts for the idea. Later that night, Walker and some of his neighbors ambushed the raiders, killing two in the process, while two others escaped into the bush. The next day or so, Rider's slave stumbled upon the men, named Ball and Lipsey. The slave advised the Walkers and Quantrill of his find. On locating them, Quantrill and Morgan Walker killed them.

George and his son John were both on Quantrill's Roster of original guerrillas. They also served together in the 8th Missouri Infantry Battalion, assigned to Company D. Joining them in the company and on the Roster were John, Ab, and Thomas Teague. George was likely at the battle of Pleasant Hill, Missouri on July 11, 1862. He survived the war and died on December 26 in either 1876 or 1880. His place of burial was in the Old Lobb Cemetery at Blue Springs. Cemetery records show the year of his death as 1880.

QUANTRILL'S THIEVES By: Joseph K. Houts, Jr.

Robert Stephenson
(Robert John Stevenson)

Robert John Stevenson was born in Ohio in 1844. Little is known about him except for his whereabouts after the war.

Due to his association with guerrilla chieftain William Clarke Quantrill, he was probably at the battle of Pleasant Hill, Missouri on July 11, 1862. There has been reference of a Captain Stevenson serving under Captain Lea in March 1864 along the Mississippi River in Louisiana. There was a list written by Captain E. E. Rogers, Provost Marshal, Lexington, Missouri, showing a Robert Stephenson surrendering to Federal authorities on May 22, 1865.

Robert J. Stevenson tombstone, Elmwood Cemetery, Mexico, Missouri
Courtesy Randy Senor

At the turn of the century, he resided in Mexico, Missouri, later moving to Oklahoma, and then Kansas City, Missouri. While in Kansas City, he lived with a grand niece. On February 26, 1922, he died following an operation. Services were held in Kansas City and the body was returned to Mexico, Missouri for burial in the Elmwood Cemetery. He was listed as a Civil War veteran in his obituary.

William D Tucker
(William)

William D. Tucker in all likelihood was the brother of James S. Tucker, who was also set forth on the Roster of William Clarke Quantrill's original riders. James was listed as an officer on the document with the title of 3rd sergeant. Both men may have been from Lafayette County, Missouri prior to the Civil War. He was at the battle of Lone Jack, Missouri on August 16, 1862 along with his brother James. In addition, he was at the battle of Pleasant Hill, Missouri on July 11, 1862, where he and George Maddox were wounded. Three other guerrillas on the Roster would be killed or subsequently die as a result of the fight; John Hampton, Jeremiah F. Doores, and Ezra Moore.

There was a report of a William Tucker being with the 1st North East Missouri Cavalry, Company A. There was also a report of a William Tucker being with the 12th Missouri Cavalry, Company A. Further there was reference to a William Tucker being killed on September 25, 1865 in Scotland County, Missouri by soldiers of the Missouri State Militia. Whether all of these Tuckers were one and the same has remained a mystery. In all probability, they may have all been the same individual.

QUANTRILL'S THIEVES   By: Joseph K. Houts, Jr.

John Teague
(John H., J. H., J., Nat, Neal Tigue, J. N. Tague)

John H. Teague was born on January 14, 1841, with his place of birth being probably in Missouri. Information concerning his family has remained somewhat clouded. Abe and T. F. Teague were also set forth on the Roll and in all likelihood were his brothers. Both John and Abe were from Shannon County, Missouri, located in the southeast quadrant of the state, within thirty miles of the northern Arkansas border. Teague may at times have been confused with, or was one and the same individual as, Nat or Neal Tigue, who rode with William T. "Bloody Bill" Anderson, in particular at the battle of Centralia, Missouri on September 27, 184. There has also been some evidence linking his brother, Abe, with Anderson's gang at the same time.

Concerning his service, it appears to have covered four distinct realms. First, he enlisted as a private into the Missouri State guard (MSG) in July 1861, at Eminence, Shannon County, Missouri. He was assigned to 2nd Regiment, infantry, under the command of Captain Shade Chilton, with Tho. Chilton as 1st Lieutenant, and Jas. Kile as 3rd Lieutenant. Apparently, after Major General Sterling Price's defeat at Pea Ridge, Arkansas on March 6-8, 1862, and with the likely expiration of his enlistment, he joined William Clarke Quantrill's guerrilla band. This interlude represented the second part of his Confederate service. In all probability, he was in several of the early skirmishes between Quantrill and Union troops in Jackson and Cass Counties, Missouri.

Following a brief association with Quantrill, he again enlisted into the regular Confederate Army on March 30, 1862. On this occasion, he was assigned to Company I of the 4th Missouri Regiment under the command of Colonel McFarland, with George Norman as captain, and 1st Lieutenant Bennet and 2nd Lieutenant Anderson. Later the regiment would be consolidated into the 1st Missouri Regiment under the command of Colonel Rice. While serving in the army, Teague's outfit became involved in the Vicksburg Campaign. He was at the battles of Corinth, Mississippi, October 3-4. 1862; Grand Gulf, Mississippi, April 29, 1863; Port Gibson, Mississippi, May 1, 1863; Champion Hill, Mississippi, May 16, 1863; and the siege of Vicksburg, Mississippi, May 18-July 4, 1863.

Union prisoner documents show that he deserted on July 7, 1863. After the surrender of Confederate forces at Vicksburg, the troops were subsequently paroled. Teague probably left the army, believing the war was played out and his participation no longer required in fighting for the "Cause." Afterwards, he most likely returned home and then ventured to Jackson County, Missouri and reestablished his association with the guerrillas. Records show that he again surrendered to Union officials on May 26, 1865, as part of guerrilla leader David Pool's gang, at Lexington, Missouri to Captain E. E. Rogers, Provost Marshal. His name was listed as J. N. Tague, but subsequent authorities have interpreted the spelling as John Teague.

On July 13, 1913, Teague applied for a Confederate ex-soldier's pension. His residence was listed as Birch Tree, Shannon County, Missouri, only a few miles to the west of his brother Abe's home in Winona, Missouri of the same county. The application stated that he was married and that he had three grown children. He claimed to be a member of Colonel J. R. Woodside's Confederate Camp No. 751 at Alton, Oregon County, Missouri, located directly south of Shannon County. Brother Abe also belonged to this camp. Teague noted on the application that he had been infected with the measles within the first six months of his enlistment, which "badly" impaired his vision to the present. The final dispensation of his application has remained a mystery, suggesting that it was denied, perhaps because he had deserted after the fall of Vicksburg.

QUANTRILL'S THIEVES By: Joseph K. Houts, Jr.

T F Teague
(Thos. F., Thomas)

    Thomas F. Teague was born around 1835, with his place of birth being Missouri. In 1860, he was living in Cass County, Missouri. The Federal Census for that year showed him residing in the household of John M. and Elizabeth F. Gains and their two children, Martha E. and Wm. M. His occupation was not set forth. Elizabeth may have been a sister, which would account for his presence. He was listed on the Roll next to John and Ab Teague, who in all probability were his brothers, tying him to William Clarke Quantrill's guerrilla band. Thomas was older, which also would have explained his not being in the same county with them.

    Teague was in all likelihood at the battle of Pleasant Hill, Missouri on July 11, 1862, along with his brothers. In a report to Union Colonel McFerran, on June 1, 1864, Captain J. A. Wells stated that a recently captured guerrilla was supposedly a member of Teague's gang. Possibly, he was operating in this part of the state. Since he was the eldest among his brothers, he may have had his own guerrilla outfit. Of further note, by this time in the war Quantrill's outfit had splintered into several different and predominately independent orbits. This factor has also lead to speculation that Teague may have been leading his own group of partisans. Other than this reference and potential link, nothing else has been uncovered concerning him.

QUANTRILL'S THIEVES By: Joseph K. Houts, Jr.

A B Teague
(Abe, Ab, Abraham)

Abe Teague was born around 1845. His place of birth has remained unknown, although it can be assumed that he was born in Missouri. In all probability, he was a brother of John and T. F. Teague, who were also set forth on the Roll, next to his name. On October 13, 1913 he submitted an application for a pension as a former Confederate soldier. He avowed being married and to have three grown children. At that time, he stated his residence to be Winona, Shannon County, Missouri.

His pension application stated that he attended Confederate reunions and was a member of Colonel J. R. Woodside's Confederate Camp No. 751, at Alton, Oregon County, Missouri, located directly south of Shannon County. Brother John was a member of the same organization. During the war he received an injury to his eyes. Apparently, powder flashed into both, thereby impairing his vision. It did not state, whether the injury prevented him from gainful employment. In all probability, he was injured while firing a musket, when the powder flared back and burned his eyes.

Teague's service record has some blanks as to all the war years. In 1862, it has been established that he and his brothers rode with William Clarke Quantrill. Most likely, he was at the battle of Pleasant Hill, Missouri on July 11, 1862. There was mention in a Union report submitted by George West, a scout, of a Teague attacking an express rider named Briggs of the Second Wisconsin Cavalry, in or around Fulton County, Arkansas. The report was dated August 2, 1863. Of some coincidence, Teague's pension application stated that he enlisted into the 47th Arkansas Cavalry at Jacksonport, Arkansas in August 1864, assigned to Company I. Although a year later, it does pinpoint his whereabouts in this area. His regimental commander was Colonel Crandall, followed by Captain Long, 1st Lieutenant J. B. Reaser, 2nd Lieutenant John Dean, and 3rd Lieutenant Harrison James. There was also a claim that he served in Company N of either the 13th or 15th Missouri Cavalry.

QUANTRILL'S THIEVES By: Joseph K. Houts, Jr.

Union prisoner records show him serving with the 15th Missouri Cavalry upon surrendering on May 11, 1865, followed by parole on June 5, 1865, at Jacksonport, Arkansas.

Concerning battles, he represented to be at Booneville, Missouri, June 17, 1861; Ironton, Missouri, October 21, 1861 or September 27, 1864; Vera Cruz, Missouri, November 7, 1862; Jefferson City, Missouri, October 9 and 11-12, 1864; Brunswick, Missouri, October 11, 1864; and Paris, Missouri, October 15, 1864. The argument can be made that he enlisted in the 47th Arkansas Cavalry in August of 1864 as part of Major General Sterling Price's last invasion of Missouri. Also, if he was at the second battle of Ironton, he may have been part of those guerrilla bands operating through the middle of Missouri in late summer and early autumn, namely those belonging to William T. "Bloody Bill" Anderson, John Thrailkill, and George Todd.

Unfortunately for Teague, he was a property owner. His pension application stated he owned 120 acres in his wife's name. Only 30 acres were under cultivation. The homestead was valued at $800.00-$700.00, with a mortgage in the amount of $327.00. The problem was that he had too many assets to be considered an indigent under the Missouri pension statute. Accordingly, on November 19, 1913, the adjutant general denied his application. Of some surprise, sixteen months to the day after the date of his rejection, he wrote the adjutant general inquiring of his application and its consideration. On March 22, 1915, the adjutant general again wrote Teague stating he that had been notified of rejection and that he could appeal the matter to Jno. Barker, Attorney General, for the state of Missouri. He retained John W. McClellan, Prosecuting Attorney for Shannon County, Missouri as his attorney. McClellan wrote the adjutant general on December 6, 1915, seeking a reconsideration of the case. However, on December 9, the adjutant general responded that the matter was closed.

Thomson
(Thompson) (James, Oscar and Oliver P. Thompson)

Thomson has no real identity, only a best guess. Although, in all likelihood there was such an individual as set forth on the Roster, there was not a first name or initial(s) attached, which could assist in this individual's true identification. Of primary importance in resolving this mystery was the probable misspelling of the name. Other lists and sources have the spelling as Thompson. As can be imagined there were countless Thomsons and Thompsons living in Missouri at the time of the Civil War. In examining those individuals bearing these two last names, one finds only men with the last name of Thompson who may have had even a remote association with guerrilla chieftain William Clarke Quantrill. From this field, three individuals from Western Missouri stood out as potential candidates, James, Oscar, and Oliver P. Thompson. Accordingly, each individual will be described as if he was the real Thompson riding with Quantrill.

James Thompson

James Thompson was born in Missouri in 1834. His wife was named Sarah J. and they had two children, Susan E. and Margaret E. The 1860 census listed his occupation as a farmer. On August 1, 1862 he enlisted at Johnson County, Missouri into the 16th Missouri Infantry, Parson's Brigade under the command of Colonels Vardaman Cockrell and Jackman. He was a private and his company commander was Captain David M. Raker. Six other guerrillas on the Roster were his neighbors. They were Obediah Strange Barnett, George McKinley Barnett, N.T. Doak, John Newton Oliphant, James H., and Lewis A. Cunningham. Of further significance, he was in Company D of the 16th Mo. Infantry, which also had nine other guerrillas on the Roster serving in this unit. Their names were Hugh L. W. Anderson, William H. Baker, James H. Cunningham, Lewis A. Cunningham, Robert Davenport, N. T. Doak, Charles L.

Longacre, Henry Warren Ogden, and Henry C. Pemberton. The Cunninghams and Doak were his neighbors. If he was the real Thompson, then in all probability he was at Pleasant Hill, Missouri on July 11, 1862. Thompson was at the battles of Lone Jack, Missouri, August 16, 1862, and Prairie Grove, Arkansas, December 7, 1862. Apparently, he deserted on February 1, 1863, but did participate in the Lawrence, Kansas raid on August 21, 1863. Unfortunately, he was killed by his comrades on their return to Missouri for unknown reasons, which may have stemmed from his earlier desertion or for some other betrayal. The body was buried in the Second Creek Baptist Church Cemetery. He was indicted posthumously by a Douglas County, Kansas's grand jury on November 18, 1863, along with thirty-five other guerrillas, for his role in the death of George Burt during the Lawrence raid. The indictment represented somewhat of an irony considering the fact he was not only under a death warrant from Kansas; but had been killed by his own. It appeared no one liked him.

Oscar Thompson

Oscar Thompson was a rider at one time with Quantrill. He was a friend of guerrilla William Napoleon "Babe" Hudspeth. Outside of this information, little has been recorded of his wartime experiences.

Oliver P. Thompson

Oliver P. Thompson was born in 1814 with his place of birth being Kentucky. His wife was named Louisa, whose place of birth was Tennessee. According to the 1860 Johnson County Census, they had seven children, six of whom were born in Kentucky with the last one being born in Missouri. Their names were William, Mary S., Mildred C., Thomas J., Elizabeth, Harriet, and Clover B. In addition, they owned 12 slaves. The family had moved to Missouri after 1850 and Oliver was listed as a farmer in 1860. If he was the real Thompson, then in all probability he was at Pleasant Hill, Missouri on July 11, 1862.

Thompson was at the battle of Lone Jack, Missouri on August 16, 1862. Later in the war he rode with guerrilla George M. Todd. On September 21, 1864, he received a mortal wound during a skirmish at Fayette, Missouri. He died three days later on September 24, 1864.

The Logical Thompson

Among all the above individuals, the best guess as to the actual Thompson having ridden with Quantrill would be James. Although later killed by his partisan comrades, James' earlier associations established a preponderance of evidence implicating him as the likely man on the Roster. In addition, the fact that many of his neighbors were riders with Quantrill strongly suggested that he was the real Thompson.

QUANTRILL'S THIEVES By: Joseph K. Houts, Jr.

Wm Vaughn
(William H. Vaughan)

William H. Vaughan was born in Illinois in 1840. Next to his name on Quantrill's Roster was James Vaughan, who would be hanged for his guerrilla activities on May 29, 1863 at Fort Leavenworth, Kansas. James and William may have been cousins. Both men lived on the same plot of land in New Santa Fe, Jackson County, Missouri, which in itself suggests that they were related somehow. The 1860 Federal Census for the county listed Vaughan as a laborer residing with a James Rees and his family.

He was in the 12th Missouri Cavalry Regiment assigned to Company E. Other guerrillas on the Roster and serving in the regiment were Oscar Hampton, Richard Maddox, James Vaughan, John Jarrette, F. M. Scott, William Campbell, James A. Hendricks, and Boone T. Muir. In all probability, he was at the battle of Pleasant Hill, Missouri on July 11, 1862. There was a report of a William Vaughan riding with William T. "Bloody Bill" Anderson later in the war, in which event he may have been at the battle of Centralia, Missouri on September 27, 1864. His life and whereabouts after the war have remained a mystery.

QUANTRILL'S THIEVES By: Joseph K. Houts, Jr.

James Vaughn
(James Vaughan, Jim)

James Vaughan was known as "a well-liked bushwhacker." His place of birth was Missouri, sometime around 1843. He was the fourth of nine children born to Josiah and Mary Vaughan. The names of his siblings were: Robert T., Thomas, Daniel, Margaret, Susan E., Sarah L., Mary, and one other daughter. Brothers Daniel and Thomas also rode with William Clarke Quantrill during the war. Also, on the Roster and living on the same tract of land was a William H. Vaughn, who was probably a cousin. Both men served together in the 12th Missouri Cavalry Regiment assigned to Company E. The Vaughan family would pay dearly for their allegiance to the South. By war's end his sister-in-law, Nancy Jane Vaughan the wife of Thomas, would die in the Gratiot Prison in St. Louis, Missouri on March 17, 1865, his mother and several sisters would be incarcerated and James would be hung at the hands of a Union executioner.

Probably more has been written about Vaughan's death than about the deaths of any of the other the guerrillas who died during the war, with the exception of the death of William T. "Blood Bill" Anderson, and of course the death of Quantrill himself. In many respects his death resulted in an escalation of the bloodshed between the guerrillas and the Missouri Union army.

Unfortunately for Vaughan, he was in need of a shave and haircut. He and another partisan went to Wyandotte, Kansas to visit a barbershop. In order to disguise their identity as guerrillas, they wore Union uniforms into the town. The two men took off their gunbelts so that they could fit into the barber's chairs, leaving themselves totally unarmed. Within a short period of time, Union troops swarmed into the shop seizing both men. Vaughan's fate now became a political issue.

In early May of 1863, Richard Yeager, also a guerrilla, raided Council Grove, Kansas, a community well beyond the Missouri state line. The reaction among Kansans and those Missouri Unionists living on the border was calamitous. Brigadier General James G. Blunt was in charge of the area along the border and received harsh criticism for not having better defenses. Because of the crisis, Blunt decided to execute Vaughan as retribution for Yeager's raid, and in general to demonstrate his frustration with the ongoing war with the guerrillas. On learning about Vaughan's sentence, Quantrill intervened personally and offered Blunt a three to one prisoner exchange for him. However, Blunt refused to negotiate and set Vaughan's execution date for May 29, to be carried out at Fort Leavenworth, Kansas.

On the day of his death, observers noted he looked saddened as he approached the gallows. However, upon ascending the platform his demeanor changed, taking on a certain air of defiance. In his last words to the gallery he asked for a respectful burial. Vaughan then proceeded to speak his peace, first warning the crowd of what was yet to come, then stating that he was not sorry for his actions. He coldly stated in reference to the guerrilla cause, "We can be killed but not conquered. Taking my life today will cost you one hundred lives, and this debt my friends will pay in a very short time." With that statement he accepted the blindfold and stepped onto the trap door. His final statement was, "This is my last look; let her slide." Fifteen minutes later he was dead and two minutes later he was cut down. The body was laid to rest roughly a hundred yards from where he had died.

As if his words spoke a prophecy, revenge was swift. Prior to his death, the news of his fate was heard by Confederate Colonel Ben Parker. The colonel threatened General Blunt by stating that if Vaughan was executed, he in turn would put four Union prisoners to death. Blunt ignored the threat, but unfortunately for Parker's captives they were soon scarified upon Parker's learning of Vaughan's execution. On June 16, the guerrillas attacked a Union column in Westport, Missouri. Many of the troops scattered and ran upon being assaulted, leaving several dead behind. Guerrilla, Will McGuire, approached one of the dead and put a note in his mouth, which stated, "Remember the dying words of Jim Vaughan." As the war continued for another two years, these words would come to haunt and torture the region.

C T Williamson
(Charles T.)

Charles T. Williamson was born in 1841 with his place of birth being Kentucky. His parents were Johnson and Susan Williamson. His father was born in 1816, Scott County, Kentucky and his mother was born in 1820, Bourbon County, Kentucky. Williamson married Ann Haun who was the daughter of Alfred and Nancy Haun. She was born in Tennesse in 1841. Between Charles and Ann, they would have five children named, William, Lula, Thomas, James, Lizzie, and Susan. These offspring produced a total of seven grandchildren: Audley Tarwater, Anna Mann, and Cassie, Herschel, Kathryn, Mollie, and Helen Williamson.

In 1862 at Eutonia, Arkansas, Williamson enlisted into Shank's Regiment as a private assigned to Company I, under the command of Major General Joseph O. Shelby. Shank's Regiment was also known as the Jackson County Regiment and the 12th Missouri Cavalry. The outfit's first commander was Colonel Upton Hays, who was on the Roster with Williamson. In all probability, he was at the battle of Pleasant Hill, Missouri on July 11, 1862. He also fought at Lone Jack, Missouri on August 16, 1862. One account has him being paroled out of service in 1864, whereas another source has placed his surrender at either Shreveport or New Orleans, Louisiana in May 1865. By the end of his service he had obtained the rank of 2nd sergeant.

Williamson attended the Confederate Veteran's Reunion on August 25, 1885 at Higginsville, Missouri. After the war he settled in Concord, Missouri where he died in 1912. His wife would live until 1923, also dying in Concord.

QUANTRILL'S THIEVES   By: Joseph K. Houts, Jr.

Coal Younger
(Thomas Coleman, Cole, "Bud" Younger)

Thomas Coleman "Bud" Younger was born on January 15, 1844 in Jackson County, Missouri. His parents were Henry Washington and Busheba Fristoe Younger. Cole's paternal great grandmother was a daughter of Revolutionary War hero General "Lighthorse Harry" Lee, the father of Confederate General Robert E. Lee. Mrs. Younger's father fought at the Battle of New Orleans under General Andrew Jackson. Through another descendant of his mother, he was distantly related to the fourth Chief Justice of the United States Supreme Court, John Marshall. Grandfather Charles Lee Younger had nineteen children, eleven of whom were illegitimate. One out of wedlock daughter, Adeline Wilson, would become the mother of Grat, Bob, and Emmett Dalton of the Dalton Gang. These brothers became infamous for their attempted double bank robbery at Coffeeville, Kansas on October 5, 1892. As for Cole, he was the seventh of fourten siblings. Brother James Henry (Jim) Younger would also serve as a partisan during the Civil War, riding with guerrilla chieftain George M. Todd.

As stated by Cole, "Mine was a happy childhood." His father was a prosperous farmer owning separate tracts in Jackson and Cass Counties Missouri. He also had a United States mail contract, which added to the family's well being. At one time his

Thomas Coleman "Cole" Younger
Used by permission, State Historical Society of Missouri

estate was estimated to be in excess of $100,000.00. Henry Younger was also known politically, serving three terms in the Missouri legislature, eight years as a Jackson County judge and lastly as mayor of Harrisonville, Missouri. Although a slaveholder, he was a devout Unionist, opposed to secession. However, as the war widened, he would not be able to escape this contradiction.

In the summer of 1861, Cole joined General Sterling Price's Missouri State Guard and participated in one of the first battles of the Civil War at Carthage, Missouri on July 5, 1861. After this brief brush with hostilities, he returned to Cass County. While home, he attended a dance hosted by Colonel Cutbert Mockbee in honor of his daughter. However, an altercation occurred that forever altered his life, and the lives of the rest of the members of the Younger family. During the course of the evening, Captain Irvin Walley of the 5th Missouri Militia Cavalry, sometimes called James, arrived at the event and proceeded to offend several of the young ladies. In particular, he bothered Cole's sister, whereupon Cole intervened and cut Walley off in his advance. Outraged, the captain accused him of being a spy, whereupon Younger knocked Walley to the floor. Walley drew his gun, but Cole's friends intervened and prevented any bloodshed. The captain threatened to kill Cole later. Upon explaining the incident to his parents, they advised him to hide out at their Jackson County farm. In the meantime, Walley secured an indictment alleging that Cole Younger was a spy. It had been his parents desire to send him to college, but now unfortunately he became committed to the life of an outlaw, for his own survival.

While Henry Younger was away in Washington, D. C. tending to business related to his government mail contract, a party of Kansas Jayhawkers lead by the notorious Dr. Charles R. "Doc" Jennison raided the Younger farm, stealing stock, and burning several buildings. On Henry's return from Washington, he went to Kansas City on a cattle-buying mission, and while he was there he protested Jennison's trespass to local authorities. However, on the way back to Harrisonville, Captain Walley and several soldiers of the 5th Missouri Militia Cavalry killed him with three shots and his body was "left bloating in the sun." Later in the day, Mrs. Washington Wells and her son Samuel came upon the scene. Mr.

Younger had also been robbed of $400.00, but $2,000.00 stashed in a money belt had been overlooked. General Ben Loan, commander for the Central District of Missouri, arrested Walley for the crime, but supposedly there were no witnesses and he was freed. Commenting on Henry's murder, noted historian John D. Edwards said, "to make tense the nerves and steel the heart of Coleman Younger, there met with his life's blood, with the white hairs of a loved father slain upon the highway."

Following his release, Walley again turned his sights on the Youngers. He arrested Cole's sister, and one snowy morning he forced Mrs. Younger to burn the family's home. She was left to wander with four of her children and the household slave, Suse. Mrs. Younger first went to Lafayette County, then Howard and Cass counties, before ending up back in Lafayette County at Waverly, Missouri. Once a week, she was required to report to Union officials in Lexington, Missouri. Thereafter, she was constantly harassed by pro-Northerners who were in search of sons Cole and Jim, as if she were an outlaw herself.

As a result of these tragedies, Coleman Younger joined Quantrill's outfit in October 1861, along with brother-in-law John Jarrette. In simple terms, he was quoted stating "the knowledge that my father had been killed in cold blood filled my heart with the lust for vengeance." He further commented the war had become, "…a personal affair after his sister imprisoned and his mother driven from her home by Union soldiers." In essence, a guerrilla was born out of these misdeeds. Later in reference to Cole and Jim's war years, it would be said, "the Youngers did bloody work."

Besides participating in the battle at Carthage, Cole was at the Tate house, March 22, 1862 and the Lowe house, April 15, 1862, skirmishes. In addition, he was at the battles of Pleasant Hill, Missouri, July 11, 1862; Independence, Missouri, August 11, 1862; Lone Jack, Missouri, August 16, 1862; Lawrence, Kansas, August 21, 1863; and Baxter Springs, Kansas, October 6, 1863. Contrary to some claims he was not at the raids on Olathe, Kansas, September 6, 1862; Shawneetown, Kansas, in October 1862; or the battle of Centralia, Missouri on September 27, 1864. On November 3, 1862, Younger did not head south for the winter with Quantrill, but instead went with Captain Joe Lea and Dick Yaeger, where they pursued cotton smugglers along the Mississippi River. In the spring of 1864, Younger and Jarrette left Quantrill for unknown reasons. Along with William H. Gregg, the three enlisted in the regular Confederate Army at Shreveport, Louisiana under General Kirby Smith and were assigned to service in the New Mexico territory. They were to recruit fresh troops for the army, but the task failed. Thereupon, Cole headed to Arizona and later Mexico. After enduring seven Apache attacks, he departed the area and arrived in Los Angeles, California, staying with an uncle. While Cole was in California, General Lee surrendered at Appomattox Court House on April 9, 1865.

Although a bushwhacker, and as he said himself his "heart" was full of "vengeance," Cole was far from the savage killer that many of his compatriots became during the war. He was noted for loyalty, bravery, and he was against the cold-blooded nature of the conflict. At the Lowe house, he returned after escaping in order to awaken George Todd, Joe Gilchrist, and Andy Blunt. His effort saved Todd and Blunt, but Gilchrist was killed in the affair. During the battle of Lone Jack, he ran ammunition to frontline troops, receiving the bravo of Union troops. Thinking they were rejoining at this being shot while dismounting, he yelled back, "hallow and be damned, you ain't killed nobody." After the battle he protected Union Major Emory S. Foster and his brother from being killed by incensed Confederate troops. At Pleasant Hill, Younger was credited with saving Kit Chiles after his horse had fallen. He stopped and placed Kit behind him, and sped away quickly to safety. Even at Lawrence, the worst of all the guerrilla's exploits, Cole was reported to have saved at least twelve civilian lives.

Younger was known for his antics and historical insight. Prior to the battle of Independence, he was sent on a reconnaissance mission dressed as an old apple woman wearing a dress and bonnet. He entered the town scouting out the position and movements of Lieutenant Colonel James T. Buel's troops. On exiting, he was stopped by a picket, questioned and upon feeling restrained, he shot him dead and galloped away. During the Lawrence raid, he noted that Quantrill had given the command not to kill any women or old men. However, in the midst of the attack a Negro woman yelled out of her window "you _ _ _ of _ _ _ _." She fell dead from a barrage of bullets before anyone realized that she was a woman. At Baxter Springs, Younger and several others opposed approaching the Union fortification. However, once engaged in the fight, he along with Jarrett almost captured Union General James G. Blunt.

Probably one of his worst experiences was the imprisonment of two of his cousins, Sue Vandiver and Armenia Gilvey, in an old dilapidated hotel at 14th and Grand in Kansas City, Missouri. At this point in the war, women suspected of aiding and abetting the guerrillas were to be incarcerated, until they could be transported away from the western regions of the state, preferably to Arkansas. Several women were related to other guerrillas, notably Jabez McCorkle and William T. "Bloody Bill" Anderson. Union officials were warned the building was unstable, but it went unattended. On August 13, 1863 the building collapsed, killing five women and maiming many others for life. Among the fatalities were his two cousins, McCorkle's sister and sister-in-law, along with Anderson's sister. This tragic event launched the raid on Lawrence. The guerrillas were convinced that the building had been intentionally undermined.

During the spring of 1864, while in Texas, Cole visited John Shirley on his farm outside Syene. During the war Shirley operated a hotel in Carthage, Missouri. On the occasion of his visit, Cole met Shirely's daughter, Myra Belle, who was fourteen years old. Younger returned to the war, and in 1868 he ran into Myra Belle again in Bates County, Missouri. She had married an old war acquaintence of Cole's named Jim Reed. Later, in 1871, Cole again met Myra Belle and Jim Reed, this time in Texas. Apparently, she took a fondness to Cole and upon discovering her feelings Cole soon departed. Several years afterwards, her husband was killed while particpating in a stage coach robbery outside of San Antonio. She then married a man named Sam or Tom Starr and started using the name of Belle as her first name. Following her marriage, she claimed that Cole had fathered her child and she even started using Younger as her last name. However, in his autobiography many years later, Younger strongly denied any liaison with her. The name "Belle Star" endures as a legendary icon of Old West folklore.

In 1866, Cole returned to Missouri hoping to start life over. The family's holdings were in shambles, but there was still the land to be farmed. Returning ex-Confederate soldiers, and in particular former guerrillas, were to be immediately confronted with Missouri's new Drake constitution an embodiment of a reconstruction government which denied many civil liberties to these once Southern patriots. Further compounding Cole's return to normal society was a false identification made of him during the war. As a result, peace would once again elude him.

Purportedly, during Quantrill's raid on Olathe and Shawneetown in 1862, a man named Judy was killed. The father was from Cass County, Missouri and moved to Kansas during the war. Afterwards, he returned to the county and became sheriff. The actual killers of his son were Dick Maddox and Joe Hall. At the time Younger was in Austin, Missouri. However, the father secured an indictment in Kansas against Younger that would plague and haunt him until 1903. Judy's father even raided Cole's farm in search of him. In part because of this writ, a vigilante group sought Younger, which eventually forced him to leave the state. Cole along with his brothers Jim and Robert Ewing (Bob) Younger left for Texas in 1868. Within this period Frank and Jesse James commenced robbing banks. In short order, they became notorious for their daring deeds and soon became famous. The Youngers were often held to be part and parcel of the James' exploits. However, in his memoirs, Cole refuted any such participation stating to have only met Jesse after the war in 1866. Even with this denial, the phrase "James-Younger Gang" became synonymous with bank and train robberies up to 1876. At the time of the Gallatin, Missouri bank robbery on December 7, 1869, according to Cole, he and his brothers were in Austin, Texas. He stayed in Texas until 1872.

The law and various former pro-Union citizens continued to hound and seek out the Younger brothers. It seemed every time the James' committed a heist, they were held to have participated in the escapade. Until his dying days, Cole disavowed ever being with the James gang. By 1875, an initiative was begun to grant amnesty to the James, Youngers, and other outlaw sorts. Upon introduction in the Missouri legislature the bill showed promise of passage. The act was in effect a compromise, whereby if these outlaws surrendered, they would be assured a fair trial, with the possibility of exoneration in some cases. However, once again fate would intercede, forever dictating the future of the Youngers. Prior to the bill, the Pinkerton Agency had long hunted the James gang, ever since their first train robbery. While the amnesty issue was being moved through government channels, they raided the James' farm at Kearny, Missouri. They launched a grenade into the house, which killed Frank and Jesse's half brother, Archie Samuel, in addition to blowing off their mother, Zerelda's, right arm at the elbow. A neighbor, Daniel A. Askew helped the agents in locating the James' homestead. To some extent, public support rallied behind the amnesty bill in light of this incident. However, Jesse purportedly killed the Pinkerton agents and Askew. As a result, both democrats and ex-Confederate legislators voted against the measure, erasing any further chance of a normal life for these men.

Shortly, after the amnesty bill's failure, Cole went to Florida, with a brief sojourn to Cuba. At some point he returned to Missouri and, contrary to general public opinion that Jesse James conceived the idea, he made plans to rob the First National Bank of Northfield, Minnesota. The reason for selecting this bank was because former Union General Benjamin F. Butler and his son-in-law J. T. Ames had a substantial amount of money on deposit. During the war, after the Union capture of New Orleans, Louisiana, Butler had been made military governor of the city. He became known as "Beast Butler" in response to his handling of the unladylike manners of the town's women towards his troops. The decree was entitled "Women Order" and was dated May 15, 1862. Accompanying Younger to Minnesota were brothers Jim and Bob, plus Clell Miller, Bill Chadwell, and three others named Pitts, Wood, and Howard. Cole stated that Frank and Jesse James were not in on the job. However, in later years Jesse would assume the name of Thomas Howard, while living in St. Joseph, Missouri, prior to his death on April 3, 1882, lending suspicion to his presence.

The attempted robbery on September 7, 1876 turned into a bust, leaving Miller and Chadwell dead. For two weeks the shot-up remnants of the gang avoided a large manhunt. Eventually, on September 21, 1876, in the proximity of Madelia, Minnesota the survivors surrendered to a posse. Bob Younger had his elbow shattered by a single bullet and Cole supposedly was shot eleven times. Instead of facing the death penalty, all of the Youngers pleaded guilty and were sentenced to life in prison. They were confined at the Stillwater Penitentiary. Cole's prison number was 699 and he would become known as a model prisoner. His jail cell was open to public viewing because of his notoriety. On September 16, 1889, Bob died of consumption.

In time, efforts were initiated for the early release of Cole and Jim. Previous wartime adversaries supported the idea. One in particular was Major Emory S. Foster, who had been saved by Cole at the battle of Lone Jack. During these efforts, Younger downplayed some of the Quantrill myths, such as the guerrillas carried a "black flag" and had to take a "black oath" before joining the gang. It has been speculated that he made these assertions in order to lessen his image, and that of the other partisans, as vicious and villainous cutthroats. Finally, on July 10, 1901, after twenty-five years of confinement the two brothers were granted a conditional parole. The terms of their release though, forbid them from leaving Minnesota.

Jim had suffered from depression while in prison. After his release, it became more pronounced, due in part to the fact that he could not leave the state and marry his sweetheart. As a result, on either October 19 or 20, 1901, he committed suicide. In view of this tragedy, Cole was given a full parole on February 4, 1903. There were several conditions attached to the release; he could not profit from his wartime and outlaw experiences, or in any way make a public performance or speech.

Younger returned to Missouri and regularly attended many of the annual Quantrill reunions. He was present at those in 1908 and 1910. Cole Younger, Frank James, and William H. Gregg were among the more noted former guerrillas in regular attendance. Cole was also listed on Captain Stephan Ragan's Jackson County United Confederate Veterans Roster of 1895.

After leaving Minnesota, he tied up with Frank James and formed the "Cole Younger and Frank James Historical Wild West Show." Since he was prevented from profiting by way of a public performance, he would sit in the audience and mingle with the spectators as a separate attraction, in effect circumventing his parole in a de facto sense. In time Frank tired of the show and quit. Thereupon, Younger merged his production into the "Greater Lew Nicholas Show."

In later years, he took to the lecture circuit, repeating often his speech entitled "What My Life Has Taught Me." The speech was of some length and set forth several virtues to be followed by all individuals. Of particular note, he emphasized the importance of women and how they should be given more equality in society. Cole frequently spoke against the vices of liquor. He blamed the botched bank robbery at Northfield, and his subsequent imprisonment, on the fact that several members of the gang were drunk.

Of ironic coincidence, Younger joined the Christian Church on August 21, 1913, the 50th anniversary of the raid on Lawrence. In his few remaining years, he lived with a niece, Nora Hall, in Lee's Summit, Missouri. For many years his residency there was memorialized by the largest annual community event held in Lee's Summit, "Cole Younger Days." In these recent years of political correctness, the event has been renamed "Old Tyme Days," the thinking being that naming their annual celebration after a notorious outlaw might not be best for the town's image.

On March 21, 1916 he died of Uremia, a disease whereby excess urea, combined with other waste products accumulates in the blood. It is an illness associated with kidney disease or its malfunction. Cole was buried in the City Cemetery at Lee's Summit. Two of his pallbearers were the sons of Frank and Jesse James. Throughout the course of his life, it was reported that he was shot between twenty-eight to thirty-six times.

QUANTRILL'S THIEVES By: Joseph K. Houts, Jr.

Richard Yeager
(Richard Younger, Dick Yager)

Richard E. Yeager was twenty-one years old at the start of the Civil War. He was one of five children born to Judge James B. and Mary J. Yeager. His father was the Presiding Judge of Jackson County, Missouri in 1840. In 1855, the Judge was elected to the state legislature serving two consecutive terms. As a side venture, he also ran a freighting business on the Santa Fe Trail. Son Richard managed one of his father's wagon trains.

On November 22, 1860, Richard married Martha J. Muir, the sister of Boone T. Muir, also on Quantrill's Roll of original guerrillas. Early in the war, he returned home only to find that the notorious Kansas Jayhawker, Dr. Charles R, "Doc" Jennison and his gang had raided the family's farm and business. Practically everything had been stolen, including the slaves. They did leave fifty head of stock and sheep. Unfortunately, several days later, the Jayhawkers returned and took these remaining possessions. Yeager was already sympathetic to the South; the Jennison raid prompted him to join Quantrill's outfit.

Richard "Dick" Yeager
Used by permission, State Historical Society of Missouri

He was at the Battle of Independence, Missouri, August 11, 1862; Lawrence, Kansas, August 21, 1863; and Baxter Springs, Kansas, October 6, 1863. At Baxter Springs, Yeager, John Jarrette, and Frank Smith almost captured Brigadier General James G. Blunt.

Luckily for the general, his horse was faster. In the winter of 1862-63, he remained in Missouri with Cole Younger and Joe Lea, instead of going to northwest Arkansas with the rest of Quantrill's gang. However, in the winter of 1863-64, he went to Sherman, Texas for quartering with his fellow guerrillas. Purportedly, he was married and his wife stayed with him during this period in Texas.

    Yeager was credited with conducting one of the most daring guerrilla raids into Kansas. With him were two dozen men. Over the course of several days, he and his men slipped into Kansas along the Santa Fe Trail, in groups of twos and threes. Soon to be famous William T. "Bloody Bill" Anderson was counted among the participants. On May 4, 1863, the intruders congregated outside Council Grove, Kansas, a distance of 130 miles from the Missouri state line. They formed up on the town's outskirts, trying to scare the inhabitants by their presence. Suddenly, a lone rider entered the square—Yeager, who was in search of a dentist to examine his toothache. The dentist, Dr. J. H. Bradford, agreed to treat the unwanted patient, but only on the condition that the guerrillas would not harm the town. He agreed, and then stated, "get this God damn tooth out." The tooth was extracted and the doctor administered some spirited medication in order to soothe the pain and soften his disposition. Yeager kept his word and proceeded to Diamond Springs, which his band plundered. A citizen named Augustus Howell was killed and his wife was wounded. This was one of the few incidents where a woman would be injured by guerrillas. From Diamond Springs, the gang advanced towards the border raiding Rock Springs, Gardner, and Black Jack.

    Following Diamond Springs, James L. McDowell, an U. S. Marshall and also a major general of the Kansas Militia, formed a twenty-man posse to pursue and capture the guerrillas. At the Cottonwood River northwest of Emporia, McDowell caught up with and attacked Yeager's force, capturing ten to twelve of his men. The marshall entrusted the prisoners to Captain John E. Stewart for transport to Fort Riley, Kansas. Stewart, at one time had ridden with Quantrill during the Missouri-Kansas border war, when supposedly he was a Jayhawker. While enroute to the fort, the captives attempted an escape, which resulted in the captain killing all of them. McDowell continued to chase Yeager, but the guerrilla chieftain and his remaining band were able to out pace the posse, returning to the sanctuary of Jackson County, Missouri outside Black Jack. Kansans were outraged at this bloody invasion of their territory. One newspaper heralded, "Guerrillas! The Boldest Raid Yet!!" Bridadier General Blunt was in charge of the Kansas military district. However, as has been previously noted about his ability, he was slow to react to the transgression. As a somewhat tempered measure of response, Blunt had 23-year-old guerrilla, James Vaughn, hung at Fort Leavenworth, Kansas on May 19. Vaughn had been taken prisoner in a Kansas City, Missouri barbershop while getting a hair cut. The venture into Kansas in many ways contributed to the Lawrence, Kansas raid three months later. Quantrill was convinced an attack on Lawrence was now possible, especially since it was only 40 miles from the border. When the guerrilla command voted on going to Lawrence, Yeager was quoted as saying, "Where my house once stood there is a heap of ashes. I haven't a neighbor that's got a house—Lawrence and the torch."

There have been several versions of Yeager's death. One account has claimed that he died between June 10-19, 1864 following a campaign led by General Egburt Brown, in an attempt to eradicate the guerrillas from Missouri. Supposedly, he was killed along with 27 others. More likely it occurred while riding with George Todd's gang in July 1864. On July 20, he and David Pool rode into Arrow Rock, Missouri, taking 40 horses and $20,000.00 worth of property. While on the return trip to the gang on the Sni-A-Bar River, he received a severe gunshot wound to the head. Unable to travel, he was left to recuperate at the Flannery house. Two weeks later a Union patrol found him at Flannery's and killed him, which would place his death around August 6. Purportedly, he killed three Federals and wounded two others during the melee. His father had been incarcerated in a St. Louis prison, in part due to his son's wartime activities. As a result of Order #11, Yeager's wife walked from Independence, Missouri to Texas. In 1866, she remarried.

Yeager was called "a young hero famed for dash and courage." He was described as being "pure as a child, simple," and "tranquil." Probably, the most pointed characterization of him was, "that he lived literally with his revolver belt buckled."

J. H. Terry
(John H.)

John H. Terry was born in 1843 with his place of birth being North Carolina. His parents were named William and Ellen and he was the first of four siblings. The entire family was from North Carolina, having arrived in Missouri around 1855 and settling in Lone Jack. In the 1860 Federal Census his father was listed as a farmer and John was documented as being a laborer living with the William Cave family. The Cave's were neighbors of the Terry household. He had apparently left home to learn a trade and become self-sufficient.

Terry was a member of the 10th Missouri Cavalry under the command of Colonel Robert R. Lawther. He was assigned to Company A. Two other guerillas on the Roster were also part of this company, John D. Brinker and William M. Haller, William Clarke Quantrill's first recruit. Brinker was a captain and Haller was a 1st lieutenant. Concerning engagements, he was at the battle of Lone Jack, Missouri, August 16, 1862, and in all probability at Pleasant Hill, Missouri, July 11, 1862. On May 28, 1865 he surrendered to Captain E. E. Rogers the Provost Marshal at Lexington, Missouri, whereupon he took the oath of allegiance to the United States government. Nine other guerrillas on the Roster also turned themselves in between May 21-28 at Lexington. They were David Pool, G. M. Barnett, Samuel L. Clifton, Sylvester Atchison, John Atchison, Wiley Atchison, R. (A.) Harris, John H. Teague, and Robert Stephenson.

Chapter V
"Micah"

"...and they shall beat their swords into plowshares, and their spears into pruning hooks, nation shall not lift up sword against nation, neither shall they learn war anymore...."

The words and revelations of the prophet Micah have long represented a warning, but yet a hope and a promise to civilization. The above passage has thundered through the ages, begging mankind to forego the evils of war and to make peace and testimony to the sanctity of God. It has appeared often in scholarly texts, Sunday sermons, and even hymnals, professing the wisdom in following the ways of the Lord. More particularly, his words have represented a form of damnation against those of old, who settled their score through bloodshed and believed in false idols, if not only in themselves. Although, considered a prophet of condemnation, salvation was foreseen in his vision of the Messiah. A person to be born in Bethlehem, who would lead the fallen to their savior, a man of peace, hallmarked the Prince of Peace, or as known today as the Christ Child - the Son of God. The most remarkable aspect in the enormity of this man's vision was its foretelling the beginning of Christianity and what it had to offer for the world's future. Of startling revelation though was that this prophecy was foretold 750 years before the birth of Christ, a reality yet to awaken humanity. However, even with all that was depicted by him, none has been more lasting than his urging warriors to cast down their weapons into tools of harvest and production, as opposed to instruments of battle and destruction. In other words, let peace conquer war and rule the land henceforth.

By the spring of 1865, not only the Civil War, but also the guerrilla war in Missouri was for all purposes played out and settling down to an uneasy conclusion. Sadly, peace had not conquered war, as sought in the words of Micah, but war had beaten war, until those still surviving cared little anymore about anything, except perhaps in its ending. However, with the end, peace did once again emerge, as if in the form of a late bloom, growing slowly, but ever mindful of the unpredictable climate in which it struggled for root and foundation. With this new emergence, slowly the men started returning home, or to what was left of their family and once proud abodes. In the words of the prophet, it was time to convert their weapons into "plow shares." Many of the regular Confederate soldiers from Missouri had surrendered in the Deep South, such as Louisiana, Texas, and Arkansas. The guerrillas on the other hand were mostly scattered about through the western environs of Missouri, except for a few Quantrill's remnants caught in Kentucky and those who had long left the partisan conflict and joined the regular service. In late May though, led by David Poole, upwards of 200 of these once proud irregulars would eventually turn themselves in at Lexington and would swear never again to bear arms against the United States. A few did not, like such notables as Richard Burns and Archie Clements. In short order, they would meet their fate. However, for the most part, those who by chance had avoided death's shadow did surrender and set out upon a course of reconciliation and peace with their one-time enemies. Even with the hardships imposed by the post Civil War Missouri Drake Constitution, most guerrilla veterans sought out new lives, where possibly they and their families could once again survive, if not thrive.

Civil unrest and wars have always been very costly, in the loss and sufferings of human lives, and in the associated material waste and destruction. By the war's end, Western Missouri had almost been totally destroyed by the ravages of Jayhawkers, guerrillas, Union troops, and the imposition of General Ewing's infamous Order #11. For many years afterward, it would be known as the "burnt district." The guerrillas themselves paid an extremely high price for their involvement. From a pure casualty standpoint, twenty-seven of Quantrill's original riders set forth on the Roll had been killed during the war. In addition, others who rode with him also met a similar end. On average, one out of seven soldiers died during the Civil War, where the attrition rate among these 93 original partisans was closer to a one in three loss ratio. The greatest death toll occurred among Quantrill's officer corps, where six out of nine had perished by the summer of 1865. Actually, this figure represented a remarkable loss, since all armies need a successive line of command in which to operate and engage the enemy. Another interesting fact was that two men were killed after the ending of general hostilities, later in 1865, but still during the last official year of the conflict and were war related. However, for the record the following list of men met their demise in the line of duty at one time or another during the conflict:

The Fallen

William H. Baker	Jeremiah F. Doores	John N. Oliphant
William M. Bledsoe	Noah Estes	Henry C. Pemberton
Andrew Blunt *	William M. Haller *	William C. Quantrill *
John D. Brinker	John Hampton	Fernando M. Scott *
William M. Burgess **	Upton Hays	James Thompson
William F. Cheatham	William F. Judd	George W. Todd *
Kit Chiles	Richard Maddox *	William D. Tucker **
John B. Dickey	Ezra Moore	James Vaughan
William T. Doak	James L. Morris	Richard Yeager

* Command Corps
** Killed after hostilities, but in 1865

The mortality rate was high. In addition, the Missouri counties that the partisans called "home" were ravaged. Areas that were once prosperous and flush with vegetation, game, and timber were turned into a barren wasteland. Jackson, Cass, and Bates counties bore the brunt of the scars of the conflict. These regions had paid the full measure of Union response for the

QUANTRILL'S THIEVES By: Joseph K. Houts, Jr.

actions of their native guerrilla fighters. The more guerrillas from a given area, the greater the devastation visited upon the region. Special note can be given to their counties of origin. As a group, they came from eight Western Missouri counties, and from two states other than Missouri. A considerable number of the men were from an unknown place of origin. The breakdown has been summarized as follows:

Place of Origin

Carroll County
James L. Morris

Cass County
Robert Hall
Thomas J. Hall
Given Horn
James Lyons
Thomas F. Teague
Cole Younger

Chariton County
Oscar Hampton

Clay County
Thomas Colesure

Howard County
William H. Butler

Jackson County
Henry Ackers
John Atchison
Wylie Atchison
Lee Ball
William C. Bell
William M. Bledsoe
Richard Burns
Kit Chiles
John B. Dickey
Jeremiah Doores
Noah Estes
John H. George
William H. Gregg
William M. Haller
William Halley
John Hampton
A. Harris
Upton Hays

Jackson County (cont.)
James A. Hendricks
John Jarrette
John W. Koger
George Maddox
Richard Maddox
Erza Moore
Boone T. Muir
Joshua Owings
George Rider
John W. Rider
Fernando M. Scott
John H. Terry
George W. Todd
James Vaughan
William Vaughan
Ridhard Yaeger

Johnson County
Hugh L. W. Anderson
William H. Baker
George M. Barnett
Obadiah S. Barnett
John D. Brinker
William Burgess
William H. Campbell
Al Cunningham
James Cunningham
Robert Davenport
William T. Doak
James G. Freeman
Nathan Houston
Matthias Houx
Michael M. Houx
Robert Houx
Charles A. Longacre
Otho Offutt
Frank M. Ogden
Harry Ogden

Johnson County (cont.)
John N. Oliphant
Henry C. Pemberton
James P. Perdee
Thomas B. Perdee
F. M. Robertson
James Thompson

Lafayette County
H. Austin
David M. Poole
James S. Tucker
William D. Tucker

Vernon County
Benjamin F. Long

Ohio
William C. Quantrill

Texas
Syrus Cockrell

Unknown
Andrew Blunt
James Barnett
J. Bowers
James H. Bowlin
William Chamblin
W. F. Cheatham
Samuel Clifton
William Colesure
James R. Dejarnett
M. H. Doores
William F. Judd
Robert Stephenson
Ab Teague
John Teague
Charles F. Williamson

224

QUANTRILL'S THIEVES By: Joseph K. Houts, Jr.

In reviewing the above breakdown, some interesting conclusions can be drawn about the guerrillas. Without question, Jackson and Johnson Counties had the combined largest contingency, representing 62 of the total, or two thirds of the group. No other region came close to this figure, except the "Unknown" category and probably most of them were from these counties. The reason that such a sizable lot evolved from these two counties, as opposed to others, can only be surmised.

Jackson County was in the lead because it bordered Kansas and was more heavily populated than neighboring counties. It was comprised of a varied, but prominent slaveholding populous. Its proximity to Kansas was important because available transportaion routes of the day made Jackson County the easiest prey for Jayhawkers, Freebooters, and other rogue bands of marauders. If any of the other counties had been in the same geographic location, then they too would have been the epicenter of not only the guerrillas, but also the attending violence.

Althouth Johnson County did not directly border Kansas, it was in easy access and openly split in its sentiment. The county had long been settled and contained a significant number of slaveholders.

In addition to the georgraphic origins of the guerrillas, another noteworthy factor that helps to explain their assemblage more than anything else was the family relationships of these men and the interconnection among one another. In other words, a majority of these riders, and those who subsequently followed them, were related, as brothers, cousins, or through marriage. An astonishing 39 out of the original 93 guerrillas were relatives, with 31 alone being brothers. Concerning the remaining eight, one was a nephew, and seven were linked by marriage. The one nephew was Robert Houx and the seven marriages were John H. George, Ezra Moore, Joshua Owings as a group; Cole Younger and John Jarrette as another; with Richard Yeager and Boone T. Muir as the last contingent. There were

QUANTRILL'S THIEVES By: Joseph K. Houts, Jr.

fourteen groups of identical names with as many as three individuals in each. Their names and the numbers were as follows:

Common Surnames

Atchison (3)	Hall (2)	Rider (2)
Barnett (2)	Houx (3)	Teague (3)
Colesure (2) *	Maddox (2)	Tucker (3)
Cunningham (2)	Ogden (2)	Vaughan (2)
Doores (2) *	Perdee (2)	

* Assumed to be brothers

    On a percentage basis 43% of them were related, which in itself could explain why so many joined Quantrill, over a relatively short period of time. It must be remembered the Civil War was a defining moment in the American family. Oftentimes, since its conclusion, it has been called the war of "brother against brother." However, for the most part families usually tended to stay together in times of crisis and conflict. In analyzing the biographical sketches of these men, it can be seen that many aligned themselves with Quantrill because of some insult or outrage committed either upon themselves, or upon a member of their family. Many had been harassed by Jayhawkers or Missouri Unionists and therefore enlisted seeking revenge, or simply personal protection. Several of them had been slave owners, although initially pro-Union in their stance. Unfortunately, their Unionist views were often overlooked or ignored, forcing several to join the Confederate cause.

    In Jackson County alone, nine of the guerrillas either owned slaves themselves, or were from slave owning families. Collectively they account for the ownership of thirty-six slaves. The names of those owning slaves, or being in a slave owner's household were as follows:

QUANTRILL'S THIEVES By: Joseph K. Houts, Jr.

Jackson County Slave Owners

Richard Burns	William M. Haller	Boone T. Muir
Kit Chiles	A. Harris	George Rider
William H. Gregg	Upton Hays	Richard Yeager

    Those from Johnson County also owned a sizable lot of slaves, thereby tainting them as Pro-Southern in the initial stages of the conflict. There are some fundamental human values that often motivate us to take action. In the case of the guerrillas, it was the sanctity of their families, and the protection of their property and liberty, which they saw as either assaulted, stolen, or destroyed. A threat to one of these elements alone has often been enough to bring a man to arms. Without question, those partisans from Jackson and Johnson Counties felt that they had been forced to take up arms out of righteous self-protection.

    There is another factor, beyond family connections, that bears some examination in terms of explaining how this particular group of men arrived on the stage of history in the same time and place. Simply stated, many of them were neighbors. In the days of the frontier, neighbors were an important part of society—an important part of each individual's and each family unit's support system. In many respects they represented lifelines, or micro systems of support for each other. The country was rural and it took a long time to travel even the shortest of distances. A neighbor could be a vital necessity in situations of danger, illness, hunger, or need. On occasion, one's neighbors would become an extension of one's family. Many times a parent would grant a son or daughter part of their acreage in order for the offspring to earn a livelihood. In Jackson County, one finds three groupings of neighbors among the partisans. When combined, they together account for twenty of the riders. The first group was clustered around the towns of Blue Springs, Pink Hill, Stony Point and Oak Grove. The second was located near Independence. And the third group was centered around Lone Jack and New Santa Fe. They were composed of the following men:

QUANTRILL'S THIEVES By: Joseph K. Houts, Jr.

Jackson County Groupings

First Group	**Second Group**	**Third Group**
John Atchison	Henry Ackers	Jeremiah Doores
Sylvester Atchison	William M. Bledsoe	James Vaughan
Wiley Atchison	Richard Burns	William Vaughan
William C. Bell		
Kit Chiles		
John H. George		
William H. Gregg		
John Hampton		
A. Harris		
James A Hendricks		
John W. Koger		
Ezra Moore		
Joshua Ownings		
George Rider		
John W. Rider		

Johnson County also had a sizable group of neighbors in various townships. The largest concentration was from Madison Township, where seven of the guerrillas lived in relatively close proximity to each other. Their names were as follows:

Johnson County Grouping

William H. Baker	Al Cunningham	John N. Oliphant
George M. Barnett	James Cunningham	William C. Pemberton
Obediah S. Barnett	Nathan Houston	

Collectively, if those guerrillas, who were related, slave owners, or neighbors, were added together, then 58 of them would have a common variable or connection. Of numerical coincidence, 5/8ths of all of them had a common bond, a remarkably high percentage for such a varied and diverse group. As a percentage, this figure accounted for roughly 62 % of all these men. It could be said that this was their true strength, not in numbers, but in the closeness of their association. Arguably, an individual will fight harder and longer when motivated by ties of family or friendship.

Sixty-six of the original guerrillas survived the war. As previously pointed out, twenty-seven of them had died, while in the service of Quantrill. The survivors may be broken down into two distinct categories; those whose post-war employed has been determined or documented, and those whose activities after the war have remained unknown. The unknowns were not necessarily destitute as some may assume or predict, but were merely undocumented as to their subsequent livelihoods. Many probably went to Texas or got caught up in the continental expansion movement and went West. Most of those whose employment can be determined would lead normal, if not exemplary, lives—a far cry from their historical legacy. Surprisingly, most all of the guerrillas became respected, and often prominent, citizens of their communities. The array of their employment was diverse and ranged from a life of crime as an outlaw, to membership in the United States Congress. These men and their employment has been set forth as follows:

Post War Employment

Carpenter
George M. Barnett
Deputy Sheriff
William H. Gregg
Doctor
M. H. Doores
Charles A. Longacre
Farmer
John Atchison
Sylvester Atchison
Wiley Atchison
Obediah Barnett
John H. George
Oscar Hampton
A. Harris
Matthias Houx
John Koger
Joshua Ownings

Farmer (cont.)
John W. Rider
George Rider
Robert Stephenson
Ab Teague
Freighter
James A. Hendricks
Justice of the Peace
Benjamin F. Long
Laborer
James H. Bowlin
J. Bowers
Livery and Stock
Otho Offutt
Outlaw
Richard Burns
Cole Younger

Policeman and Bartender
Samual Clifton
William Halley
Prison Guard
George Maddox
Rancher
John Jarrette
Rancher & Policeman
William Halley
Revolutionary & Artist
William H. Campbell
Scout
David Poole
Traveler
Syrus Cockrell
U. S. Congressman
Henry Ogden

QUANTRILL'S THIEVES By: Joseph K. Houts, Jr.

The thirty-three men of unknown post-war employment, for the most part, were probably farmers, laborers or ranchers. Some of them may have worked on the building of the transcontinental railroad, or even joined the United States Cavalry and fought in the country's Indian Wars. Their names were as follows:

Unknown Post-War Employment

Hugh L. W. Anderson	James Cunningham	Boone T. Muir
Henry Ackers	Robert Davenport	Frank Ogden
H. Austin	James R. Dejarnett	James P. Perdee
Lee Ball	James G. Freeman	Thomas B. Perdee
James Barnett	Robert J. Hall	F. M. Robertson
William C. Bell	Thomas Hall	John Teague
William H. Butler	Given Horn	Thomas F. Teague
William Chamlin	Nathan Houston	John H. Terry
Thomas Colesure	Michael M. Houx	James S. Tucker
William Colesure	Robert Houx	William Vaughan
Al Cunningham	James Lyons	Charles T. Williamson

A Chosen Few

Of all of the former guerrillas, a few have stood out more than the others. This handful gained notoriety, not so much for their post war activities, but in the context of an ironic twist of events.

The most obvious within this group was the ultimate bad guy among the original ninety-three—George Todd. A man possessed of fire in battle, a person who tended to have a chip on his shoulder, and an individual of cunning, greed for power and revenge. It could be said that he was the best of the worst, perhaps even more dangerous, powerful, and charismatic than Quantrill himself. In the end, Todd challenged and eventually wrestled control of the guerrilla gang from his leader, just as Quantrill had deceived and turned on his associates at the Morgan Walker farm in December 1860.

The next notable was William C. Bell. After the war, he signed a petition, along with his neighbors, protesting excess violence in his township and seeking the outlaw of guns. This was an amazing turn around for a former gun-toting guerrilla.

One man stayed the course of violence and insurrection, even following the war. He was William H. Campbell, who was reported to have been associated with Generalissimo Maximillian, and afterwards participated in the Cuban revolution. In his twilight years, he became an artist of some notoriety. He turned away from destroying things, and spent his final years creating them.

Samuel Clifton represents an even more acute change of direction. In order to prove his loyalty to the gang, he had clubbed a man to death en route to the raid on Lawrence. After the war he became a policeman and a bartender, counterbalancing his wartime lawlessness with peacetime law enforcement, and throwing in a measure of good cheer.

M. H. Doores and Charles A. Longacre both became doctors after the war. How strange for these two men to have participated in the bloodiest combat of the war, then profess the Hippocratic Oath as their standard of behavior in saving the lives of others.

William Halley, too, was a peculiarity in that he was reported to have been a very fierce fighter while a guerrilla, but afterwards he served as a policeman. In the end, he was committed to an insane asylum. Many of the guerrilla's victims during the war must have thought that the guerillas were all crazy, but this individual was the only one for whom insanity was actually documented.

There is irony too in the post-war careers of Benjamin Long and George Maddox; both spent their latter years in law enforcement. Long was a justice of the peace, and Maddox was a prison guard at the Missouri state penitentiary. Immense ironies, given the fact that they had been labeled criminals themselves and would have been imprisoned or hung, if caught while fighting as an irregular.

The best of the lot though, or ultimate success story, was Henry Ogden, who became a Louisiana politician. In time, he would serve several terms as a United States Congressman, absolutely an incredible twist for a man who once raised arms against his country. In each of these cases, life changed and took on new meaning. A climate of peace and prosperity returned to Missouri as well as among its citizens. Wounds would remain, but time would eventually heal the scars.

The Destitute

There were a few of the guerrillas, who in their later years, fell upon hard times and had to seek the help of others. Most notable was Cole Younger, who after his release from prison, traveled about the Midwest espousing the benefits of leading a virtuous life. He ended up residing with a niece until his dying days.

Syrus Cockrell is of interest in that he never settled down. He was not necessarily destitute, but he spent the rest of his life roaming about the West, with all of his possessions in a wagon.

Seven former guerrillas sought refuge in the Confederate State Memorial Home at Higginsville, Missouri. Those seeking asylum at the facility were Obediah S. Barnett, James H. Bowling, William H. Butler, John W. Koger, Boone T. Muir, Ab Teague, and John Teague. Unfortunately, only Barnett and Koger were granted admittance. Both of them eventually died there, and were buried in the Home's cemetery. A peculiar oddity is that a portion of Qauntrill's body was interned in the same graveyard on October 24, 1992. The rest of his remains, or more specifically his skull, was laid to rest in the 4th Street Cemetery at Dover, Ohio on October 30, 1992. One can only guess whatever may have happened to those former guerrillas who were turned away by the Home, in all probability they died penniless and forgotten men.

The Prophecy

As this chapter began so must it end, with the words of the prophet Micah. Enormous issues were confronting the young American nation in 1860. Unfortunately, talk and diplomacy gave way to war. A terrible experience was visited upon the country, where both sides felt a compelling justification in the righteousness of their individual points of view. But when it was over, what had we learned and what had been gained? In all honesty, the answer to both questions was probably nothing. It could be said that all hell had broken loose and devastated the land for four horrible years, all in fear of an anticipated, but dreaded change. A change that in the end won out and for all intents and purposes was destined to win from the start. The nation remained united, and finally all men were now free and equal under the law, correcting a misstatement of fact set forth in the Declaration of Independence that had haunted the nation since its founding.

The South gained nothing in declaring its independence, and the suffering of her citizens was immense. The North expended a huge store of resources, both human and economic, in restoring the Union, and in the end merely brought the nation back to the point of beginning. War represents the failure of human wisdom. According to a German proverb, that a great war leaves a country with three armies—an army of cripples, an army of mourners, and an army of thieves. The aftermath of the War Between the States poignantly verifies the truth in those words.

Sydney Smith, English clergyman and essayist of the late 18th and early 19th centuries, said, "The greatest curse that can be entailed on mankind is a state of war. All the atrocious crimes committed in years of peace, all that is spent in peace by the secret corruptions, or by the thoughtless extravagance of nations, are mere trifles compared with the gigantic evils which stalk over this world in a state of war. God is forgotten in war; every principle of Christianity is trampled upon." We can only hope and pray that someday our species will finally heed the words of Micah and put the notion of warfare behind us. Life is precious above all else; above all deeds and words, especially those that lead to waste and war.

QUANTRILL'S THIEVES By: Joseph K. Houts, Jr.

General Order No. 2
St. Louis, Mo., March 13, 1862

     1. Martial Law has never been legally declared in Missouri except in the city of St. Louis, and on and in the immediate vicinity of the railroads and telegraph lines and even in these localities military officers are specially directed not to interfere with the lawful process of any loyal civil court. It is believed that the time will soon come when the rebellion in Missouri may be considered as terminated, and when even the partial and temporary military restraint which has been exercised in particular places, may be entirely withdrawn. By none is this more desired than by the General commanding.

     2. It must, however, be borne in mind that in all places subject to the incursions of the enemy, or to the depredations of insurgents and guerrilla bands, the military are authorized, without any formal declaration of martial law, to adopt such measures as may be necessary to restore the authority of the Government, and to punish all violations of the laws of war. This power will be exercised only where the peace of the country and the success of the Union cause absolutely require it.

     3. Evidence has been received at these Headquarters that Major General Sterling Price has issued commissions or licenses to certain bandits in this State authorizing them to raise "Guerrilla forces," for the purpose of plunder and marauding. Gen. Price ought to know that such a course is contrary to the rules of civilized warfare, and that every man who enlists in such an organization forfeits his life, and becomes an outlaw. All persons are hereby warned that, if they join any guerrilla band, they will not, if captured, be treated as ordinary prisoners of war, but will be hung as robbers and murderers. Their lives shall atone for the barbarity of their General.

By Command of Maj. Gen. Halleck
N. H. McLean, Assistant Adjutant General

General Order No. 9
Head Quarters District of the Border
Kansas City, Mo., August 18, 1863

    I. Lieut. Col. Walter King, 4th Regiment. M.S.M., will, as often as necessary, visit the several military stations in that part of Missouri included in the District, and ascertain what negroes are there who desire escort out of Missouri, and were the slaves of persons who, since the 17th day of July 1862, have been engaged in the rebellion, or have in any way given aid or comfort thereto. He will make and certify a list of all such negroes at each of station, and of the persons by whom the disloyalty of their masters can be shown and will deliver one copy of each list to the Commander of such stations, and forward one to the Head-Quarters. Before preparing such list, he will give due public notice of the time at which he will be aided in such duty at each station. He will be aided in the discharge of his duties by special instructions received from or through, these Head-Quarters.

    II. Commanders of such stations will furnish from time to time, as they may be called or by commanders of escorts, copies of the lists so prepared and filed with them; and will issue rations, where necessary, to negroes named in each list who are unable to move from such stations or to earn a living there, until escort can be furnished them to a place of safety, where they can support themselves.

    III. Commanders of companies and detachments serving in that part of Missouri included in the District, will give escort and subsistence, where practicable, to all negroes neared in such certified lists, to Independence, Kansas City, Westport, or the State of Kansas - sending direct to these Head-Quarters all such negroes fit for military duty, and willing to enlist.

By order of Brigadier General Ewing
P.B. Plumb, Major and Chief of Staff

QUANTRILL'S THIEVES By: Joseph K. Houts, Jr.

General Order Number 10
Headquarters District of the Border
Kansas City, Mo, August 18, 1863

I. Officers commanding companies and detachments, will give escort and subsistence, as far as practicable, through that part of Missouri included in the District, to all loyal free persons desiring to remove to the state of Kansas or to a permanent military stations in Missouri-including all persons who have been ascertained, in the manor provided in General Order No. 9 of this District, to have been the slaves of persons engaged in aiding the rebellion since July 17, 1862. Where necessary, the teams of persons engaged in aiding the rebellion since July 23, 1862, will be taken to help such removal and after being used for that purpose, will be turned over to the officer commanding the nearest military station, who will at once report them to an Assistant Provost Marshall, or to the District Provost Marshall and hold them subject to this order.

II. Such officers will arrest and send to the District Provost Marshall for punishment, all men (and all women, not heads of families) who willfully aid and encourage guerrillas; with a written statement of the names and residence of such persons and of the proof against them. They will discriminate as carefully as possible between those who are compelled by threats or fears to aid the rebels and those who aid them from disloyal motives. The wives and the children of known guerrillas, and also women who are heads of families and are willfully engaged in aiding guerrillas, will be notified by such officers to move out of this district and out of the State of Missouri forthwith. They will be permitted to take unmolested, their stock, provisions and household goods. If they fail to remove promptly they will be sent by such officers under escort to Kansas City for shipment South, with their cloths and such necessary household furniture as may be worth removing.

III. Persons who have borne arms against the Government and voluntarily lay them down and surrender themselves at a military station, will be sent under escort to the District Provost Marshall at these Head Quarters. Such persons will be banished with their families to such State or district out of this department as the General Commanding the Department may direct, and will there remain exempt from other military punishment or account of their past disloyalty, but not exempt from civil trial for treason.

    IV. No officer or enlisted man, without special instructions from these Head Quarters will burn or destroy any buildings, fences, crops or other property. But all furnaces and fixtures of blacksmith shops in that part of Missouri included in the District, not at military stations, will be destroyed and the tools either removed to such stations or destroyed.

    V. Commanders of companies and detachments serving in Missouri will not allow persons not in the military service of the United States to accompany them on duty except when employed as guides, and will be held responsible for the good conduct of such men employed as guides and for their obedience to orders.

    VI. Officers and enlisted men belonging to regiment or companies, organized or unorganized, are prohibited going from Kansas to the District of Northern Missouri without written permission or order from these Head Quarters or from the Assistant Provost Marshal at Leavenworth City or the Commanding officer at Fort Leavenworth or some Officer commanding a military station in the District of Northern Missouri.

By Order of Brigadier General Ewing
P.B. Plumb, Major and Chief of Staff

QUANTRILL'S THIEVES By: Joseph K. Houts, Jr.

General Order Number 11
Headquarters District of the Border
Kansas City, Mo., August 25, 1863

First, ___ All persons living in Jackson, Cass and Bates Counties, Missouri, and in that part of Vernon included in this district, except those living within one mile of the limits of Harrisonville, Hickman Mills, Independence and Pleasant Hill and Harrisonville, and except those in the part of Kaw Township, Jackson County, north of Brush Creek and west of the Big Blue, embracing Kansas City and Westport, are hereby ordered to remove from their present places of residence within fifteen days from the date hereof. Those who, within that time, establish their loyalty to the satisfaction of the commanding officer of the military station nearest their present places of residence will receive from him certificates stating the fact of their loyalty, and the names of the witnesses by whom it can be shown. All who receive such certificates will be permitted to remove to any military station in the district, or to any part of the State of Kansas except the counties on the eastern border of the State. All others shall remove out of the district. Officers commanding companies and detachments serving in the counties named will see that this paragraph is promptly obeyed.

Second, ___ All hay and grain in the field, or under shelter in the district, from which the inhabitants are required to remove, within the reach of the military stations, after the 9th of September, next, will be taken to such stations and turned over to the proper officers there; and reports of the amounts so turned over made to district headquarters, specifying the name of all loyal owners and the amount of such produce taken from them. All grain and hay found in such district after the 9th of September, next, not convenient to such stations, will be destroyed.

Third, ___ The provisions of General Order No. 10 from these headquarters will be at once vigorously executed by officers commanding in the parts of the district, and at the stations not subject to the operations of paragraph first of this order, especially in the towns of Independence, Westport and Kansas City.

Fourth, ___ Paragraph 3, General Order No. 10, is revoked as to all who have borne arms against the government in the district since August 20, 1863.

By order of the Brigadier General Ewing,
H. Hannahs, Adjutant

QUANTRILL'S THIEVES By: Joseph K. Houts, Jr.

ENDNOTES

Introduction Endnotes

Richard S. Brownlee, <u>Gray Ghosts of the Confederacy</u> (Richmond, Virginia: The William Byrd Press, Inc., 1958), p. 99.

Albert Castel, <u>William Clarke Quantrill: His Life and Times</u> (New York: Frederick Fell, Inc., 1962), pp. 24, 29, 92-93.

Joanne Chiles Eakin and Donald R. Hale, <u>Branded As Rebels</u> (Independence, Mo.: Print America, 1995), p. 491.

John N. Edwards, <u>Noted Guerrillas</u> (Shawnee, Kansas: Two Trails Publishing, 1996), p. 53-54, 110.

Edward E. Leslie, <u>The Devil Knows How to Ride</u> (New York: Random House, 1996), p. 141.

"Roll of Quantrell's Company of Thieves," Major Thomas W. Houts, unsigned and undated.

"Roll of 93 of Quantrell's Gang of Outlaws," copy sent for information of Brig. Genl. Schofield signed Henry J. Stierlin, Capt. Co. "A" 1 Mo Cav., 16 July 1862 (United States National Archives, Washington, D.C.).

"Quantrell's Muster Roll," notations attached setforth Quantrill's Co. Mo., one irregular roll not dated or signed. Copy of this or similar roll, shows the copy forwarded to Maj. Genl. Schofield July 16, 1862, 92 names, see memo on index (United States National Archives, Washington, D.C.).

Larry Wood, "They Rode with Quantrill," <u>America's Civil War</u>, November 1996, pp. 58-64.

"Quantrill's Men," Compiled from reliable sources for Robt. Curran, Charles E. Bell, 1st Sgt. U.S.M.C. (Ret), undated.

Don Hoog, "Letter to Mr. Brownlee," containing 600 Quantrill riders, 2 Nov. 1969.

Chapter 1. "... To Wage War" Endnotes

Richard S. Brownlee, <u>Gray Ghosts of the Confederacy</u> (Richmond, Virginia: The William Byrd Press, Inc., 1958), pp. 5-8, 10-11, 19-27, 30, 32, 36-39, 46-47, 51-52, 64-65, 77,79-81, 83-86, 110-113, 115-117, 120-121, 125-127, 142, 146, 152-155, 157-158, 163, 165, 169, 170, 173-175, 177-178.

Albert Castel, <u>William Clarke Quantrill: His Life and Times</u> (New York: Frederick Fell, Inc., 1962), pp. 1-4, 61-63, 74, 87, 118-119, 122, 145, 150, 187-199, 216.

William Elsey Connelley, <u>Quantrill and the Border Wars</u> (New York, N.Y.: Konecky & Konecky, 1909), pp. 206-207, 236-237.

John N. Edwards, <u>Noted Guerrillas</u> (Shawnee, Kansas: Two Trails Publishing, 1996), pp. 14, 18, 19, 100, 293, 296, 299-302.

Michael Fellman, Inside War (New York, Oxford: Oxfor University Press, 1989, pp. 3, 5, 7, 13, 15, 19

Thomas Goodrich, <u>Black Flag</u> (Bloomington and Indianapolis: Indiana University Press, 1995), pp. 97, 100, 139-145.

Thomas Goodrich, Bloody Dawn: The Story Of The Lawrence Massacre (Kent, Ohio and London, England: The Kent State University Press, 1991), pp. 159-161.

Edward E. Leslie, <u>The Devil Knows How to Ride</u> (New York: Random House, 1996), pp. 5, 19-20, 83, 95-96, 112-113, 119-120, 137, 173, 199, 258, 260-262, 267, 357, 378-380.

QUANTRILL'S THIEVES By: Joseph K. Houts, Jr.

Notes to Pages 28-40

    Jay Monaghan, <u>Civil War on the Western Border, 1854-1865</u> (Lincoln and University of Nebraska Press, 1955), pp. 133-135, 319.

    Stuart W. Sanders, "Bloody Bill's Centralia Massacre," <u>America's Civil War</u>, March 2000, pp. 34-40, 82.

Chapter II. "Nefarious Business . . . Murdering Loyal Men" Endnotes

    Albert Castel, <u>William Clarke Quantrill: His Life and Times</u> (New York: Frederick Fell, Inc., 1962), pp. 53, 83, 87, 105-107.

    Alfred Castel, <u>A Frontier State at War: Kansas 1861-1865</u> (Lawrence, Kansas: Kansas Heritage Press, 1958), pp. 61-63.

    William E. Crissy, "A Romance of the Civil War 1861-5 Uncle Mat Houx," Western Historical Manuscript Collection, University of Missouri – Columbia, January 1921, pp. 1-2.

    "Death of Matthias Houx," without author and name of paper, Houx Genealogical Papers, Alice Kinyoun Houts, 21 July 1900.

    J. L. Ferguson, "Houx Family Had Large Part in Settling and Developing County," <u>Daily Star-Journal</u>, Warrensburg, MO, 4 March 1932.

    J. L. Ferguson, "The Pioneer Houts Family Has Been Represented Well in Johnson County," <u>Daily Star-Journal</u>, Warrensburg, MO, 22 July 1935.

    J. L. Ferguson, "Walnut Box Holds Memories, Reminiscences of Days Past," <u>Daily Star-Journal</u>, Warrensburg, MO, undated.

    Thomas Goodrich, <u>Bloody Dawn: The Story of the Lawrence Massacre</u> (Kent, Ohio and London, England: The Kent State University Press, 1991), pp. 1-8

    William A. Gregg, "A Little Dab of History Without Embellishment," Western Historical Manuscript Collection, University of Missouri-Columbia, p. 15.

    Anne Bennett Houx, <u>Book of Houx Stories</u> (Warrensburg, Missouri, 1995), pp. 25-36.

    Houts Genealogy List, Houts Genealogical Papers, Alice Kinyoun Houts.

    Thomas W. Houts, "Certificate of Discharge," 14 March1891.

    Matthias Houx, Application for Membership to the National Society of the Daughters of the American Revolution, Alice Kinyoun Houts, Houx Genealogical Papers, Washington, D.C., Approved, 25 July 1925.

    Houx Genealogical Papers, Alice Kinyoun Houts.

    Matthias Houx, Record of Missouri Confederate Veterans, United Daughters of the Confederacy, Missouri Division, Western Historical Manuscript Collection, University of Missouri-Columbia, pp. 1-3.

    "Matthias Houx, Son of John Jacob Houx," Houx Genealogical Papers, Alice Kinyoun Houts, p. 1.

    Interview with Joseph Kinyoun Houts, Sr., St. Joseph, Missouri, 20 February 1996.

    "Last Will and Testament of Jacob Houx," Houx Genealogical Papers, Alice Kinyoun Houts, 20 October 1853.

    Edward E. Leslie, <u>The Devil Knows How to Ride</u> (New York: Random House, 1996), pp. 106-108.

    Letter from Alice Kinyoun Houts to Tennie, Houx Genealogical Papers, 20 March 1961.

    Letter from Thirza (Houx) to Alice Kinyoun Houts, Houx Genealogical Papers, 26 March 1961.

    Letter from Thirza (Houx) to Alice Kinyoun Houts, Houx Genealogical Papers, 6 May 1961.

QUANTRILL'S THIEVES By: Joseph K. Houts, Jr.

Notes to Pages 28-53

Portrait and Biographical Records of Johnson and Pettis Counties, Missouri, "Major Thomas W. Houts," Chapman Publishing Co., Chicago, 1899, pp. 1-5.

"Roll of Quantrell's Company of Thieves," Major Thomas W. Houts, Houts Genealogical Papers, Alice Kinyoun Houts.

"Roll of 93 of Quantrell's Gang of Outlaws," Copy sent for in formation of Brig. Genl. Schofield signed Henry J. Sterlin, Capt. Co. A 1 Mo. Cav., 16 July 1862 (United States National Archives, Washington, D.C.)

"The State of Missouri," Commission Appointment to Captain Thomas W. Houts, signed William P. Hall, Acting Governor, 3 March 1862.

"The State of Missouri," Commission Appointment No. 802 to Major Thomas W. Houts, signed H. R. Gamble, Adjutant General, 27 March 1863.

U. S. Congress, House, Thomas W. Houts, H.R. Report No. 2494 to Accompany H.R. 2968 51st Cong., 1st Sess., 19 June 1890, pp. 1-3.

United States War Department, The War of Rebellion: A Compilation of the Official Records of the Union and Confederate Armies, Series I., Vol. VIII. (130 Volumes, Washington, D.C., 1880-1902), pp. 352-354, 356-358.

Ibid, Series I. Vol. XIII., pp. 154-160, 307.

Ibid, Series I. Vol. XLIII., p. 565.

Ibid, Series II., Vol. I., p. 273.

Chapter III. "The Many Wild Birds Were Caroling" Endnotes

Carl W. Breihan, Quantrill and His Civil War Guerrillas (Denver: Sage Books, 1959), p. 107.

Richard S. Brownlee, Gray Ghosts of the Confederacy (Richmond, Virginia: The William Byrd Press, Inc., 1958), pp. 71-75.

William Elsey Connelley, Quantrill and the Border Wars (New York, N. Y.: Konecky & Konecky, 1909), pp. 256-258.

John N. Edwards, Noted Guerrillas (Shawnee, Kansas: Two Trails Publishing, 1996), p. 89.

William H. Gregg, "A Little Dab of History Without Embellishment," Western Historical Manuscript Collection, University of Missouri-Columbia, pp. 12-23.

Edward E. Leslie, The Devil Knows How to Ride (New York: Random House, 1996), pp. 122-128.

United States War Department, The War of the Rebellion: A Compilation of the Official Records of the Union and Confederate Armies, Series I., Vol. XIII. (Washington, D.C., 1880-1902), pp. 154-160.

Chapter IV. ". . . Company of Thieves." Endnotes

W C Quantrell Endnotes

Richard S. Brownlee, Gray Ghosts of the Confederacy (Richmond, Virginia: The William Byrd Press, Inc., 1958), pp. 63, 103.

Albert Castel, A Frontier State at War: Kansas 1861-1865 (Lawrence, Kansas: Kansas Heritage Press, 1992), pp. 159-161.

Albert Castel, William Clarke Quantrill: His Life and Times (New York: Frederick Fell, Inc., 1962), pp. 23-45, 155-166, 201-203.

QUANTRILL'S THIEVES By: Joseph K. Houts, Jr.

Notes to Pages 53-64

Albert Castel, "William Clarke Quantrill: Terror of the Border," Civil War, January-February 1992, pp. 8-14, 22, 60.
William Elsey Connelley, Quantrill and the Border Wars (New York: Konecky & Konecky, 1909), pp. 42-45, 172, 421-434, 449-450, 483.
Joanne Chiles Eakin and Donald R. Hale, Branded as Rebels (Independence, Mo.: Print America, 1995), p. 361.
John N. Edwards, Noted Guerrillas (Shawnee, Kansas: Two Trails Publishing, 1996), pp. 30-31, 33-36, 435, 549.
Thomas Goodrich, Bloody Dawn: The Story of the Lawrence Massacre (Kent, Ohio and London, England: The Kent State University Press, 1991), pp. 81-122.
Edward E. Leslie, The Devil Knows How to Ride (New York: Random House, 1996), pp. 36-43, 86-97, 106, 113-119, 122-128, 137, 144, 149-150, 186-187, 343-347, 364-369, 407-420, 432, 436.
Larry Wood, "They Rode with Quantrill," America's Civil War, November 1996, pp. 58-64.

Wm Haller 1st Lieutenant Endnotes

Albert Castel, William Clark Quantrill: His Life and Times (New York: Frederick Fell, Inc., 1962), pp. 67, 92.
William Elsey Connelley, Quantrill and the Border Wars (New York, N.Y.: Konecky & Konecky, 1909), pp. 270, 275.
Joanne Chiles Eakin and Donald R. Hale, Branded as Rebels (Independence, Mo.: Print America, 1995), p. 184.
John N. Edwards, Noted Guerrillas (Shawnee, Kansas: Two Trails Publishing, 1996), pp. 52, 78, 87-91, 122-127, 164.
Edward E. Leslie, The Devil Knows How to Ride (New York: Random House, 1996), pp. 137, 141.
Hattie E. Poppino, Jackson County, Missouri Census of 1860 (1964), p. 97.
Larry Wood, "They Rode with Quantrill," America's Civil War, November 1996, pp. 60-61.

G W Todd 2nd Lieutenant Endnotes

Richard S. Brownlee, Gray Ghosts of the Confederacy (Richmond, Virginia: The William Byrd Press, Inc., 1958), pp. 122, 140.
Albert Castel, William Clarke Quantrill: His Life and Times (New York: Frederick Fell, Inc., 1962), pp. 87, 92, 126, 137-138.
William Elsey Connelley, Quantrill and the Border Wars (New York, NY: Konecky & Konecky, 1909), p. 455.
Joanne Chiles Eakin and Donald R. Hale, Branded as Rebels (Independence, Mo.: Print America, 1995), p. 433-434.
Thomas Goodrich, Black Flag (Bloomington and Indianapolis: Indiana University Press, 1995), pp. 137-138, 152.
William H. Gregg, "The Lawrence Raid," Kansas State Historical Society, Topeka, Kansas.
Edward E. Leslie, The Devil Knows How to Ride (New York: Random House, 1996), 300, 310, 316, 334-345.
Hattie Poppino, Jackson County Missouri Census of 1860 (1964), p. 246.

QUANTRILL'S THIEVES By: Joseph K. Houts, Jr.

Notes to Pages 65-70

W H Gregg 1st Sergeant Endnotes

Richard S. Brownlee, Gray Ghosts of the Confederacy (Richmond, Virginia: The William Byrd Press, Inc., 1958), p 122.
Albert Castel, William Clarke Quantrill: His Life and Times (New York: Frederick Fell, Inc., 1962), pp. 157-159.
William Elsey Connelley, Quantrill and the Border Wars (New York, N.Y.: Konecky & Konecky, 1909), pp. 189, 281.
Joanne Chiles Eakin and Donald R. Hale, Branded as Rebels (Independence, Mo.: Print America, 1995), pp. 175-176.
John N. Edwards, Noted Guerrillas (Shawnee, Kansas: Two Trails Publishing, 1996), pp. 54, 90, 110, 201, 218, 254 and 328.
William H. Gregg, "A Little Dab of History Without Embellishment," Western Historical Manuscript Collection, University of Missouri-Columbia, p. 1, 67.
Donald R. Hale, We Rode with Quantrill (1992), pp. 96-105.
Edward E. Leslie, The Devil Knows How to Ride (New York: Random House, 1996), pp. 178, 231, 248-251, 288-290 and 387-388.
John McCorkle, Three Years with Quantrill (Norman and London: University of Oklahoma Press, 1992), pp. 179-180.
Larry Wood, "They Rode With Quantrill," America's Civil War, November 1996, p. 60.

John Jarrette 2nd Sergeant Endnotes

Albert Castel, William Clarke Quantrill: His Life and Times (New York: Frederick Fell, Inc., 1962), pp. 139, 151, 159, 223.
William Elsey Connelley, Quantrill and the Border Wars (New York, N.Y.: Konecky & Konecky, 1909), pp. 317, 445.
Joanne Chiles Eakin and Donald R. Hale, Branded as Rebels (Independence, Mo.: Print America, 1995), p. 236.
John N. Edwards, Noted Guerrillas (Shawnee, Kansas: Two Trails Publishing, 1996), pp. 54, 60-62, 161, 181, 183, 189, 197, 213, 281, 460.
John N. Edwards, Shelby and His Men (Waverly, Missouri: General Joseph Shelby Memorial Fund, 1993), pp. 142-144.
Donald R. Hale, They Called Him Bloody Bill (Clinton, MO: The Printery, 1992), p. 54.
Edward E. Leslie, The Devil Knows How to Ride (New York: Random house, 1996), pp. 99, 250.
Hattie Poppino, Jackson County, Missouri Census of 1860 (1964), p. 124.
John McCorkle, Three Years with Quantrill (Norman and London: University of Oklahoma Press, 1992), pp. 78, 96-98.
James R. Ross, I, Jesse James (Dragon Publishing Corp., 1988), p. 92.
Larry Wood, "They Rode with Quantrill," America's Civil War, November 1996, p. 60.

J L Tucker 3rd Sergeant Endnotes

Richard S. Bownlee, Gray Ghosts of the Confederacy (Richmond, Virginia: The William Byrd Press, Inc., 1958), pp. 253-261.
Joanne Chiles Eakin and Donald R. Hale, Branded as Rebels (Independence, Mo.: Print America, 1995), p. 437.

QUANTRILL'S THIEVES By: Joseph K. Houts, Jr.

Notes to Pages 70-75

   John N. Edwards, Noted Guerrillas (Shawnee, Kansas: Two Trails Publishing, 1996), pp. 84, 90, 99, 110, 272-282.

Andrew Blunt 4th Sergeant Endnotes

   Richard S. Brownlee, Gray Ghosts of the Confederacy (Richmond, Virginia: The William Byrd Press, Inc., 1958), pp. 182-183.
   Albert Castel, William Clarke Quantrill: His Life and Times (New York: Frederick Fell, Inc., 1962), pp. 79, 95, 101, 122, 174, 174n.
   William Elsey Connelley, Quantrill and the Border Wars (New York, NY: Konecky & Konecky, 1909), pp. 156, 251-252, 278.
   Joanne Chiles Eakin and Donald R. Hale, Branded as Rebels (Independence, Mo.: Print America, 1995), p. 32.
   John N. Edwards, Noted Guerrillas (Shawnee, Kansas: Two Trails Publishing, 1996), pp. 64, 83-84, 87, 91, 110, 118, 157, 189-190, 207, 360, 363.
   Edward E. Leslie, The Devil Knows How to Ride (New York: Random House, 1996), pp. 202, 253.
   John McCorkle, Three Years with Quantrill (Norman and London: University of Oklahoma Press, 1992), p. 65.

F M Scott Commissary Endnotes

   Carl W. Breihan, Quantrill and His Civil War Guerrillas (Denver: Sage Books, 1959), pp. 166-174.
   Richard S. Brownlee, Gray Ghosts of the Confederacy (Richmond, Virginia: The William Byrd Press, Inc., 1958), pp. 253-261.
   Joanne Chiles Eakin and Donald R. Hale, Branded as Rebels (Independence, Mo.: Print America, 1995), p. 386.
   John N. Edwards, Noted Guerrillas (Shawnee, Kansas: Two Trails Publishing, 1996), pp. 110, 112, 156, 177, 178.
   Thomas Goodrich, Black Flag (Bloomington and Indianapolis: Indiana University Press, 1995), pp. 70-71.
   Edward E. Leslie, The Devil Knows How to Ride (New York: Random House, 1996), p. 185.

Richard Madox Quartermaster Endnotes

   Carl W. Breihan, Quantrill and His Civil War Guerrillas (Denver: Sage Books, 1959), pp. 166-174.
   Richard S. Brownlee, Gray Ghosts of the Confederacy (Richmond, Virginia: The William Byrd Press, Inc., 1958), pp. 253-261.
   Albert Castel, William Clarke Quantrill: His Life and Times (New York: Frederick Fell, Inc., 1962), pp. 131, 161.
   William Elsey Connelley, Quantrill and the Border Wars (New York, N.Y.: Konecky & Konecky, 1909), p. 384.
   Joanne Chiles Eakin and Donald R. Hale, Branded As Rebels (Independence, Mo.: Print America, 1995), p. 279.
   John N. Edwards, Noted Guerrillas (Shawnee, Kansas: Two Trails Publishing, 1996), pp. 176, 189, 328, 460.

QUANTRILL'S THIEVES By: Joseph K. Houts, Jr.

Notes to Pages 74-79

Edward E. Leslie, The Devil Knows How to Ride (New York: Random House, 1996), pp. 284, 287-290.

Letter from Amos Vannarsdall to Joseph K. Houts, Jr., 12 February 2000.

Hattie Poppino, Jackson County, Missouri Census of 1860 (1964), p. 158

Henry Akers Endnotes

William Elsey Connelley, Quantrill and the Border Wars (New York, N.Y.: Konecky & Konecky, 1909), pp. 457-458.

Joanne Chiles Eakin and Donald R. Hale, Branded as Rebels (Independence, Mo.: Print America, 1995), pp. 2-3.

Donald R. Hale, We Rode with Quantrill (Shawnee, Kansas: Two Trails Publishing, 1996), p. 80.

Edward E. Leslie, The Devil Knows How to Ride (New York: Ramdom House, 1996), p. 341.

Irene Spainhour, Quantrell's Men Veterans of the Civil War Battle of Lone Jack, Mo (1998), pp. 18, 25.

Hattie E. Poppino, Jackson County, Missouri Census of 1860 (1964), p. 2.

U L Anderson Endnotes

Joanne Chiles Eakin and Donald R. Hale, Branded as Rebels (Independence, Mo.: Print America, 1995), p. 6.

Joanne Chiles Eakin, Confederate Records from the United Daughters of the Confederacy Files, Vol. 1. (Independence, Mo: Two Trails Genealogy Shop, 1996), p. 21.

Hazel Tyler, Compiler, Johnson County, Missouri 1860 Federal Census with the 1860 Mortality Schedule (Springfield, Mo.: Ozarks Genealogical Society, Inc., 1997), p. 81.

Sylvester Atchison Endnotes

Joanne Chiles Eakin and Donald R. Hale, Branded As Rebels (Independence, Mo.: Print America, 1995), p. 11.

1870 Jackson County, Missouri Census, Mid-Continent Public Library, Genealogy & Local History Branch, Independence, Missouri, Courtesy Verna Gail Johnson, p. 156.

Jackson Co. Genealogical Society, Marriage Records of Jackson Co., Mo. Book 6 Mid-Continent Public Library, Genealogy & Local History Branch, Independence, Missouri, Courtesy Verna Gail Johnson, p. 1.

Hattie E. Poppino, Jackson County, Missouri Census of 1860 (1964), p. 7.

Irene Spainhour, Quantrell's Men Veterans of the Civil War Battle of Lone Jack, Mo (1998), p. 2.

Wiley Atchison Endnotes

1870 Jackson County, Missouri Census, Mid-Continent Public Library, Genealogy & Local History Branch, Independence, Missouri, Courtesy Verna Gail Johnson, p. 155.

QUANTRILL'S THIEVES By: Joseph K. Houts, Jr.

Notes to Pages 79-83

Jackson Co. Genealogical Society, <u>Marriage Records of Jackson Co., Mo. Book 4</u> Mid-Continent Public Library, Genealogy & Local History Branch, Independence, Missouri, Courtesy Verna Gail Johnson, p. 1.

Hattie E. Poppino, <u>Jackson County, Missouri Census of 1860</u> (1964), p. 7.

John Atchison Endnotes

<u>1870 Jackson County, Missouri Census</u>, Mid-Continent Public Library, Genealogy & Local History Branch, Independence, Missouri, Courtesy Verna Gail Johnson, p. 156.

Jackson Co. Genealogical Society, <u>Marriage Records of Jackson Co., Mo. Book 4</u> Mid-Continent Public Library, Genealogy & Local History Branch, Independence, Missouri, Courtesy Verna Gail Johnson, p. 1.

Hattie E. Poppino, <u>Jackson County, Missouri Census of 1860</u> (1964), p. 7.

H Austin Endnotes

Joanne Chiles Eakin and Donald R. Hale, <u>Branded As Rebels</u> (Independence, Mo.: Print America, 1995), pp. 272, 325.

Genealogical Society of Liberty, Inc., <u>1860 Federal Census Clay County, Missouri</u> (Liberty, Mo., 1985), p. 3.

Mary Helm Burnetti , Compiler and Publisher, <u>1860 Federal Census Lafayette County, Missouri</u> (Odessa, Missouri, 1982), p. 160.

J D Brinker Endnotes

Richard S. Brownlee, <u>Gray Ghosts of the Confederacy</u> (Richmond, Virginia: The William Byrd Press, Inc., 1958), pp. 253-261.

Joanne Chiles Eakin, <u>Confederate Records from the United Daughters of the Confederacy Files</u>, Vol. I. (Shawnee Mission, Kansas: Two Trails Genealogy Shop, 1996), p. 150.

Joanne Chiles Eakin and Donald R. Hale, <u>Branded As Rebels</u> (Independence, Mo.: Print America, 1995), p. 43.

John N. Edwards, <u>Noted Guerrillas</u> (Shawnee, Kansas: Two Trails Publishing, 1996), pp. 76-78, 86-89.

John N. Edwards, <u>Shelby and His Men</u> (Waverly, Missouri: General Joseph Shelby Memorial Fund, 1993), p. 496.

<u>The History of Johnson County, Missouri</u> (Kansas City, Mo.: Kansas City Historical Company, 1881), pp. 689-690.

Hazel Tyler, Compiler, <u>Johnson County, Missouri 1860 Federal Census with the 1860 Mortality Schedule</u> (Springfield, Mo.: Ozarks Genealogical Society, Inc., 1997), p. 88.

United States War Department, <u>The War of the Rebellion: A Compilation of the Official Records of the Union and Confederate Armies</u>, Series I., Vol. VIII. (Washington, D.C., 1890-1900), pp. 344-345.

<u>Ibid</u>, Series I., Vol. XIII., p. 125.

<u>Ibid</u>, Series I., Vol. XXII, pp. 700-701.

QUANTRILL'S THIEVES By: Joseph K. Houts, Jr.

Notes to Pages 84-91

Jas H Bowling Endnotes

James Bowlin, "Application for Admission to the Confederate Soldier's Home at Higginsville, Missouri," Attachments Thereto, Confederate Memorial State Historical Site, Higginsville, Missouri, 27 January 1913.

James Bowlin, "Pension for Ex-Confederate Soldiers," Attachments Thereto, Confederate Memorial State Historical Site, Higginsville, Missouri, 21 June 1913.

Richard Burns Endnotes

Carl W. Breihan, Quantrill and His Civil War Guerrillas (Denver: Sage Books, 1959), pp. 166-174.

Richard S. Brownlee, Gray Ghosts of the Confederacy (Richmond, Virginia: The William Byrd Press, Inc., 1958), pp. 244, 253-261.

Albert Castel, William Clarke Quantrill: His Life and Times (New York: Frederick Fell, Inc., 1962), p. 222.

William Elsey Connelley, Quantrill and the Border War (New York, N.Y.: Konecky & Konecky, 1909), p. 457.

Joanne Chiles Eakin and Donald R. Hale, Branded as Rebels (Independence, Mo.: Print America, 1995), pp. 54-55.

John N. Edwards, Noted Guerrillas (Shawnee, Kansas: Two Trails Publishing, 1996), pp. 53, 54, 56, 110, 459-460.

Edward R. Leslie, The Devil Knows How to Ride (New York: Random House, 1996), pp. 343, 394.

Hattie E. Poppino, Jackson County, Missouri Census of 1860 (1964), p. 31.

Irene Spainhour, Quantrell's Men Veterans of the Civil War Battle of Lone Jack, Mo (1998), p. 3.

Warren Welch, Warren Welch Remembers Transcribed by Joanne Chiles Eakin (Independence, Missouri: Two Trails Publishing, 1997), p. 2.

Cole Younger, The Story of Cole Younger by Himself (Springfield, Mo.: Oak Hills Publishing, 1996), p. 50.

W M Burges Endnotes

Burgess Genealogical Papers, Michael Burgess, Johnson County Historical Society, Inc., Warrensburg, Missouri, undated.

Letter from Michael Burgess to Joseph K. Houts, Jr., 12 January 2000.

United States War Department, The War of the Rebellion: A Compilation of the Official Records of the Union and Confederate Armies, Series I, VIII. (Washington, D.C., 1890-1900), pp. 344-345.

Ibid, Series I., VIII., pp. 356-358.

Ibid, Series II., Vol. III., pp. 426-427.

W A Baker Endnotes

W. H. Baker, Missouri Confederate Unit Rosters, 16th Missouri Cavalry CSA, Missouri–Sons of Confederate Unit Rosters, http://missouri-scv.org/mounits/rosters.html.

Joanne Chiles Eakin, Confederate Records from the United Daughters of the Confederacy Files, Vol. I. (Independence, Mo: Two Trails Publishing, 1996), p. 49.

QUANTRILL'S THIEVES   By: Joseph K. Houts, Jr.

Notes to Pages 90-97

    Joanne Chiles Eakin and Donald R. Hale, Branded As Rebels (Independence, Mo: Print America, 1995), pp. 14-15.
    "Copy Muster Roll of Capt. W. C. Quantrell", Head Quarters Department of the Mo., St. Louis, Mo. November 5, 1864.
    Hazel Tyler, Compiler, Johnson County, Missouri 1860 Census with the 1860 Mortality Schedule (Springfield, Mo: Ozark Genealogical Society, Inc., 1997), pp. 34, 113, 124.

W H Butler Endnotes

    W H Butler, "Pension for Ex-Confederate Soldiers," attachments thereto, Confederate Memorial State Historical Site, Higginsville, Missouri, 20 June 1913.

G N Burnett Endnotes

    Joanne Chiles Eakin and Donald R. Hale, Branded as Rebels (Independence, Mo.: Print America, 1995), pp. 17-18, 402.
    Donald R. Hale, We Rode with Quantrill (1992), pp. 82-83.
    Marilyn Bailiff King, "Family History Report" George McKinley Barnett, King Genealogical files, undated, pp. 1-6.
    S. D. Kirfner, "George Barnett Rode with Men of Quantrell," Topeka Daily, Topeka, Kansas, 25 January, 1931.
    Irene Spainhour, Quantrell's Men Veterans of the Civil War Battle of Lone Jack, Mo (1998), p. 2.

James Barnett Endnotes

    Joanne Chiles Eakin, Confederate Records from the United Daughters of the Confederacy Files, Vol. I. (Shawnee Mission, Kansas: Two Trails Genealogy Shop, 1996), p. 60.
    Joanne Chiles Eakin and Donald R. Hale, Branded as Rebels (Independence, Mo.: Print America, 1995), p. 18.

O. S. Barnett Endnotes

    Obadiah Strange Barnett, "Application for Admission to the Confederate Home at Higginsville, Missouri," Confederate Memorial State Historical Site. Higginsville, Missouri, undated.
    Joanne Chiles Eakin and Donald R. Hale, Branded As Rebels (Independence, Mo.: Print America, 1995), p. 18.
    Joanne Chiles Eakin, Confederate Records From the United Daughters of the Confederacy Files, Vol. I. (Independence, Mo.: Two Trails Genealogy Shop, 1996), p. 62.
    John N. Edwards, Shelby and His Men (Waverly, Missouri: General Joseph Shelby Memorial Fund, 1993), pp. 165-167, 287.
    Letter from Kay Russell, Tourist Assistant Confederate Memorial State Historical Site to Joseph K. Houts, Jr., 12 June 1999.
    Phillip W. Steele and Steve Cottrell, Civil War in the Ozarks (Gretna: Pelican Publishing Company, 1994), p. 60.

Notes to Pages 98-103

Lee Ball Endnotes

Hattie E. Poppino, Jackson County, Missouri Census of 1860 (Kansas City, Mo.:1964), p. 9.

W M Bledsoe Endnotes

Bledsoe Genealogy Chart, Family Internet Connection, Bledsoe@Sprintmail.com, 12 December 2000.
Carl W. Breihan, Quantrill and His Civil War Guerrillas (Denver: Sage Books, 1959), pp. 166-174.
Richard S. Brownlee, Gray Ghosts of the Confederacy (Richmond, Virginia: The William Byrd Press, Inc., 1958), pp. 253-261.
Albert Castel, William Clarke Quantrill: His Life and Times (New York: Frederick Fell, Inc., 1962), pp. 152-153, 168.
William Elsey Connelley, Quantrill and the Border Wars (New York, N.Y.: Konecky & Konecky, 1909), pp. 254, 429, 432.
Joanne Chiles Eakin and Donald R. Hale, Branded as Rebels (Independence, Mo.: Print America, 1995), p. 31.
John N. Edwards, Noted Guerrillas (Shawnee, Kansas: Two Trails Publishing, 1996), p. 75.
Edward R. Leslie, The Devil Knows How to Ride (New York: Random House, 1996), p. 276.
Letter from Bob Bledsoe to Joseph K. Houts, Jr., Relating Bledsoe Family Genealogy and History of William and Mabel Melton Bledsoe, 23 December 2000.
Letter from Bob Bledsoe to Joseph K. Houts, Jr., 24 December 2000.
John McCorkle, Three Years with Quantrill (Norman and London: University of Oklahoma Press, 1992), pp. 139, 141-142.
Irene Spainhour, Quantrell's Men Veterans of the Civil War Battle of Lone Jack, Mo (1998), p. 3.
Warren Welch, Warren Welch Remembers, Transcribed by Joanne Chiles Eakin (Independence, Missouri: Two Trails Publishing, 1997), p. 7.
Cole Younger, The Story of Cole Younger by Himself (Springfield, Mo.: Oak Hills Publishing, 1996), p. 18.

W C Bell Endnotes

Joanne Chiles Eakin, Confederate Records From the United Daughters of the Confederacy Files, Vol. I. (Independence, Mo.: Two Trails Genealogy Shop, 1996), p. 80.
Hattie E. Poppino, Jackson County, Missouri Census of 1860 (1964), p. 15.
The History of Jackson County, Missouri (Kansas City, Mo.: Union Historical Company, Birdsall, William & Co., 1881), p. 325.

J Bowers Endnotes

Mary Helm Burnetti, 1860 Federal Census Lafayette County, Missouri (Odessa, Missouri, 1982), p. 94.
http://missouri-scv.org/mounits/rosters.num, 2nd Missouri Cavalry Regiment, Company G.

QUANTRILL'S THIEVES   By: Joseph K. Houts, Jr.

Notes to Pages 102-107

http://missouri-scv.org/mounits/rosters.num, 5th Missouri Cavalry Regiment, Company G.

http://missouri-scv.org/mounits/rosters.num, 3rd Missouri Cavalry Regiment, Company F.

"Quantrell's Muster Roll", Notations Attached Setforth Quantrell's Co. Mo. 2 One Irregular Roll Not Dated or Signed. Copy of this or similar roll shows the copy forwarded to Maj. Genl. Schofield July 16, 1862, 92 names, see memo on index (United States National Archives, Washington, D.C.)

W H Campbell Endnotes

James A. Browning, "Confederate Guerrillas and Those Who Rode with the James Gang," Confederate Memorial State Historic Site, Higginsville, Missouri, Courtesy Kay Russell, p. 5.

Joanne Chiles Eakin and Donald R. Hale, Branded As Rebels (Independence, Mo.: Print America, 1995), p. 60.

Hazel Tyler, Compiler, Johnson County, Missouri 1860 Federal Census with the 1860 Mortality Schedule (Springfield, Mo.: Ozarks Genealogical Society, Inc., 1997), pp. 70, 116, 122.

JJR Dejarnatt Endnotes

http://missouri-scv.org/mounits/rosters.num, 10th Missouri Cavalry Regiment, Company D.

James Cunningham Endnotes

Joanne Chiles Eakin, Confederate Records from the Daughters of the Confederacy Files, Vol. II. (Independence, Mo.: Two Trails Publishing, 1996), pp. 135-137.

Carmichael Cemetery, Centerview, Johnson County, Missouri.

Hazel Tyler, Compiler, Johnson County, Missouri 1860 Federal Census with the 1860 Mortality Schedule (Springfield, Mo.: Ozarks Genealogical Society, Inc., 1997), p. 124.

Al Cunningham Endnotes

Carl W. Breihan, Quantrill and His Civil War Guerrillas (Denver: Sage Books, 1959), pp. 166-174.

Richard S. Brownlee, Gray Ghosts of the Confederacy (Richmond, Virginia: The William Byrd Press, Inc., 1962), pp. 253-261.

Joanne Chiles Eakin, Confederate Records from the United Daughters of the Confederacy Files, Vol. II. (Independence, Mo.: Two Trails Publishing, 1996), pp. 134-136.

Joanne Chiles Eakin and Donald R. Hale, Branded as Rebels (Independence, Mo.: Print America, 1995), p. 102.

John N. Edwards, Noted Guerrillas (Shawnee, Kansas: Two Trails Publishing, 1996), pp. 135, 138-140, 142, 162, 164-165.

Irene Spainhour, Quantrell's Men Veterans of the Civil War Battle of Lone Jack, Mo. (1998), p. 4.

Notes to Pages 106-112

    Hazel Tyler, Compiler, <u>Johnson County Missouri 1860 Federal Census with the 1860 Mortality Schedule</u> (Springfield, Mo.: Ozarks Genealogical Society, Inc., 1997), p. 124.
    Cole Younger, <u>The Story of Cole Younger by Himself</u> (Springfield, Mo.: Oak Hills Publishing, 1996), p. 146.

W Collesure Endnotes

    Genealogical Society of Liberty, Inc., <u>1860 Federal Census Clay County, Missouri</u>: (Liberty, Mo., 1985), p. 16.

Thomas Collesure Endnotes

    Genealogical Society of Liberty, Inc., <u>1860 Federal Census Clay County, Missouri</u>, (Liberty, Mo.: 1985), p. 16.
    Rose Mary Lankford, <u>The Encyclopedia of Quantrill's Guerrillas</u> (Evening Shade, Ar.: 1999), p. 45.

Kit Chiles Endnotes

    Carl W. Breihan, <u>Quantrill and His Civil Was Guerrillas</u> (Denver: Sage Books, 1959), p. 167.
    Richard S. Brownlee, <u>Gray Ghosts of the Confederacy</u> (Richmond, Virginia: The William Byrd Press, Inc., 1958), pp. 70, 103, 254.
    William Elsey Connelley, <u>Quantrill and the Border Wars</u> (New York, N.Y.: Konecky & Konecky, 1909), pp. 259, 262-263.
    Joanne Chiles Eakin and Donald R. Hale, <u>Branded as Rebels</u> (Independence, Mo.: Print America, 1995), pp. 70, 74.
    Joanne Chiles Eakin, <u>Walter Chiles of Jamestown and Some of His Descendants</u> (Independence, MO: Wee Print, 1983), pp. 99-102, 165-168.
    <u>History Andrew and DeKalb Counties</u> (St. Louis and Chicago: The Goodspeed Publishing Co., 1888), pp. 128-129.
    Edward E. Leslie, <u>The Devil Knows How to Ride</u> (New York: Random House, 1996), pp. 147-148.
    James R. Ross, <u>I Jesse James</u> (Dragon Publishing Corp., 1988), pp. 79-80.

Samuel Clifton Endnotes

    Albert Castel, <u>William Clarke Quantrill: His Life and Times</u> (New York: Frederick Fell, Inc., 1962), pp. 104, 126.
    Joanne Chiles Eakin and Donald R. Hale, <u>Branded as Rebels</u> (Independence, Mo.: Print America, 1995), pp. 80-81.
    John N. Edwards, <u>Noted Guerrillas</u> (Shawnee, Kansas: Two Trails Publishing, 1996), p. 99.
    Interview with Dr. Philip R. Acuff, St. Joseph, Missouri, 9 July 1999.
    <u>Webster's Seventh New Collegiate Dictionary</u> (Springfield, Massachusetts, U.S.A.: G&C Merriam Company, Publishers, 1963), p. 105.

QUANTRILL'S THIEVES By: Joseph K. Houts, Jr.

Notes to Pages 112-121

Wm Chamblin Endnotes

Joanne Chiles Eakin and Donald R. Hale, <u>Branded as Rebels</u> (Independence, Mo.: Print America, 1995), p. 66.

Syrus Cockrell Endnotes

Joanne Chiles Eakin, <u>Confederate Records From the United Daughters of the Confederacy Files</u>, Vol. II. (Independence, Mo.: Two Trails Publishing, 1966), pp. 76-77.
Joanne Chiles Eakin and Donald R. Hale, <u>Branded as Rebels</u> (Independence, Mo.: Print America, 1995), p. 84.
Cockrell Family File, Johnson County Historical Society, Warrensburg, Missouri.
Michael Fellman, <u>Inside War</u> (New York, Oxford: Oxford University Press, 1989), p. 137.
J. L. Ferguson, "County Records Hidden in Thicket Near Centerview During Civil War," <u>Daily Star-Journal</u>, Warrensburg, Mo., 14 May 1933.
Letter from Bella Hughes to Joseph K. Houts, Jr., 10 July 2000.
Letter from Bella Hughes to Joseph K. Houts, Jr., 11 July 2000.
Letter from Bella Hughes to Joseph K. Houts, Jr., 12 July 2000.
"Senator Cockrell's Brother." <u>Weekly Standard</u>, Warrensburg, Missouri, 28 July, 1899.

W F Cheatham (Dead) Endnotes

http://missouri-scv.org/mounits/rosters.num, William's Regiment, Company F.

W H Campbell Endnotes

James A. Browning, "Confederate Guerrillas and Those Who Rode with the James Gang," Confederate Memorial State Historic Site, Higginsville, Missouri, Courtesy Kay Russell, p. 5.
Joanne Chiles Eakin and Donald R. Hale, <u>Branded As Rebels</u> (Independence, Mo.: Print America, 1995), p. 60.
Hazel Tyler, Compiler, <u>Johnson County, Missouri 1860 Federal Census with the 1860 Mortality Schedule</u> (Springfield, Mo.: Ozarks Genealogical Society, Inc., 1997), pp. 70, 116, 122.

Robert Davenport Endnotes

Joanne Chiles Eakin, <u>Confederate Records from the United Daughters of the Confederacy Files</u>, Vol. II. (Shawnee Mission, Kansas: Two Trails Publishing, 1996), p. 149.
Joanne Chiles Eakin and Donald R. Hale, <u>Branded as Rebels</u> (Independence, Mo.: Print America, 1995), pp. 105-106.
Hazel Tyler, Compiler, <u>Johnson County, Missouri 1860 Federal Census with the 1860 Mortality Schedule</u> (Springfield, Mo.: Ozarks Genealogical Society, Inc., 1997), p. 36.
<u>Ibid</u>, Houx Family, p. 36.

Notes to Pages 120-126

United States War Department, The War of the Rebellion: A Compilation of the Official Records of the Union and Confederate Armies, Series I., Vol. XIII. (Washington, D.C., 1890-1900), p. 125.

N F Doak Endnotes

Joanne Chiles Eakin, Confederate Records from the United Daughters of the Confederacy Files, Vol. II. (Shawnee Mission, Kansas: Two Trails Publishing, 1996), pp. 180-181.

Joanne Chiles Eakin and Donald R. Hale, Branded as Rebels (Independence, Mo.: Print America, 1995), p. 114.

http://missouri-scv.org/mounits/rosters.num, 16th Missouri Infantry.

The History of Johnson County, Missouri (Kansas City, Mo.: Kansas City Historical Company, 1881), pp. 842-843.

"Rader Led Warrensburg's Confederates." Daily Star-Journal, Warrensburg, Missouri, 20 August 1976, Reprinted The Blue & Gray Chronicle, Independence, Missouri, June 2001.

Hazel Tyler, Compiler, Johnson County, Missouri 1860 Federal Census with the 1860 Mortality Schedule (Springfield, Mo.: Ozark Genealogical Society, Inc., 1997), p. 110.

J N Dickers Endnotes

Joanne Chiles Eakin and Donald R. Hale, Branded as Rebels (Independence, Mo.: Print America, 1995), p. 113.

History of Saline County, Missouri, (St. Louis: Missouri Historical Company, 1881), pp. 318-319.

Hattie E. Poppino, Jackson County, Missouri Census of 1860 (Kansas City, Mo.:1964), pp. 60, 223.

M H Doors Endnotes

Joanne Chiles Eakin, Confederate Records from the United Daughters of the Confederacy Files, Vol. II. (Independence, Mo.: Two Trails Publishing, 1996, pp. 184-185.

Joanne Chiles Eakin and Donald R. Hale, Branded As Rebels (Independence, Mo.: Print America, 1995), p. 115.

http://missouri-scv.org/mounits/rosters.num, 10th Missouri Cavalry Regiment, Company H.

Hattie E. Poppino, Jackson County, Missouri Census of 1860 (Kansas City, Mo.:1964), p. 63.

Hazel Tyler, Compiler, Johnson County, Missouri 1860 Federal Census with the 1860 Mortality Schedule (Springfield, Mo.: Ozarks Genealogical Society, Inc., 1997), p. 27.

J F Doores Endnotes

Joanne Chiles Eakin and Donald R. Hale, Branded As Rebels (Independence, Mo.: Print America, 1995), p. 115.

Edward R. Leslie, The Devil Knows How to Ride (New York: Random House, 1996), pp. 127-128.

QUANTRILL'S THIEVES   By: Joseph K. Houts, Jr.

Notes to Pages 126-130

   Hattie E. Poppino, Jackson County, Missouri Census of 1860 (1964), pp. 47, 63.

Noah Estes Endnotes

   Carolyn M. Bartels, Missouri Confederate Deaths Union Prisons & Hospitals (Transcribed, Independence, Mo.: Distributed Blue & Gray Book Shoppe), p. 6.
   Carl W. Breihan, Quantrill and His Civil War Guerrillas (Denver: Sage Books, 1959), pp. 166-174.
   Richard S. Brownlee, Gray Ghosts of the Confederacy (Richmond, Virginia: The William Byrd Press, Inc., 1958), pp. 253-261.
   Joanne Chiles Eakin, Confederate Records From the United Daughters of the Confederacy Files Vol. III. (Independence, Mo.: Two Trails Publishing, 1996), p. 25.
   Joanne Chiles Eakin, Quantrill's Company (transcription of National Archives Microfilm, 1997), 109, M322, Roll #193, pp. 1, 11.
   Joanne Chiles Eakin and Donald R. Hale, Branded as Rebels (Independence, Mo.: Print America, 1995), pp. 135-136.
   John N. Edwards, Noted Guerrillas (Shawnee, Kansas: Two Trails Publishing, 1996), p. 188.
   Letter from Ralph E. Church, Cemetery Administrator, Jefferson Barracks National Cemetery, Department of Veteran's Affairs to Joseph K. Houts, Jr., 15 May 2000.
   Hattie E. Poppino, Jackson County, Missouri Census of 1860 (1964), p. 71.
   Irene Spainhour, Quantrell's Men Veterans of the Civil War Battle of Lone Jack, Mo (1998), p. 4.

J G Freeman Endnotes

   Hazel Tyler, Compiler, Johnson County, Missouri 1860 Federal Census with the 1860 Mortality Schedule (Springfield, Mo.: Ozarks Genealogical Society, Inc., 1997), pp. 105, 107.

J H George Endnotes

   Richard S. Brownlee, Gray Ghosts of the Confederacy (Richmond, Virginia: The William Byrd Press, Inc., 1959), pp. 253-261.
   William Elsey Connelley, Quantrill and the Border Wars (New York, N.Y.: Konecky & Konecky, 1909), p. 302.
   Joanne Chiles Eakin, Confederate Records from the United Daughters of the Confederacy Files, Vol. III., (Independence, Mo.: Two Trails Publishing, 1996), p. 104.
   Joanne Chiles Eakin and Donald R. Hale, Branded as Rebels (Independence, Mo.: Print America, 1995), pp. 161-162.
   John N. Edwards, Noted Guerrillas (Shawnee, Kansas: Two Trails Publishing, 1996), pp. 58, 75, 86-87, 99, 161, 182-183.
   John N. Edwards, Shelby and His Men (Waverly, Missouri: General Joseph Shelby Memorial Fund, 1993), p. 556.
   B. James George, Sr. "The Q-Men of Jackson County," The Oak Grove Banner, Oak Grove, Missouri, 9 October 1959.

Notes to Pages 129-137

William H. Gregg, "A Little Dab of History Without Embellishment," Western Historical Manuscript Collection, University of Missouri-Columbia, 1906, p. 15.
Donald R. Hale, We Rode with Quantrill (1992), pp. 95-96.
Jay Monaghan, Civil War on the Western Border 1854-1865 (Lincoln and London: University of Nebraska Press, 1955), p. 321.
Hattie E. Poppino, Jackson County, Missouri Census of 1860 (1964), p. 86.
Irene Spainhour, Quantrell's Men Veterans of the Civil War Battle of Lone Jack, Mo (1998), pp. 5, 16, 24.

Mike Houx Endnotes

Richard S. Brownlee, Gray Ghosts of the Confederacy (Richmond, Virginia: The William Byrd Press, Inc., 1958), p. 136.
Albert Castel, A Frontier State at War: Kansas 1861-1865 (Lawrence, Kansas: Kansas Heritage Press, 1958), p. 159.
William E. Crissy, "A Romance of the Civil War 1861-65 Uncle Mat Houx," Western Historical Manuscript Collection, University of Missouri-Columbia, January, 1921, pp. 1-2.
J. L. Ferguson, "Houx Family Had Part in Settling and Developing County," Daily Star-Journal Warrensburg, Mo., 4 March 1932.
Ann Bennett Houx, Book of Houx Stories (Warrensburg, Missouri, 1995), pp. 20, 26, 29, 43, 48.
Last Will and Testament of Jacob Houx, Houx Genealogical Papers, Alice Kinyoun Houts, 20 October 1853.
Letter from Alice Kinyoun Houts to Tennie, 20 March 1961.
Letter from Thirza (Houx) to Alice Kinyoun Houts, 6 May 1961.
Letter from A. Pauline Houx Hall to Joseph K. Houts, Jr. concerning Michael Morningstar Houx, 29 June 1999.

Mat Houx Endnotes

Albert Castel, William Clarke Quantrill: His Life and Times (New York: Frederick Fell, Inc., 1962), p. 87.
Joanne Chiles Eakin, Confederate Records From the United Daughters of the Confederacy Files, Vol. IV. (Independence, Mo. Two Trails Publishing, 1997), p. 84.
Joanne Chiles Eakin and Donald R. Hale, Branded As Rebels (Independence, Mo.: Print America, 1995), p. 215.
William E. Crissy, "A Romance of the Civil War 1861-5 Uncle Mat Houx," Western Historical Manuscript Collection, University of Missouri-Columbia, January, 1921, pp. 1-2.
"Death of Matthias Houx," without author and name of newspaper, 21 July 1900.
J. L. Ferguson, "County Records Hidden in Thicket Near Centerview During Civil War," Daily Star-Journal, Warrensburg, Mo., 14 May 1933.
J. L. Ferguson, "Houx Family Had Large Part in Setting and Developing County," Daily Star-Journal, Warrensburg, Mo., 4 March 1932.
J. L. Ferguson, "Miss Mary Houx Has Government Papers Seeking Confiscation of Father's Land," Daily Star-Journal, Warrensburg, Mo., 30 September 1930.

QUANTRILL'S THIEVES By: Joseph K. Houts, Jr.

Notes to Pages 133-143

L. Ferguson, "Walnut Boy Holds Memories, Reminiscences of Days Past," Daily Star-Journal, Warrensburg, Mo.

Ann Bennett Houx, Book of Houx Stories (Warrensburg, Missouri, 1995), pp. 20, 23-31.

Houx Genealogical Papers, Alice Kinyoun Houx.

Matthias Houx, Record of Missouri Confederate Veterans, United Daughters of the Confederacy, Missouri Division, Western Historical Manuscript Collection, University of Missouri-Columbia.

Hazel Tyler, Compiler, Johnson County, Missouri 1860 Federal Census with the 1860 Mortality Schedule (Springfield, Mo.: Ozarks Genealogical Society, Inc., 1997), p. 36.

Interview with Margaret Bardgett, Warrensburg, Missouri, 10 April 1999.

United States War Department, The War of the Rebellion: A Compilation of the Official Records of the Union and Confederate Armies, Series 11. Vol. 1. (Washington, D.C., 1880-1902), p. 273.

Robert Houx Endnotes

Joanne Chiles Eakin and Donald R. Hale, Branded as Rebels (Independence, Mo.: Print America, 1995), pp. 215 491.

William H. Gregg, "A Little Dab of History Without Embellishment," Western Historical Manuscript Collection, University of Missouri-Columbia, 1906, p. 15.

Ann Bennett Houx, Book of Houx Stories (Warrensburg, Missouri, 1995), pp. 26, 31, 33.

Interview with Margaret Bardgett, Warrensburg, Missouri, 10 April 1999.

"Passing of a Pioneer," Daily Star-Journal, Warrensburg, Mo., without author's name and date.

W Halley Endnotes

Joanne Chiles Eakin and Donald R. Hale, Branded as Rebels (Independence, Mo.: Print America, 1995), pp. 184-185.

Hallie E. Poppino, Jackson County, Missouri Census of 1860 (1964), p. 98.

Irene Spainhour, Confederate Veterans of the Civil War Battle of Lone Jack, Mo (1998), p. 6.

Interview with Jerry Russell, Heaton, Bowman, Smith and Sidenfaden Chapel, concerning Halley's funeral service and costs, 16 February 2000.

Interview with St. Joseph Police Department, concerning Halley's police service and discharge, 16 February 2000.

"Member of the Quantrell Band," St. Joseph Daily Gazette-Herald, St. Joseph, Missouri, 19 December 1900, courtesy of St. Joseph, Missouri Public Library.

"Mixed Up", Lee's Summit Journal, Lee's Summit, Jackson County, Mo., 8 February 1901, courtesy Dee Mathews, Mid-Continent Public Library.

John Hampton Endnotes

Carl W. Breihan, Quantrill and His Civil War Guerrillas (Denver: Sage Books, 1959), pp. 165-174.

Notes to Pages 143-146

    Richard S. Brownlee, <u>Gray Ghosts of the Confederacy</u> (Richmond, Virginia: The William Byrd Press, Inc., 1958), pp. 253-261.
    William Elsey Connelley, <u>Quantrill and the Border Wars</u> (New York, N.Y.: Konecky & Konecky, 1909), p. 257.
    Joanne Chiles Eakin, <u>Confederate Records from the United Daughters of the Confederacy Files</u>, Vol. III. (Independence, Mo.: Two Trails Publishing, 1996), p. 176.
    Joanne Chiles Eakin and Donald R. Hale, <u>Branded as Rebels</u> (Independence, Mo.: Print America, 1995), p. 187.
    John N. Edwards, <u>Noted Guerrillas</u> (Shawnee, Kansas: Two Trails Publishing, 1996), p. 52.
    Edward R. Leslie, <u>The Devil Knows How to Ride</u> (New York: Random House, 1996), p. 126.
    Hattie E. Poppino, <u>Jackson County, Missouri</u> Census of 1860 (1964), p. 99.

O Hampton Endnotes

    <u>History of Howard and Chariton Counties</u> (1884), pp. 485, 1145-1146.
    Mary (Bartee) Couch, Compiler, <u>1860 Federal Census for Chariton County, Missouri</u> (Marceline, Missouri: 1887).
    http://missouri-scv.org/mounits/rosters.num, 12th Missouri Cavalry Regiment, Company D.

G N Horn Endnotes

    James A. Browning, "Confederate Guerrillas and Those Who Rode with the James Gang," Confederate Memorial State Historical Site, Higginsville, Missouri, Courtesy Kay Russell, p. 18.
    Thomas E. Clatworthy, Transcriber, <u>Cass County, Missouri 1860 Federal Census</u> (Harrisonville, Missouri: The Cass County Historical Society, 1982), p. 68.
    Joanne Chiles Eakin, "Warrants Issued After the Burning of Lawrence," (1997), pp. 1-2.
    Joanne Chiles Eakin and Donald R. Hale, <u>Branded As Rebels</u> (Independence, Mo.: Print America, 1995), pp. 214, 499.
    John N. Edwards, <u>Noted Guerrillas</u> (Shawnee, Kansas: Two Trails Publishing, 1996), p. 367.
    Horn Ancestry, Ancestry.com, http://pedigree.ancestry.com/cgn-dim/preview. uh/h.

J J Hall Endnotes

    Richard S. Brownlee, <u>Gray Ghosts of the Confederacy</u> (Richmond, Virginia: The William Byrd Press, Inc., 1958), pp. 253-261.
    Thomas E. Clatworthy, Transcriber, <u>Cass County, Missouri 1860 Federal Census</u> (Harrisonville, Missouri: The Cass County Historical Society, 1982), p. 86.
    William Elsey Connelley, <u>Quantrill and the Border Wars</u> (New York, N.Y.: Konecky & Konecky, 1909), pp. 302-303.
    Joanne Chiles Eakin and Donald R. Hale, <u>Branded As Rebels</u> (Independence, Mo.: Print America, 1995), pp. 182-183.
    John N. Edwards, <u>Noted Guerrillas</u> (Shawnee, Kansas: Two Trails Publishing, 1996), pp. 185, 387.

QUANTRILL'S THIEVES By: Joseph K. Houts, Jr.

Notes to Pages 146-153

   Edward R. Leslie, The Devil Knows How to Ride (New York: Random House, 1996), p. 344.
   Cole Younger, The Story of Cole Younger by Himself (Springfield, Mo.: Oak Hills Publishing, 1996), p. 34.

M Houston Endnotes

   Mary Helm Burnetti, 1860 Federal Census Lafayette County, Missouri (Odessa, Missouri, 1982), p. 12.
   http://missouri-scv.org/mounits/rosters.num, 1st North East Missouri Cavalry Regiment, Company H.
   http://missouri-scv.org/mounits/rosters.num, 4th Missouri Cavalry Regiment, Company I.
   http://missouri-scv.org/mounits/rosters.num, Clark's Regiment Missouri Infantry, Company B.
   Hazel Tyler, Compiler, Johnson County, Missouri 1860 Federal Census with the 1860 Mortality Schedule (Springfield, Mo.: Ozarks Genealogical Society, Inc. 1997), pp. 121-122, 124.

A Harris Endnotes

   Carl W. Breihan, Quantrill and His Civil War Guerrillas (Denver: Sage Books, 1959), pp. 166-174.
   Joanne Chiles Eakin, Confederate Records from the United Daughters of the Confederacy Files, Vol. IV. (Independence, Mo.: Two Trails Publishing, 1997), p. 7.
   Joanne Chiles Eakin and Donald R. Hale, Branded As Rebels (Independence, Mo.: Print America, 1995), pp. 191-192.
   William Elsey Connelley, Quantrill and the Border Wars (New York: Konecky & Konecky, 1909), p. 250.
   John N. Edwards, Noted Guerrillas (Shawnee, Kansas: Two Trails Publishing, 1996), pp. 69, 81, 142, 307, 309.
   Hattie E. Poppino, Jackson County, Missouri Census of 1860 (1964), pp. 102-103.
   The History of Jackson County, Missouri (Kansas City, Mo.: Union Historical Company, Birdsall, Williams & Co., 1881), pp. 297, 368.

U Hays Endnotes

   Joe Anderson, "The Civil War & Slavery in Missouri," Public Presentation Speech, Pony Express Museum Archives Video, Pony Express Museum, St. Joseph, Missouri, 8 February 2000.
   Richard S. Brownlee, Gray Ghosts of the Confederacy (Richmond, Virginia: The William Byrd Press, Inc., 1958), pp. 101-165.
   Albert Castel, A Frontier State of War: Kansas 1861-1865 (Lawrence, Kansas: Kansas Heritage Press, 1992), p. 58.
   Albert Castel, William Clarke Quantrill: His Life and Times (New York: Frederick Fell, Inc., 1962), pp. 58-61, 81, 93-95.
   William Elsey Connelley, Quantrill and the Border Wars (New York, N.Y.: Konnecky & Konnecky, 1909), pp. 79, 266.

Notes to Pages 150-155

    Joanne Chiles Eakin, Confederate Records From the United Daughters of the Confederacy Files, Vol. IV. (Shawnee Mission, Kansas: Two Trails Publishing Shop, 1997), pp. 25-26.
    Joanne Chiles Eakin, Warren Welch Remembers (Independence, Missouri: Two Trails Publishing, 1998), pp. 2-3.
    Joanne Chiles Eakin and Donald R. Hale, Branded As Rebels (Independence, Mo.: Print America, 1995), pp. 198-199.
    John N. Edwards, Noted Guerrillas (Shawnee, Kansas: Two Trails Publishing, 1996), pp. 92-93, 96, 106-109.
    John N. Edwards, Shelby and His Men (Waverly, Missouri: General Joseph Shelby Memorial Fund, 1993), pp. 73-74, 83-86.
    William H. Gregg, "A Little Dab of History Without Embellishment," Western Historical Manuscript Collection, University of Missouri-Columbia, 1906, pp. 25-29.
    Thomas Goodrich, Bloody Dawn: The Story of the Lawrence Massacre (Kent, Ohio and London, England: The Kent State University Press, 1991), pp. 71-72.
    Margaret J. Hays, Letters, Article About Three Letters From Margaret to Mother in California, Higginsville, Missouri: Confederate Memorial State Historical Site, Untitled Without Author and Undated.
    Edward E. Leslie, The Devil Knows How to Ride (New York: Random House, 1996), pp. 130, 135, 139.
    John McCorkle, Three Years With Quantrill (Norman and London: University of Oklahoma Press, 1992), pp. 58-63, 218 nn. 3, 219 n. 8.
    Jay Monaghan, Civil War on the Western Border, 1854-1865 (Lincoln and London: University of Nebraska Press, 1955), pp. 255-257.
    Hattie E. Poppino, Jackson County, Missouri Census of 1860 (1964), p. 105.
    Irene Spainhour, Confederate Veterans of the Civil War Battle of Lone Jack, Mo (1998), p. 8.
    Cole Younger, The Story of Cole Younger by Himself (Springfield, Mo.: Oak Hills Publishing, 1996), pp. 20-21, 23-25, 34.

Robert Hall Endnotes

    Carl W. Breihan, Quantrill and His Civil War Guerrillas (Denver: Sage Books, 1959), pp. 166-174.
    Richard S. Brownlee, Gray Ghosts of the Confederacy (Richmond, Virginia: The William Byrd Press, Inc., 1958), pp. 253-261.
    Albert Castel, William Clarke Quantrill: His Life and Times (New York: Frederick Fell, Inc., 1962), p. 220.
    Thomas E. Clatworthy, Transcriber, Cass County, Missouri 1860 Federal Census (Harrisonville, Missouri: The Cass County Historical Society, 1982), p. 86-87.
    William Elsey Connelley, Quantrill and the Border Wars (New York, N.Y.: Konecky & Konecky, 1909), pp. 303, 449-450, 457, 478-479.
    Joanne Chiles Eakin and Donald R. Hale, Branded As Rebels (Independence, Mo.: Print America, 1995), pp. 182-183.
    John N. Edwards, Noted Guerrillas (Shawnee, Kansas: Two Trails Publishing, 1996), pp. 390, 401, 408, 411-412, 428, 430, 435.
    Becky L. Horvath, Hall Census Papers, Nelson County, Kentucky.
    Irene Spainhour, Quantrell's Men Veterans of the Civil War Battle of Lone Jack, Mo (1998), p. 6.

QUANTRILL'S THIEVES   By: Joseph K. Houts, Jr.

Notes to Pages 156-161

J A Hendricks Endnotes

Carl W. Breihan, Quantrill and His Civil War Guerrillas (Denver: Sage Books, 1959), pp. 166-174.

Richard S. Brownlee, Gray Ghosts of the Confederacy (Richmond, Virginia: The William Byrd Press, Inc., 1958), pp. 58, 253-261.

William Elsey Connelley, Quantrill and the Border Wars (New York, N.Y.: Konecky & Konecky, 1909), p. 221.

"Death Ends His Illness," Montana Daily Record, 11 April 1904.

Joanne Chiles Eakin, Confederate Records From the United Daughters of the Confederacy Files, Vol. IV. (Independence, Mo.: Two Trails Genealogy Shop, 1997), p. 37.

Joanne Chiles Eakin and Donald R. Hale, Branded as Rebels (Independence, Mo.: Print America, 1995), p. 200.

John N. Edwards, Noted Guerrillas (Shawnee, Kansas: Two Trails Publishing, 1996), pp. 328, 331.

Edward R. Leslie, The Devil Knows How to Ride (New York: Random House, 1996), pp. 96-97, 290.

Joaquin Miller, An Illustrated History of the State of Montana (Chicago: The Lewis Publishing Co., 1894), pp. 585-587.

R. L. Polk & Co.'s, Helena City Directory (Helena, Montana: Independent Press, 1900), p. 224.

Hattie E. Poppino, Jackson County, Missouri Census of 1860 (1964), p. 107.

Cole Younger, The Story of Cole Younger By Himself (Springfield, Mo.: Oak Hill Publishing, 1996), p. 61.

Irene Spainhour, Quantrell's Men Veterans of the Civil War Battle of Lone Jack, Mo (1998), p. 22.

W F Judd Endnotes

Carolyn M. Bartels, Missouri Confederate Deaths Union Prisons & Hospitals (transcribed, Independence, Mo.: Distributed Blue & Gray Book Shoppe), p. 10.

Joanne Chiles Eakin, Confederate Records From the United Daughters of the Confederacy Files, Vol. IV. (Independence, Mo.: Two Trails Publishing, 1997), p. 161.

Joanne Chiles Eakin and Donald R. Hale, Branded as Rebels (Independence, Mo.: Print America, 1995), p. 244.

Letter from Ralph E. Church, Cemetery Administrator, Jefferson Barracks National Cemetery, Department of Veterans Affairs to Joseph K. Houts, Jr., 7 February 2000.

Letter from Stephanie Young to Joseph K. Houts, Jr., 7 November 1999.

J W Koger Endnotes

Carl W. Breihan, Quantrill and His Civil War Guerrillas (Denver: Sage Books, 1959), pp. 166-174.

Richard S. Brownlee, Gray Ghosts of the Confederacy (Richmond, Virginia: The William Byrd Press, Inc., 1958), pp. 58, 219.

Albert Castel, William Clarke Quantrill: His Life and Times (New York: Frederick Fell, Inc., 1962), pp. 66, 77-78, 151-152, 158, 202.

QUANTRILL'S THIEVES By: Joseph K. Houts, Jr.

Notes to Pages 159-164

William Elsey Connelley, Quantrill and the Border Wars (New York, N.Y.: Konecky & Konecky, 1909), pp. 248-250, 281, 430, 435, 458.

Joanne Chiles Eakin and Donald R. Hale, Branded as Rebels (Independence, Mo.: Print America, 1995), pp. 256-257.

John N. Edwards, Noted Guerrillas (Shawnee, Kansas: Two Trails Publishing, 1996), pp. 53-54, 89-91, 99.

Donald R. Hale, We Rode with Quantrill (1992), pp. 116-117.

"Kincheloe to Mathis," Confederate Memorial State Historical Site, Higginsville, Missouri, Microfilm Roll No. RG, 33, 439.

John William Koger, "Application for Admission to the Confederate Soldier's Home of Missouri at Higginsville, Missouri," Confederate Memorial State Historical Site, Higginsville, Missouri, 11 August 1909.

Edward E. Leslie, The Devil Knows How to Ride (New York: Random House, 1996), pp. 116, 325, 343-344, 413.

Hattie Poppino, Jackson County, Missouri Census of 1860 (1964), p. 138

John McCorkle, Three Years with Quantrill (Norman and London: University of Oklahoma Press, 1923), pp. 139, 185.

Irene Spainhour, Confederate Veterans of the Civil War Battle of Lone Jack, Mo (1998), p. 10.

Irene Spainhour, Quantrell's Men Veterans of the Civil War Battle of Lone Jack, Mo (1998), p. 26.

C A Longacre Endnotes

Joanne Chiles Eakin, Confederate Records From the United Daughters of the Confederacy Files, Vol. V (Independence, Mo.: Two Trails Publishing, 1998), p. 78.

Joanne Chiles Eakin and Donald R. Hale, Branded as Rebels (Independence, Mo.: Print America, 1995), p. 273.

Letter from Barbara McCormick to Joseph K. Houts, Jr., outlining Charles A. Longacre's medical and family history, 10 April 2000.

Letter from Barbara McCormick to Joseph K. Houts, Jr., outlining Charles A. Longacre's later years and medical practice, 15 April 2000.

Letter from Barbara McCormick to Joseph K. Houts, Jr., outlining Charles A. Longacre's family lineage, 16 April 2000.

Letter from Barbara McCormick to Joseph K. Houts, Jr., outlining Charles A. Longacre's family connection to Cole Younger, 17 April 2000.

Letter from Barbara McCormick to Joseph K. Houts, Jr., outlining Charles A. Longacre's Civil War connections, 19 April 2000.

C. A. Longacre Military File, Missouri State Archives, 3 February 2000.

Longacre Genealogical File, Barbara McCormick, Wilmington, North Carolina.

B L Long Endnotes

History of Vernon County, Missouri (St. Louis: Brown & Co., 1887; Reprint, Clinton, Mo.: The Printery, 1974), pp. 345-346, 349.

http://missouri-scv.org/mounits/rosters.num, 5th Missouri Cavalry Regiment, Company B.

QUANTRILL'S THIEVES   By: Joseph K. Houts, Jr.

Notes to Pages 165-169

James Lyon Endnotes

    James A. Browning, "Confederate Guerrillas and Those Who Rode with the James Gang," Confederate Memorial State Historical Site, Higginsville, Missouri, Courtesy Kay Russell, p. 24
    Carolyn M. Bartels, Transcriber, Missouri Confederate Surrender Shreveport & New Orleans, May 1865, (1991), p. 47.
    Thomas E. Clatworthy, Transcriber, Cass County, Missouri 1860 Federal Census (Harrisonville, Missouri: The Cass County Historical Society, 1982), pp. 37, 39.
    Joanne Chiles Eakin and Donald R. Hale, Branded As Rebels (Independence, Mo.: Print America, 1995), p. 277.
    James Lyon, Missouri Confederate Unit Rosters 12th Missouri Cavalry CSA, Missouri Sons of Confederate Unit Rosters, http://missouri-scv.org/memorials/rosters.htrl.

B T Muir Endnotes

    Joanne Chiles Eakin and Donald R. Hale, Branded as Rebels (Independence, Mo.: Print America, 1995), p. 317.
    John N. Edwards, Noted Guerrillas (Shawnee, Kansas: Two Trails Publishing, 1996), pp. 94-95.
    Interview with Jan Toms and Muir Family material concerning B. T. Muir 11 May 2001.
    Boon T. Muir, "Application for Admission to the Confederate Soldier's Home of Missouri at Higginsville, Missouri." Attachments thereto, Confederate Memorial State Historical Site, Higginsville, Missouri, 10 May 1910.
    Hattie Poppino, Jackson County, Missouri Census of 1860 (1964), pp. 174-175.
    Warden Welch, Warren Welch Remembers, transcribed by Joanne Chiles Eakin (Independence, Missouri: Two Trails Publishing, 1997), p. 21.
    Cole Younger, The Story of Cole Younger by Himself (Springfield, Mo.: Oak Hills Publishing, 1996), pp. 20, 24.

J L Morris Endnotes

    Carl W. Breihan, Quantrill and His Civil War Guerrillas (Denver: Sage Books, 1959), pp. 166-174.
    James A. Browning, "Confederate Guerrillas and Those Who Rode with the James Gang," Confederate Memorial State Historical Site, Higginsville, Missouri, Courtesy Kay Russell, p. 27.
    Richard S. Brownlee, Gray Ghosts of the Confederacy (Richmond, Virginia: The William Byrd Press, Inc., 1958), pp. 253-261.
    Carroll County, Missouri 1850 Federal Census, p. 37A.
    Joanne Chiles Eakin, Confederate Records from the United Daughters of the Confederacy Files, Vol. VI. (Independence, Mo.: Two Trails Publishing, 1999), p. 19.
    John N. Edwards, Noted Guerrillas (Shawnee, Kansas: Two Trails Publishing, 1996), pp. 89-90, 99, 145, 216, 234.
    Irene Spainhower, Quantrell's Men Veterans of the Civil War Battle of Lone Jack, Mo (1998), p. 9.

QUANTRILL'S THIEVES By: Joseph K. Houts, Jr.

Notes to Pages 170-174

George Madox Endnotes

   Richard S. Brownlee, Gray Ghosts of the Confederacy (Richmond, Virginia: The William Byrd Press, Inc., 1958), pp. 253-261.
   Albert Castel, William Clarke Quantrill: His Life and Times (New York: Frederick Fell, Inc., 1962), pp. 66, 131.
   William Elsey Connelley, Quantrill and the Border Wars (New York: Konecky & Konecky, 1909), p. 357.
   "Deaths" Lee's Summit Journal, Lee's Summit, Jackson County, Mo, 8 February, 1901, Mid Continent Public Library, Independence, Mo.
   Joanne Chiles Eakin, Confederate Records from the United Daughters of the Confederacy Files, Vol. V. (Independence, Missouri: Two Trails Publishing, 1998), p. 134.
   Joanne Chiles Eakin and Donald R. Hale, Branded as Rebels (Independence, Mo.: Print America, 1995), pp. 278-279.
   John N. Edwards, Noted Guerrillas (Shawnee Kansas: Two Trails Publishing, 1996), pp. 89-90, 99, 175, 460.
   Edward R. Leslie, The Devil Knows How to Ride (New York: Random House, 1996), pp. 126, 242-244.
   Letter from Amos Vannarsall to Joseph K. Houts, Jr., 15 February 2000.
   John McCorkle, Three Years With Quantrill (Norman and London: University of Oklahoma Press, 1992), pp. 137-142.
   Hattie E. Poppino, Jackson County, Missouri Census of 1860 (1964), p. 158.
   Irene Spainhour, Quantrell's Men Veterans of the Civil War Battle of Lone Jack, MO (1998), p. 8.
   "Still Lives" Lee's Summit Journal, Lee's Summit, Jackson County, Mo, 5 April 1901. Mid Continent Public Library, Independence, Mo.
   Vannarsall Genealogical Papers, Amos Vannarsall.

Erzy Moore Endnotes

   Albert Castel, William Clarke Quantrill: His Life and Times (New York: Frederick Fell, Inc., 1962), p. 83.
   Joanne Chiles Eakin, Confederate Records from the United Daughters of the Confederacy Files, Vol. VI. (Independence, Mo.: Two Trails Publishing, 1999), p. 9.
   Joanne Chiles Eakin and Donald R. Hale, Branded as Rebels (Independence, Mo.: Print America, 1995), pp. 312-313.
   John N. Edwards, Noted Guerrillas (Shawnee, Kansas: Two Trails Publishing, 1996), p. 89.
   Edward E. Leslie, The Devil Knows How to Ride (New York: Random House, 1996), p. 127.
   Hattie E. Poppino, Jackson County, Missouri Census of 1860 (1964), p. 171.
   B. James George, Sr., "The Q-Men of Jackson County," The Oak Grove Banner, Oak Grove, Missouri, 9 October 1959.

J N Olliphant Endnotes

   Richard S. Brownlee, Gray Ghosts of the Confederacy (Richmond, Virginia: The William Byrd Press, Inc., 1958), pp. 253-261.

QUANTRILL'S THIEVES   By: Joseph K. Houts, Jr.

Notes to Pages 174-178

    Joanne Chiles Eakin, <u>Branded As Rebels</u> (Independence, Mo.: Print America, 1995), p. 331.
    John N. Edwards, <u>Noted Guerrillas</u> (Shawnee, Kansas: Two Trails Publishing, 1996), pp. 337, 356.
    Irene Spainhour, <u>Quantrell's Men Veterans of the Civil War Battle of Lone Jack, Mo</u> (1998), p. 9.
    Hazel Tyler, Compiler, <u>Johnson County, Missouri 1860 Census with the 1860 Mortality Schedule</u> (Springfield, Mo.: Ozark Genealogical Society, Inc., 1997), pp. 105, 122.

J Owings Endnotes

    Joanne Chiles Eakin, <u>Confederate Records from the United Daughters of the Confederacy Files</u>, Vol. VI. (Independence, Mo.: Two Trails Publishing, 1999), pp. 67-68.
    Hattie E. Poppino, <u>Jackson County, Missouri</u> Census of 1860 (1964), p. 184.

Harry Ogden Endnotes

    <u>Biographical Directory of the American Congress 1774-1971</u> (United States Government Printing Office, 1971), p. 1486.
    Richard S. Brownlee, <u>Gray Ghosts of the Confederacy</u> (Richmond, Virginia: The William Byrd Press, Inc., 1958), pp. 253-261.
    Joanne Chiles Eakin and Donald R. Hale, <u>Branded as Rebels</u> (Independence, Mo.: Print America, 1995), p. 18.
    Glenn R. Conrad, <u>Dictionary of Louisiana Biography</u>, Vol. II. N-Z (New Orleans, Louisiana: Louisiana Historical Press, 1988), p. 615.
    "Death of Hon. H. W. Ogden," <u>The Bossier Banner</u>, Benton, Louisiana, 27 July 1905.
    John N. Edwards <u>Noted Guerrillas</u> (Shawnee, Kansas: Two Trails Publishing, 1996), pp. 76, 86, 90.
    Cole Younger, <u>The Story of Cole Younger by Himself</u> (Springfield, Mo.: Oak Hills Publishing, 1996), p. 60-61.

F M Ogden Endnotes

    <u>Biographical Directory of the American Congress 1774-1971</u> (United States Government Printing Office, 1971), p. 1486.
    Richard S. Brownlee, <u>Gray Ghosts of the Confederacy</u> (Richmond, Virginia: The William Byrd Press, Inc., 1958), pp. 253-261.
    Joanne Chiles Eakin and Donald R. Hale, <u>Branded as Rebels</u> (Independence, Mo.: Print America, 1995), p. 18.
    Glenn R. Conrad, <u>Dictionary of Louisiana Biography</u>, Vol. II. N-Z (New Orleans, Louisiana: Louisiana Historical Press, 1988), p. 615.
    "Death of Hon. H. W. Ogden," <u>The Bossier Banner</u>, Benton, Louisiana, 27 July 1905.
    John N. Edwards <u>Noted Guerrillas</u> (Shawnee, Kansas: Two Trails Publishing, 1996), pp. 76, 86, 90.
    Hazel Tyler, Compiler, <u>Johnson County Missouri, 1860 Federal Census with the 1860 Mortality Schedule</u> (Springfield, Mo.: Ozarks Genealogical Society, Inc., 1997), p. 84.

Notes to Pages 178-188

Cole Younger, <u>The Story of Cole Younger by Himself</u> (Springfield, Mo.: Oak Hills Publishing, 1996), p. 60-61.

Otho Offutt Endnotes

Joanne Chiles Eakin and Donald R. Hale, <u>Branded As Rebels</u> (Independence, Mo.: Print America, 1995), pp. 329, 491.
John N. Edwards, <u>Shelby and His Men</u> (Waverly, Missouri: General Joseph Shelby Memorial Fund, 1993), p. 575.
Donald R. Hale, <u>We Rode with Quantrill</u> (1992), pp. 138-142.
Offutt Family Papers, <u>Johnson County Star</u> 30 December 1893, Johnson County Historical Society, Warrensburg, Missouri.
Irene Spainhour, <u>Quantrell's Men Veterans of the Civil War Battle of Lone Jack, Mo</u> (1998), pp. 10, 18, 23.
http://missouri-scv.org/mounits/rosters.num, 5th Missouri Cavalry Regiment, 9th Missouri Battalion Sharp Shooters, 11th Missouri Infantry.

T D Perdee Endnotes

Albert Castel, <u>William Clarke Quantrill: His Life And Times</u> (New York: Frederick Fell, Inc., 1962), pp. 124, 149.
"Columbus Township", Johnson County Historical Society, Warrensburg, Missouri.
Joanne Chiles Eakin and Donald R. Hale, <u>Branded As Rebels</u> (Independence, Mo.: Print America, 1995), pp. 344, 492.
Interview with Homer Jarmen, Warrensburg, Missouri 10 April 1999.
Betty Harvey Williams, <u>Johnson County, Missouri 1860 Federal Census</u> (Warrensburg, Mo.: 1965), p. 81.
Edward R. Leslie, <u>The Devil Knows How To Ride</u> (New York: Random House, 1996), pp. 199, 270.

J R Perdee Endnotes

Albert Castel, <u>William Clarke Quantrill: His Life And Times</u> (New York: Frederick Fell, Inc., 1962), pp. 124, 149.
"Columbus Township", Johnson County Historical Society, Warrensburg, Missouri.
Joanne Chiles Eakin and Donald R. Hale, <u>Branded As Rebels</u> (Independence, Mo.: Print America, 1995), pp. 344, 492.
Interview with Homer Jarmen, Warrensburg, Missouri 10 April 1999.
Betty Harvey Williams, <u>Johnson County, Missouri 1860 Federal Census</u> (Warrensburg, Mo.: 1965), p. 81.
Edward R. Leslie, <u>The Devil Knows How To Ride</u> (New York: Random House, 1996), pp. 199, 270.

D M Pool Endnotes

Carl W. Breihan, <u>Quantrill and His Civil War Guerrillas</u> (Denver: Sage Books, 1959), pp. 166-174.
Richard S. Brownlee, <u>Gray Ghosts of the Confederacy</u> (Richmond, Virginia: The William Byrd Press, Inc., 1958), pp. 53, 127, 220, 227, 238, 241, 253-261.

QUANTRILL'S THIEVES   By: Joseph K. Houts, Jr.

Notes to Pages 185-191

Albert Castel, William Clarke Quantrill His Life and Times (New York, N.Y.: Frederick Fell, Inc., 1962), pp. 120, 150, 158, 219, 212.

William Elsey Connelley, Quantrill and the Border Wars (New York: Konecky & Konecky, 1909), p. 424

Joanne Chiles Eakin, Warren Welch Remembers (Transcribed, Independence, Mo.: Two Trails Publishing, 1997), p. 21.

Joanne Chiles Eakin and Donald R. Hale, Branded as Rebels (Independence, Mo.: Print America, 1995), p. 491-492.

John N. Edwards, Noted Guerrillas (Shawnee, Kansas: Two Trails Publishing, 1996), pp. 54, 84-91, 270, 277, 335-336.

John N. Edwards, Shelby and His Men (Waverly, Missouri: General Joseph Shelby Memorial Fund, 1993), pp. 421-423.

Edward E. Leslie, The Devil Knows How to Ride (New York: Random House, 1996), pp. 317, 325, 335, 374-376, 393.

Letter from Virginia Metheny to Joseph K. Houts, Jr., establishing date and place of Pool's birth, 4 May 2000.

Letter from Virginia Metheny to Joseph K. Houts, Jr., establishing Pool ancestry, 28 May 2000.

John McCorkle, Three Years with Quantrill (Norman and London: University of Oklahoma Press, 1992), pp. 150-151, 159, 172-173, 223.

United States War Department, The War of the Rebellion: A Compilation of the Official Records of the Union and Confederate Armies, Series I., Vol. XXIII, (Washington, D.C., 1880-1902), pp. 700-701.

Cole Younger, The Story of Cole Younger by Himself (Springfield, Mo.: Oak Hills Publishing, 1996), pp. 50-51.

H C Pemberton Endnotes

Joanne Chiles Eakin, Confederate Records from the United Daughters of the Confederacy Files, Vol. VI. (Independence, Mo.: Two Trails Publishing, 1999), p. 92.

Joanne Chiles Eakin and Donald R. Hale, Branded as Rebels (Independence, Mo.: Two Trails Publishing, 1995), p. 343.

D. C. Pemberton, "Record of Missouri Confederate Veterans Compiled for the United Daughters of the Confederacy Missouri Division," Courtesy of William T. Stolz, Manuscript Specialist Western Historical Manuscript Collector, Columbia, Missouri.

Irene Spainhour, Quantrell's Men Veterans of the Civil War Battle of Lone Jack, Mo (1998), p. 10.

Hazel Tyler, Compiler, Johnson County, Missouri 1860 Federal Census with the 1860 Mortality Schedule (Springfield, Mo.: Ozark Genealogical Society, Inc., 1997), p. 116.

F M Robinson Endnotes

Hazel Tyler, Compiler, Johnson County, Missouri 1860 Federal Census with the 1860 Mortality Schedule (Springfield, Mo.: Ozarks Genealogical Society, Inc., 1997), p. 107.

Joanne Chiles Eakin and Donald R. Hale, Branded as Rebels (Independence, Mo.: Print America, 1995), p. 373.

Notes to Pages 192-195

J W Rider Endnotes

Ancestry.com, John Winiard Rider.
Albert Castel, William Clarke Quantrill: His Life and Times (New York: Frederick Fell, Inc., 1962), pp. 38-39.
Joanne Chiles Eakin and Donald R. Hale, Branded as Rebels (Independence, Mo.: Print America, 1995), p. 370.
http://missouri-scv.org/mounits/rosters.num, 8th Missouri Infantry Battalion, Company D.
Hattie E. Poppino, Jackson County, Missouri Census of 1860 (Kansas City, Mo.: 1964), p. 202.

George Rider Endnotes

Ancestry.com, George W. Rider.
Albert Castel, William Clarke Quantrill: His Life and Times (New York: Frederick Fell, Inc., 1962), pp. 38-39.
Joanne Chiles Eakin and Donald R. Hale, Branded as Rebels (Independence, Mo.: Print America, 1995), p. 370.
http://missouri-scv.org/mounits/rosters.num, 8th Missouri Infantry Battalion, Company D.
Hattie E. Poppino, Jackson County, Missouri Census of 1860 (Kansas City, Mo.: 1964), p. 202.

Robert Stephenson Endnotes

Joanne Chiles Eakin and Donald R. Hale, Branded as Rebels (Independence, Mo.: Print America, 1995), pp. 414, 491, 492.
John N. Edwards, Noted Guerrillas (Shawnee, Kansas: Two Trails Publishing, 1996), pp. 273-274, 276.
Letter from Randy Senor to Joseph K. Houts, Jr. outlining information concerning Robert John Stevenson from his obituary and out of this information the author concluded named spelled Stevenson as opposed to Stephenson, 1 September 2000.
1860 Federal Census Clay County, Missouri (Liberty, Mo.: Genealogical Society of Liberty, Inc. 1985), p. 21.
Letter from Calvin W. Hawkins, Research Volunteer, Clay County Archives & Historical Library, concerning Robert R. and Robert T. Stephenson 16 May, 2001.
Letter from Calvin W. Hawkins, Research Volunteer, Clay County Archives & Historical Library, concerning Robert Stephenson 6 June 2001.

W D Tucker Endnotes

Carl W. Breihan, Quantrill and His Civil War Guerrillas (Denver: Sage Books, 1959), pp. 166-174.
Richard S. Brownlee, Gray Ghosts of the Confederacy (Richmond, Virginia: The William Byrd Press, Inc., 1958), pp. 253-261.
William Elsey Connelley, Quantrill and the Border Wars (New York, N.Y.: Konecky & Konecky, 1909), pp. 257.

QUANTRILL'S THIEVES   By: Joseph K. Houts, Jr.

Notes to Pages 195-203

   Joanne Chiles Eakin and Donald R. Hale, Branded as Rebels (Independence, Mo.: Print America, 1995), p. 438.
   Edward E. Leslie, The Devil Knows How to Ride (New York: Random House, 1996), p. 126.
   Irene Spainhour, Quantrell's Men Veterans of the Civil War Battle of Lone Jack, Mo (1998), p. 13.

John Teague Endnotes

   John H. Teague, "Pension for Ex-Confederate Soldiers," attachments thereto, Confederate Memorial State Historical Site, Higginsville, Missouri 7, July 1923.

T F Teague Endnotes

   Thomas E. Clatworthy, Transcriber, Cass County, Missouri 1860 Federal Census (1982), p. 11.
   United States War Department, The War of the Rebellion: A Compilation of the Official Records of the Union and Confederate Armies, Series I, Vol. XXXIV, (Washington, D.C., 1890-1900), p. 167.

A B Teague Endnotes

   Abe Teague, "Pension for Ex-Confederate Soldiers," attachments thereto, Confederate Memorial State Historical Site, Higginsville, Missouri, 13 October 1913.
   United States War Department, The War of the Rebellion: A Compilation of the Official Records of the Union and Confederate Armies, Series I., Vol. XXII (Washington, D.C., 1880-1902), p. 426.

Thomson Endnotes

   James A. Browning, "Confederate Guerrillas and Those Who Rode with the James Gang," Confederate Memorial State Historical Site, Higginsville, Missouri, Courtesy Kay Russell, p. 37.
   Richard S. Brownlee, Gray Ghosts of the Confederacy (Richmond, Virginia: The William Byrd Press, Inc., 1958), pp. 253-261.
   Joanne Chiles Eakin, Confederate Records from the United Daughters of the Confederacy Files, Vol. VI. (Independence, Mo.: Two Trails Publishing, 2000), p. 123.
   Joanne Chiles Eakin and Donald R. Hale, Branded As Rebels (Independence, Mo.: Print America, 1995), pp. 427-428.
   Hattie E. Poppino, Jackson County, Missouri Census of 1860 (Kansas City, Mo.: 1964), p. 202.
   Irene Spainhour, Quantrell's Men Veterans of the Civil War Battle of Lone Jack, Mo (1998), p. 12.
   Hazel Tyler, Compiler, Johnson County, Missouri 1860 Federal Census with the 1860 Mortality Schedule (Springfield, Mo.: Ozark Genealogical Society, Inc., 1997), p. 93.

Notes to Pages 204-216

Wm Vaughn Endnotes

http://missouri-scv.org/mounits/rosters.num, 12th Missouri Cavalry Unit, Company E.
Hattie E. Poppino, Jackson County, Missouri Census of 1860 (Kansas City, Mo.:1964), p. 251.

James Vaughn Endnotes

Albert Castel, William Clarke Quantrill: His Life and Times (New York: Frederick Fell, Inc., 1962), pp. 106-107, 116.
Joanne Chiles Eakin, "The Story Behind the Letter," The Blue & Gray Chronicle, Independence, Missouri, October 2000.
Joanne Chiles Eakin and Donald R. Hale, Branded as Rebels (Independence, Mo.: Print America, 1995), p. 442.
John N. Edwards, Noted Guerrilla (Shawnee, Kansas: Two Trails Publishing, 1996), pp. 84-85.
Thomas Goodrich, Black Flag (Bloomington and Indianapolis: Indiana University Press, 1995), pp. 65-66.
Thomas Goodrich, Bloody Dawn: The Story of the Lawrence Massacre (Kent, Ohio and London, England: The Kent State University Press, 1991), p. 77.
John McCorkle, Three Years with Quantrill (Norman and London: University of Oklahoma Press, 1992), pp. 100-102.
Hattie E. Poppino, Jackson County, Missouri Census of 1860 (1964), p. 251.

C T Williamson Endnotes

Carolyn M. Bartels, Transcribed, Missouri Confederate Surrender Shreveport & New Orleans May 1865 (1991), p. 79.
Joanne Chiles Eakin, Confederate Records from the United Daughters of the Confederacy Files, Vol. III. (Independence, Mo.: Two Trails Publishing, 2000), p. 73.
Joanne Chiles Eakin and Donald R. Hale, Branded as Rebels (Independence, Mo.: Print America, 1995), p. 470.
John N. Edwards, Shelby and His Men (Waverly, Missouri: General Joseph Shelby Memorial Fund, 1993), p. 563.
Irene Spainhour, Quantrell's Men Veterans of the Civil War Battle of Lone Jack, Mo (1998), p. 16

Coal Younger Endnotes

Carl W. Breihan, Quantrill and His Civil War Guerrillas (Denver: Sage Books, 1959), pp. 166-174.
Richard S. Brownlee, Gray Ghosts of the Confederacy (Richmond, Virginia: The William Byrd Press, Inc., 1958), pp. 43, 61, 100, 118, 147, 244-246.
Albert Castel, A Frontier State at War: Kansas 1861-1865 (Lawrence, Kansas: Kansas Heritage Press, 1992, p. 104.
Albert Castel, William Clarke Quantrill: His Life and Times (New York: Frederick Fell, Inc., 1962), pp. 69, 93-94, 99, 119-120, 158-159, 222-231.
Albert Castel, "William Clarke Quantrill: Terror of the Border," Civil War, January- February 1992, p. 11.

QUANTRILL'S THIEVES By: Joseph K. Houts, Jr.

Notes to Pages 208-219

   William Elsey Connelley, Quantrill and the Border Wars (New York, N.Y.: Konecky & Konecky, 1909), pp. 251-252, 275, 317, 385, 445-446.
   Joanne Chiles Eakin and Donald R. Hale, Branded as Rebels (Independence, Mo.: Print America, 1995), p. 485.
   John N. Edwards, Noted Guerrillas (Shawnee, Kansas: Two Trails Publishing, 1996), pp. 70-72, 90-91, 98-99, 110, 137, 196, 202, 209, 218-219, 221-225, 281-282.
   Michael Fellman, Inside War (New York Oxford: Oxford University Press, 1989), p. 262.
   Thomas Goodrich, Black Flag (Bloomington and Indianapolis: Indiana University Press, 1995), p. 35.
   Thomas Goodrich, Bloody Dawn: The Story of the Lawrence Massacre (Kent, Ohio and London England: The Kent State University Press, 1991), pp. 15-16, 149.
   Donald R. Hale, We Rode with Quantrill (1992), p. 172.
   Robert Paul Jordan, The Civil War (Washington, D.C.: the National Geographic Society, 1969), pp. 87-90.
   Edward E. Leslie, The Devil Knows How to Ride (New York: Random House, 1996), pp. 100-103, 115, 118, 121, 141-142, 223, 290, 292, 379, 392, 401-403.
   Letter from William E. Parrish to Joseph K. Houts, Jr. concerning Cole Younger, 21 January 2001.
   John McCorkle, Three Years with Quantrill (Norman and London: University of Oklahoma Press, 1992), pp. 10, 116.
   Jay Monaghan, Civil War on the Western Border, 1854-1865 (Lincoln and London: University of Nebraska Press, 1955), pp. 280-281.
   Irene Spainhour, Confederate Veterans of the Civil War Battle of Lone Jack, Mo (1998), p. 17.
   Irene Spainhour, Quantrell's Men Veterans of the Civil War Battle of Lone Jack, Mo (1998), pp. 13, 24-25.
   Larry Wood, "They Rode with Quantrill," America's Civil War, November 1996, pp. 60-63.
   Cole Younger, The Story of Cole Younger by Himself (Springfield, Mo.: Oak Hills Publishing, 1996), pp. 1-3, 11, 14, 17-18, 21, 30, 47, 50-51, 56, 59, 62, 78-81, 85-86, 91, 93, 96, 99, 103, 108, 114, 122, 137.

Richard Yeager Endnotes

   Richard S. Brownlee, Gray Ghosts of the Confederacy (Richmond, Virginia: The William Byrd Press, Inc., 1958), p. 194.
   Albert Castel, A Frontier State at War: Kansas 1861-1865 (Lawrence, Kansas: Kansas Heritage Press, 1992), p. 116.
   Albert Castel, William Clarke Quantrill: His Life and Times (New York: Frederick Fell, Inc., 1962), pp. 99, 104-105, 123, 179.
   William Elsey Connelley, Quantrill and the Border Wars (New York, N.Y.: Konecky & Konecky, 1909), p. 275.
   Joanne Chiles Eakin and Donald R. Hale, Branded as Rebels (Independence, MO.: Print America, 1995), pp. 482-483.
   John N. Edwards, Noted Guerrillas (Shawnee, Kansas: Two Trails Publishing, 1996), pp. 189, 233-234.

Notes to Pages 217-233

Thomas Goodrich, Black Flag (Bloomington and Indianapolis: Indiana University Press, 1995), p. 127.

Thomas Goodrich, Bloody Dawn: The Story of the Lawrence Massacre (Kent, Ohio and London, England: The Kent State University Press, 1991), pp. 39, 77.

Edward E. Leslie, The Devil Knows How to Ride (New York: Random House, 1996), p. 310.

John McCorkle, Three Years with Quantrill (Norman and London: University of Oklahoma Press, 1992), p. 155.

The History of Jackson County, Missouri (Kansas City, MO: Union Historical Company, Birdsall, Williams & Co., 1881), reprint (Cape Girardeau, Mo.: Ramfre Press, 1966), p. 898.

Jan Toms, Muir Family Papers, concerning Yeager's marriage to Boone T. Muir's sister, Martha J. Muir.

Larry Wood, "They Rode With Quantrill," America's Civil War, November 1996, p. 60.

J H Terry Endnotes

Hattie E. Poppino, Jackson County, Missouri Census of 1860 (1964), p. 241.

Irene Spainhour, Quantrell's Men Veterans of the Civil War Battle of Lone Jack, Mo (1998), p. 12.

John H. Terry, Missouri Confederate Unit Rosters, 10th Missouri Cavalry CSA, Missouri – Sons of Confederate Unit Rosters, http://Missouri-SCV.org/mounits/rosters.html.

Chapter V. "Micah" Endnotes

Interview with Major Mark Martsolf, The Salvation Army, St. Joseph, Missouri 19 May 2001.

Interview with Reverend Robert Wollenburg, First Presbyterian Church, St. Joseph, Missouri 19 May 2001.

Micah, 4:3, 5:1-6.

QUANTRILL'S THIEVES By: Joseph K. Houts, Jr.

Bibliography

PRIMARY SOURCES

CEMETERIES:
Blackwater Cemetery. Centerview, Johnson County, Missouri.
Carmichael Cemetery. Centerview, Johnson County, Missouri.
Houx Cemetery. Centerview, Johnson County, Missouri.

GENEALOGICAL:
Burgess, Michael. Burgess Genealogical Papers.
Houts, Alice Kinyoun. Houts Genealogical Papers.
Houts, Alice Kinyoun. "Portrait and Biographical Record." Matthias Houx.
Houts, Alice Kinyoun. Houx Genealogical Papers.
Houts, Alice Kinyoun. Kinyoun Genealogical Papers.
Houts, Alice Kinyoun. "Nathan Washington Perry," Perry Genealogical Papers.
Johnson County Historical Society. Cockrell Family File. Warrensburg, MO.
Johnson County Historical Society. Offutt Family Papers. Warrensburg, MO.
King, Marilyn Baliff. "Family History Report." George McKinley Barnett. King Genealogical Papers.
Toms, Jan. Muir Family Papers.
McCormick, Barbara. Longacre Genealogical Papers.
Vannarsall, Amos. George Maddox. Vannarsall Genealogical Papers.
Vannarsall, Amos. Richard Maddox. Vannarsall Genealogical Papers.

INTERNET:
ancestry.com.johnwinlandrider.
ancestry.com.georgewrider.
bledsoe@sprintmail.com.bledsoefamilychart.
http://missouri-scv.org/mounits/rosters.htmc.
http://pedigree.ancestry.com/cgn-dim/preview.uh/h, Horn Ancestry.
http://missouri-scv.org/mounits/rosters.num.

INTERVIEWS:
Acuff, Dr. Phillip A. St. Joseph, Missouri; 9 July 1999.
Bardgett, Margaret. Warrensburg, Missouri; 10 April 1999.
Houts, Joseph Kinyoun. St. Joseph, Missouri; 20 February 1996.
Jarmen, Homer. Warrensburg, Missouri; 10 April 1999.
Martsolf, Major Mark. The Salvation Army, St. Joseph, MO; 19 May 2001.
Russell, Jerry. Heaton, Bowman, Smith and Sidenfaden Chapel. St. Joseph, MO; 16 February 2000.
St. Joseph Police Department. St. Joseph, MO; 16 February 2000.
Vaughn, Steve. Ocala, FL; 16 October 1998.
Wollenburg, Robert. First Presbyterian Church, St. Joseph, MO; 19 May 2001.

LETTERS:
Bledsoe, Bob. Letter to Joseph K. Houts, Jr. concerning W. M. Bledsoe. 23 December 2000.
Bledsoe, Bob. Letter to Joseph K. Houts, Jr. concerning W. M. Bledsoe. 24 December 2000.
Burgess, Michael. Letter to Joseph K. Houts, Jr. concerning W. M. Burgess. 12 January 2000.
Church, Ralph E. Cemetery Administrator, Jefferson National Barracks

QUANTRILL'S THIEVES By: Joseph K. Houts, Jr.

Cemetery. Letter to Joseph K. Houts, Jr. concerning Noah Estes, 15 May 2000.

Church, Ralph E. Cemetery Administrator, Jefferson National Barracks Cemetery. Letter to Joseph K. Houts, Jr. concerning W. F. Judd, 7 February 2000.

Crittendon, Thos. T. Late Lt. Co. 7th Cav. M.S.M. "To the Committee on Military Affairs." House of Representatives. Washington, D.C. Letter. 30 November 1889.

Hawkins, Calvin W. Letter to Joseph K. Houts, Jr. concerning Robert R. and Robert T. Stephenson. 16 May 2001.

Hawkins, Calvin W. Letter to Joseph K. Houts, Jr. concerning Robert Stephenson. 6 June 2000.

Hays, Margaret J. Letters. Three to her mother. Confederate Memorial State Historical Site. Higginsville, Missouri. Undated.

Higgins, William. Secy. of State of Kansas. "To the Committee on Military Affairs." House of Representatives. Washington, D.C. Letter.

Hoog, Dan. Letter to Mr. Brownlee containing 600 Quantrill riders. 2 November 1969.

Houts, Alice Kinyoun. "Dr. John Hendricks Kinyoun." Letter, Joseph K. Houts, Jr., 6 March 1968.

Houts, Alice Kinyoun. Letter to Tennie. 20 March 1961.

(Houx), Thirza. Letter to Alice Kinyoun Houts. 26 March 1961.

Houx, Thirza. Letter to Alice Kinyoun Houts. 6 May 1961.

Hughes, Bella. Letter to Joseph K. Houts, Jr. concerning Syrus Cockrell. 10 July 2000.

Hughes, Bella. Letter to Joseph K. Houts, Jr. concerning Syrus Cockrell. 11 July 2000.

Hughes, Bella. Letter to Joseph K. Houts, Jr. concerning Syrus Cockrell. 12 July 2000.

Lazear, B. F. Late Lt. Col. 1st Cav. M.S.M. "To Committee on Military Affairs." H.R. Washington, D.C. 27 November. Letter.

McCormick, Barbara. Letter to Joseph K. Houts, Jr. concerning C. A. Longacre. 10 April 2000.

McCormick, Barbara. Letter to Joseph K. Houts, Jr. concerning C. A. Longacre. 15 April 2000.

McCormick, Barbara. Letter to Joseph K. Houts, Jr. concerning C. A. Longacre. 16 April 2000.

McCormick, Barbara. Letter to Joseph K. Houts, Jr. concerning C. A. Longacre. 17 April 2000.

McCormick, Barbara. Letter to Joseph K. Houts, Jr. concerning C. A. Longacre. 19 April 2000.

Metheny, Virginia. Letter to Joseph K. Houts, Jr. concerning D. M. Pool. 4 May 2000.

Metheny, Virginia. Letter to Joseph K. Houts, Jr. concerning D. M. Pool. 28 May 2000.

Parrish, William E. Letter to Joseph K. Houts, Jr. concerning Cole Younger. 21 January 2001.

Phillips, J. H. Late 1st Lieut. Co. C. 15th Kans. Cav. "To the Committee on Military Affairs." House of Representatives. Washington, D. C. Letter.

Phillips, Jno F. "Hon. F. M. Cockrell." U. S. Senate. Kansas City, Mo., Letter. 30 November 1889.

Quantrill, W. C. Two Letters to His Mother. Kansas Collection. University of Kansas Libraries. Lawrence, Kansas. 26 January, 1860. 23 June, 1860. Two signatures.

Russell, Kay. Confederate Memorial State Historical Site. Letter to Joseph K. Houts, Jr. concerning O. S. Barnett. 12 June 1999.

QUANTRILL'S THIEVES By: Joseph K. Houts, Jr.

Senor, Randy. Letter to Joseph K. Houts, Jr. concerning Robert John Stevenson. 1 September 2000.
Simpson, B. F. Late Maj. 15th K.C.V. "To the Committee on Military Affairs." House of Representatives. Washington, D.C. Letter.
Survivors of the 7th Cal., M.S.M. "To the President." Petition.
Vannarsall, Amos. Letter to Joseph K. Houts, Jr. concerning Richard Maddox. 12 February 2000.
Vannarsall, Amos. Letter to Joseph K. Houts, Jr. concerning George Maddox. 15 February 2000.
Young, Stephanie. Letter to Joseph K. Houts, Jr. concerning W. F. Judd, 7 November 1999.

MAGAZINES

Allmon, William B. "Sneak Attack At Lone Jack." <u>Civil War Times Illustrated</u>. April 1996, pp. 62-71.
Castel, Albert. "William Clarke Quantrill: Terror of the Border." <u>Civil War</u>, January- February 1992, p. 11.
Sanders, Stuart W. "Bloody Bill's Centralia Massacre." <u>America's Civil War</u>, March 2000, pp. 34-40, 82.
Sword, Wiley. "The Other Stonewall." <u>Civil War Times Illustrated</u>. February 1998, pp. 36-44.
Wood, Larry. "They Rode With Quantrill." <u>America's Civil War</u>. November 1996, pp. 58-64.

MANUSCRIPTS

Browning, James A. "Confederate Guerrillas and Those Who Rode With the James Gang." Higginsville, Missouri: Confederate Memorial State Historical Site.
Crissy, William E. "A Romance of the Civil War 1861-5 Uncle Mat Houx." University of Missouri-Columbia: Western Historical Manuscript Collection, 1921.
Eakin, Joanne Chiles. "Warrants Issued After the Burning of Lawrence." 1997.
Gregg, William H. "A Little Dab of History Without Embellishment." University of Missouri-Columbia: Western Historical Manuscript Collection, 1906.
Gregg, William H. "The Lawrence Raid." Topeka, Kansas: Kansas State Historical Society.

MILITARY DOCUMENTS

Barnett, Obadiah Strange. Application for Admission to the Confederate Soldier's Home At Higginsville, Missouri. Confederate Memorial State Historical Site. Higginsville, Missouri. Undated.
Bell, Charles E. Quantrell's Men. Undated.
Bowlin, James. Application for Admission to the Confederate Soldier's Home at Higginsville, Missouri. Confederate Memorial State Historical Site. Higginsville, Missouri. 27 February 1913.
Bowlin, James. Pension for Ex-Confederate Soldiers. Confederate Memorial State Historical Site. Higginsville, Missouri. 21 June 1913.
Butler, W. H. Pension for Ex-Confederate Soldiers. Confederate Memorial State Historical Site. Higginsville, Missouri. 20 June 1913.
Castelle, Capt. Edg. And Foster, Maj. U. Oath of Allegiance. N. W. Perry, 5 May 1861.

Christian, A. M. Missouri State Military Furlough Pass. N. W. Perry, 2 August 1862.
Cockrell, Capt. F. M. Missouri State Guard Military Pass. N. W. Perry,

QUANTRILL'S THIEVES By: Joseph K. Houts, Jr.

11 July 1861.
Copy Muster Roll of Capt. W. C. Quantrell. Head Quarters (sic) Department of the Mo. St. Louis, Mo. 5 November 1864.
Copy of Quantrell's Muster Roll. United States National Archives, Washington, D.C. 5 November 1864.
Gamble, H. R. The State of Missouri Commission Appointment No. 802. Major Thomas W. Houts. 27 March 1863.
Hall, William P. The State of Missouri Commission Appointment. Captain Thomas W. Houts. 13 March 1862.
Houts, Thomas W. Certificate of Discharge. 14 March 1891.
Houts, Captain Th. W. Missouri State Militia Quartermaster Report No. 52. 30 June 1862.
Houts, Major Thomas W. Roll of Quantrell's Company of Thieves.
Houx, Matthias. Record of Missouri Confederate Veterans. The United Daughters of the Confederacy. Missouri Division. Fitzhugh Lee Chapter. University of Missouri-Columbia: Western Historical Manuscript Collection.
Houx, Matthias. Record of Missouri Confederate Veterans. The United Daughters of the Confederacy. Missouri Division. Warrensburg Chapter. University of Missouri-Columbia: Western Historical Manuscript Collection.
Kincheloe to Martin, Microfilm Roll No. RG, 33, 439. Confederate Memorial State Historical Site. Higginsville, Missouri.
Koger, John William. Application for Admission to the Confederate Soldier's Home at Higginsville, Missouri. Confederate Memorial State Historical Site. Higginsville, Missouri. 11 August 1909.
Longacre, C. A. Military File. Missouri State Archives. 3 February 2000.
Muir, Boon T. Application for Admission to the Confederate Soldier's Home at Higginsville, Missouri. Confederate Memorial State Historical Site. Higginsville, Missouri. 10 May 1910.
Pemberton, D. C. Record of Missouri Confederate Veteran's Compiled for the United Daughters of the Confederacy, Missouri Division Western Historical Manuscript Collection. Columbia, Missouri.
Quantrell's Muster Roll. United States National Archives. Washington, D.C. 16 July 1862.
Stierlin, Capt. Henry J. Roll of 93 of Quantrell's Gang of Outlaws. United States National Archives, Washington, D.C. 16 July 1862.
Teague, Abe. Pension for Ex-Confederate Soldiers. Confederate Memorial State Historical Site. Higginsville, Missouri, 13 October 1913.
Teague, John H. Pension for Ex-Confederate Soldiers. Confederate Memorial State Historical Site. Higginsville, Missouri. 7 July 1923.
U. S. Congress. House. Thomas W. Houts. H.R. Report No. 2494 to Accompany H.R. 2968 51st Cong., 1st Sess., 19 June 1890.

NEWSPAPERS

The Belton Herald. Belton, Missouri. 18 May 1916.
"Columbus Township." Johnson County Historical Society. Warrensburg, Missouri Undated.
"County Records Hidden in Thicket Near Centerview During Civil War." Daily Star- Journal. Warrensburg, Missouri. 14 May 1933.
"Death Ends Illness." Montana Daily Record. 11 April 1904.

"Death of Hon. H. W. Ogden." The Bossier Banner. Benton, Louisiana. 27 July 1905.
"Death of Matthias Houx." Without Newspaper and Undated.
"George Barnett Rode With Men of Quantrell." Topeka Daily. Topeka, Kansas.

QUANTRILL'S THIEVES   By: Joseph K. Houts, Jr.

25 January 1931. Globe-Democrat. Untitled and Undated.

"Houx Family Had Large Part in Settling and Developing County." Daily Star-Journal. Warrensburg, Missouri. 4 March 1932.

"Many Familiar Names Found Among Activities Reported in 1869 Paper." Daily Star-Journal. Warrensburg, Missouri, Undated

"Member of the Quantrell Band." St. Joseph Daily Gazette-Harold. St. Joseph, Missouri. 19 December 1900.

"Miss Mary Houx Has Government Papers Seeking Confiscation of Father's Land." Daily Star-Journal. Warrensburg, Missouri. 30 September 1930.

"Mixed Up." Lee's Summit Journal. Lee's Summit, Missouri. 8 February 1901.

"Offutt." Johnson County Star. 30 December 1893.

"Passing of a Pioneer." Daily Star-Journal. Warrensburg, Missouri. Undated.

"The Pioneer Houts Family Has Been Represented Well in Johnson County." Daily Star-Journal. Warrensburg, Missouri. 22 July 1935.

"The Q-Men of Jackson County." The Oak Grove Banner. Oak Grove, Missouri. 9 October 1959.

"Rader Led Warrensburg's Confederate." Daily Star-Journal. Warrensburg, Missouri. 20 August 1976. Reported The Blue & Gray Chronicle. Independence, Missouri. June 2001.

"Senator Cockrell's Brother." Weekly Standard. Warrensburg, Missouri. 28 July 1899.

"Still Lives." Lee's Summit Journal. Lee's Summit, Missouri. 5 April 1901.

"Tardy Justice," Globe Democrat, Partially Dated 13 June

"Walnut Box Holds Memories, Reminiscences of Days Past. Daily Star-Journal. Warrensburg, Missouri. Undated.

PERIODICALS

Eakin, Joanne Chiles. "The Story Behind the Letter." The Blue & Gray Chronicle. Independence, Missouri. October 2000.

The Blue & Gray Chronicle. Reported. Independence, Missouri. June 2001.

PETITIONS

Higgins, Wm. "For the Relief of Thomas W. Houts." Petition. 1889.

Post, T. A. "Hon. Francis M. Cockrell." Washington, D.C. Petition. 22 March 1889.

Steger, J. H. Late A.A.G. Vols. "To Hon. F. M. Cockrell." U. S. Senate. Washington, D. C. Letter. 12 March 1889.

SPEECH

Anderson, Joe. "The Civil War & Slavery in Missouri." Pony Express Museum, St. Joseph, Missouri. 8 February 2000.

QUANTRILL'S THIEVES By: Joseph K. Houts, Jr.

SECONDARY SOURCES

BOOKS:
Bartels, Carolyn. <u>Missouri Confederate Deaths Union Prisons & Hospitals</u>. Independence, Mo.: Blue & Gray Book Shoppe.
Bartels, Carolyn. <u>Missouri Confederate Surrender Shreveport & New Orleans May 1865</u>. 1991.
<u>Biographical Directory of the American Congress 1774-1971</u>. United States Government Printing Office, 1971.
Breihan, Carl W. <u>Quantrill and His Civil War Guerrillas</u>. Denver, Colorado: Sage Books, 1959.
Brownlee, Richard S. <u>Gray Ghosts of the Confederacy</u>. Richmond, Virginia: The William Byrd Press, Inc., 1958.
Castel, Albert. <u>A Frontier State at War: Kansas</u>. Lawrence, Kansas: Kansas Heritage Press, 1958.
Castel, Albert. <u>William Clarke Quantrill: His Life and Times</u>. New York, N.Y.: Frederick Fell, Inc., 1962.
Connelley, William Elsey. <u>Quantrill and the Border Wars</u>. New York: Konecky & Konecky, 1909.
Conrad, Glen R. <u>Dictionary of Louisiana Biography Volume II</u>. New Orleans, Louisiana Historical Press, 1988.
Conrad, Howard L. <u>Encyclopedia of the History of Missouri</u>. Volume III. New York, Louisville, St. Louis: The Southern History Company. St. Joseph Museum, St. Joseph, Missouri, 1901.
Eakin, Joanne Chiles. <u>Confederate Records from the United Daughters of the Confederacy Files Volume I</u>. Independence, Mo.: Two Trails Publishing, 1996.
Eakin, Joanne Chiles. <u>Confederate Records from the United Daughters of the Confederacy Files Volume II</u>. Independence, Mo.: Two Trails Publishing, 1996.
Eakin, Joanne Chiles. <u>Confederate Records from the United Daughters of the Confederacy Files Volume III</u>. Independence, Mo.: Two Trails Publishing, 1996.
Eakin, Joanne Chiles. <u>Confederate Records from the United Daughters of the Confederacy Files Volume IV</u>. Independence, Mo.: Two Trails Publishing, 1997.
Eakin, Joanne Chiles. <u>Confederate Records from the United Daughters of the Confederacy Files Volume V</u>. Independence, Mo.: Two Trails Publishing, 1998.
Eakin, Joanne Chiles. <u>Confederate Records from the United Daughters of the Confederacy Files Volume VI</u>. Independence, Mo.: Two Trails Publishing, 1999.
Eakin, Joanne Chiles. <u>Confederate Records from the United Daughters of the Confederacy Files Volume VII</u>. Independence, Mo.: Two Trails Publishing, 2000.
Eakin, Joanne Chiles. <u>Confederate Records from the United Daughters of the Confederacy Files Volume VIII</u>. Independence, Mo.: Two Trails Publishing, 2001.
Eakin, Joanne Chiles. <u>Quantrell's Company</u>. 1997.
Eakin, Joanne Chiles. <u>Walter Chiles of Jamestown and Some of His Descendants</u>. Independence, Mo.: Wee Print, 1983.
Eakin, Joanne C. and Hale, Donald R. <u>Branded as Rebels</u>. Independence, Mo.: Print America, 1995.
Edwards, John N. <u>Noted Guerrillas</u>. Shawnee, Kansas: Two Trails Publishing, Reprint, 1996.
Edwards, John N. <u>Shelby and His Men</u>. Waverly, Missouri: General Joseph Shelby Memorial Fund, Reprint, 1993.
Fellman, Richard. <u>Inside War</u>. New York, Oxford: Oxford University Press, 1989.
Goodrich, Thomas. <u>Bloody Dawn: The Story of the Lawrence Massacre</u>. Kent, \ Ohio and London, England: The Kent State University Press, 1991.

Goodrich, Thomas. <u>Black Flag</u>. Bloomington and Indianapolis: Indiana

QUANTRILL'S THIEVES   By: Joseph K. Houts, Jr.

University Press, 1995.
Hale, Donald R. <u>They Called Him Bloody Bill</u>. 1992.
Hale, Donald R. <u>We Rode with Quantrill</u>. 1992.
Houx, Anne Bennett. <u>Book of Houx Stories</u>. Warrensburg, Missouri: 1995.
Jackson Co. Genealogical Society. <u>Marriage Records of Jackson County, Mo. Book 486</u>. Mid Continent Public Library, Independence, Mo. Genealogy & Local History Branch.
Jordan, Robert Paul. <u>The Civil War</u>. Washington, D.C.: The National Geographic Society, 1969.
Lankford, Rose Mary. <u>The Encyclopedia of Quantrill's Guerrillas</u>. Evening Shade, AR: 1999.
Leslie, Edward E. <u>The Devil Knows How to Ride</u>. New York: Random House, 1996.
McCorkle, John. <u>Three Years with Quantrill</u>. Norman and London: University of Oklahoma Press, 1992.
Micah
Miller, Joaquin. <u>An Illustrated History of the State of Montana</u>. Chicago: The Lewis Publishing Co., 1894.
Monaghan, Jay. <u>Civil War on the Western Border 1854-1865</u>. Lincoln and London: University of Nebraska Press, 1955.
Parrish, William E. <u>A History of Missouri Volume III 1860 to 1875</u>. Columbia, Missouri: University of Missouri Press, 1973.
Polk & Co.'s, R. L. <u>Helena City Directory</u>. Helena, Montana: Independent Press, 1900.
Settle, Jr., William A. <u>Jesse James was His Name</u>. Lincoln and London: University of Nebraska Press, 1966.
Shoemaker, Floyd Calvin. <u>Missouri and Missourians</u>. Volume I. Chicago: The Lewis Publishing Company, 1943.
Spainhour, Irene. <u>Confederate Veterans of the Civil War Battle of Lone Jack, Mo</u>. 1998.
Spainhour, Irene. <u>Quantrell's Men Veterans of the Civil War Battle of Lone Jack, Mo</u>. 1998.
Steele, Phillip W. and Cottrell, Steve. <u>Civil War in the Ozarks</u>. Gretna: Pelican Publishing Company, 1994.
United States War Department. <u>The War of the Rebellion: A Compilation of the Official Records of the Union and Confederate Armies</u>. 130 Volumes. Washington, D.C.: 1880-1912.
<u>Webster's Seventh New Collegiate Dictionary</u>. Springfield, Massachusetts, U.S.A.: G&C Merriam Company, Publishers, 1963.
Welch, Warren. <u>Warren Welch Remembers</u>. Independence, Missouri: Two Trails Publishing, 1997.
Younger, Cole. <u>The Story of Cole Younger by Himself</u>. Springfield, Mo.: Oak Hills Publishing, 1996.

CENSUS
<u>1870 Jackson County, Missouri Census</u>. Mid-Continent Public Library, Genealogy & Local History Branch, Independence, Mo.
Burnetti, Mary Helm. <u>1860 Federal Census Lafayette County, Missouri</u>. Odessa, Missouri, 1982.
<u>Carroll County, Missouri 1850 Federal Census</u>.
Chatworthy, Thomas E. <u>Cass County, Missouri 1860 Federal Census</u>. Harrisonville, Missouri: The Cass County Historical Society, 1982.
Couch, Mary (Bartee). <u>1860 Federal Census for Chariton County, Missouri</u>. Marceline, Missouri: 1887.
Genealogical Society of Liberty, Inc. <u>1860 Federal Census Clay County, Missouri</u>.

Liberty, Mo.: 1985.
Horvath, Becky C. Hall Census Papers. Nelson County, Kentucky.
Poppino, Hattie E. Jackson County, Missouri Census of 1860. 1964.
Tyler, Hazel. Johnson County, Missouri 1860 Federal Census with the 1860 Mortality Schedule. Springfield, Mo.: Ozarks Genealogical Society, Inc., 1997.
Williams, Betty Harvey. Johnson County, Missouri 1860 Federal Census. Warrensburg, Mo.: 1965.

COUNTY HISTORIES
History of Andrew and DeKalb Counties. St. Louis and Chicago: The Goodspeed Publishing Co., 1888.
History of Howard and Chariton Counties. 1884.
History of Saline County, Missouri. St. Louis: Missouri Historical Company, 1881.
History of Vernon County, Missouri. St. Louis: Brown & Co., 1887; Reprint Clinton, Mo.: The Printery, 1974.
Portrait and Biographical Records of Johnson and Pettis Counties, Missouri. Chicago: Chapman Publishing Co., 1899.
The History of Jackson County, Mo. Kansas City, Mo.: Union Historical Company, Birdsall, William & Co., 1881; Reprint Cape Girardeau, Mo.: Ramfire Press, 1966.
The History of Johnson County, Missouri: Kansas City, Mo.: Kansas City Historical Company, 1881.

QUANTRELL'S THIEVES By: Joseph K. Houts, Jr.

Index

10th Missouri Cavalry, 82, 119, 125, 182, 220
10th Missouri Infantry, 83
11th Missouri Infantry, 179
12th Missouri Cavalry, 70, 144, 165, 167, 195, 204, 205, 207
15th Kansas Cavalry, 36
15th Missouri Cavalry, 199
16th Missouri Infantry, 77, 83, 90, 91, 92, 96, 104, 118, 120, 122, 162, 189, 201
1890 Shelby Veterans Reunion, 181
1895 Jackson County United Confederate Veteran's Roster, 67, 161
1904 Quantrill Reunion, 181
1919 Treaty of Versailles, 26
1st Iowa Cavalry, 34, 42, 45, 46
1st Missouri Cavalry, 42, 46, 79
1st North East Missouri Cavalry, 147, 195
27th Infantry Missouri Volunteers, 34
2nd Arkansas Mounted Rifles, 163
2nd Colorado, 64
2nd Missouri Cavalry, 95, 102, 129, 151, 158, 175
2nd Missouri Infantry, 101
2nd United States Cavalry, 71
2nd Wisconsin Cavalry, 199
39th Missouri State Militia, 2
3rd Missouri Cavalry, 93
3rd Missouri Infantry, 102
47th Arkansas Cavalry, 199, 200
4th Missouri Cavalry, 59, 147, 196
4th Street Cemetery, Dover, Ohio, 60, 232
53rd United States Congress, 176
5th Missouri Cavalry, 102, 164, 179
5th Missouri Militia Cavalry, 209
6th Missouri Infantry, 101
7th Cavalry Post, 41
7th Cavalry, Missouri State Militia, 34, 82
7th Kansas Cavalry, 151
7th Missouri Cavalry, 42, 45
8th Missouri Infantry Battalion, 84, 192, 193
9th Missouri Battalion Sharp Shooters, 179
9th Missouri Infantry, 84
Abingdon, Virginia, 176
Acres, Henry, 76
Akers, Eliza J., 76
Akers, Henry H., 76, 224, 228, 230
Akers, Mark, 76
Akers, Matilda Mead, 76

Akers, Solomon, 76
Akers, Sylvester, 76
Alexander, John, 122
Alexandria, Louisiana, 84
Alpha Pi Fraternity, 60
Alpha Pi Fraternity, Zeta Chapter, 60
Alton, Illinois, 130
Alton, Oregon County, Missouri, 197, 199
American Civil War, 2, 6, 9, 52, 54
Ames, J. T., 214
Anderson, 2, 3, 22, 59, 64, 69, 77, 155, 163, 164, 174, 186, 196, 205, 212
Anderson, F. P., 164
Anderson, Hugh L. W., 77, 90, 122, 201, 224, 230
Anderson, Jeanie, 22
Anderson, Josephine, 22
Anderson, Mary, 22
Anderson, William T., 2, 22, 27, 57, 63, 72, 74, 146, 154, 166, 169, 174, 180, 186, 196, 200, 204, 205, 212, 218
Ankeny, William H., 42
Anne, Lawrence, 120
Anne, Rebecca F., 120
Annie Burns, 129
Anthony, Daniel R., 151
Anthony, Susan B., 151
Apperson, Elfreda Hays, 153
Appleton City, Missouri, 106
Appomattox Court House, Virginia, 26, 52, 211
Arizona, 69, 188, 211
Army of Northern Virginia, 59, 76, 159
Arnold, Moses B., 72
Arrow Rock, Missouri, 64, 219
Askew, Daniel A., 214
Atchison, David Rice, 10
Atchison, John, 80, 220, 224, 228, 229
Atchison, Sylvester, 78, 220, 228, 229
Atchison, Wiley, 79, 220, 228, 229
Atchison, Willis G., 79
Atchison, Wylie, 224
Atlanta, Georgia, 2
Aubry, Kansas, 17, 56
Austin, H., 81, 224, 230
Austin, Steve, 72
Austin, Texas, 213
Baily, W. W., 46
Baker, Elizabeth, 91
Baker, Emma A., 90
Baker, Henry S., 91
Baker, James C., 90
Baker, Maria L., 90
Baker, John and Myra, 91

QUANTRILL'S THIEVES By: Joseph K. Houts, Jr.

Baker, Maria L., 90
Baker, W A, 90
Baker, William H., 90, 91, 122, 201, 223, 224, 228
Ball, Leander, 98, 192, 193, 224, 230
Ball, Nancy J, 98, 106, 205
Ball, Sarah, 98
Ballew, Dorcas, 144
Banny, John, 141
Barker, John, 66, 200
Barnett, Absolem, 95
Barnett, Ada Cleveland, 94
Barnett, Anna Lee, 94
Barnett, Dora Belle, 94
Barnett, Dr. James J., 95
Barnett, Emiline, 94
Barnett, G. M., 220
Barnett, George Harrison, 93
Barnett, George M., 224, 228, 229
Barnett, George McKinley, 78, 79, 80, 93, 95, 96, 201
Barnett, Georgia Alice, 94
Barnett, James Monroe, 95, 224, 230
Barnett, Jennie Maud, 94
Barnett, Lee, 95
Barnett, Martha Ann, 96
Barnett, Martha Elizabeth, 94
Barnett, Mary Etna, 94
Barnett, Mary Frances Strange, 93
Barnett, Minnie Myrtle, 94
Barnett, Obediah Strange (O. S.), 90, 93, 95, 96, 147, 201, 224, 228, 229, 232
Barnett, Oscar Lee, 94
Barnett, Robert P., 95
Barnett, Samuel J., 95
Barnett, William Francis, 95
Barnette, Barbara Ann, 79
Basham, Solomon, 143
Bateman, Martha Elizabeth, 94
Bates City, Missouri, 72
Bates County, Missouri, 24
Baton Rouge, Louisiana, 84, 96
Battalion Loyal Militia of Missouri, 39
Battle of New Orleans, 208
Battle of Pleasant Hill, Missouri, 41, 131, 134, 138, 176
Battle of the Thames, 150
Battle of Westport, Missouri, 64
Battle of Wilson's Creek, Missouri, 122
Baxter Springs, Kansas, 58, 63, 65, 68, 74, 82, 99, 129, 132, 139, 159, 170, 179, 182, 183, 186, 210, 217
Beecher, Henry Ward, 8
Beeson, Harmon V., 53
Beeson, Harmond C., 54
Begole, George, 140

Belcher, Emeline, 170
Bell, Keziah, 101
Bell, Samuel R., 101
Bell, Sarah, 101
Bell, Susan C, 101
Bell, Tolmon, 101
Bell, William C. (W. C.), 101, 224, 228, 230
Belt, M. L., 161
Belton Cemetery, 168
Belton Masonic Lodge No. 450, 168
Belton, Cass County, Missouri, 168
Benton County, Missouri, 158
Benton, Bossier Parish, Louisiana, 176
Bernard, Seletha A., 80
Big Cedar, Jackson County, Missouri, 68, 170
Big Creek, 43
Bill of Rights, 16, 19
Bingham, George Caleb, 24
Birch Tree, Shannon County, Missouri, 197
Blachand, Newton C., 176
Black Flag, 186
Black Jack, 218, 219
Blackwater River, 34, 132, 134, 182, 183, 191
Blair, Frank, 11
Bledsoe, Bi, 99
Bledsoe, Charles Thomas, 99
Bledsoe, Elizabeth, 99
Bledsoe, George, 99
Bledsoe, James Carrol, 99
Bledsoe, Jim, 72
Bledsoe, Joel Joseph, 99
Bledsoe, John, 99
Bledsoe, Loving, 99
Bledsoe, Mary Ann, 99
Bledsoe, Millicent Head, 99
Bledsoe, William Harvey, 99
Bledsoe, William M. (W. M.), 99, 223, 224, 228
Blue River, 46, 148, 151
Blue Springs, Missouri, 55, 57, 112, 130, 146, 149, 151, 154, 161, 193, 227
Blue Township, Missouri, 148
Blunt, Andrew, 57, 71, 72, 99, 123, 223, 224
Blunt, James G., 36, 58, 69, 100, 152, 160, 171, 187, 205, 212, 217
Bond, Melvin, 111
Boone, Daniel, 104, 106, 150, 163
Boone, Rebecca, 163
Booneville, Missouri, 200
Border Ruffians, 10
Boswell, Mary, 170

QUANTRELL'S THIEVES By: Joseph K. Houts, Jr.

Bourbon County, Kentucky, 207
Bouse, Ann Burris, 163
Bower, W. R., 102, 103
Bowers, Joseph, 102, 103, 224, 229
Bowers, Thomas B., 102
Bowers, W T, 102
Bowlin, James H., 84, 224, 229, 232
Bowling Green, Kentucky, 95
Bowling, Jas H, 84
Bowman, Elizabeth, 161
Bowman, Reverend, 161
Bradford, J. H., 218
Breckenridge and Jackson, 150
Bredett, Eliphant, 41
Brinker, Abraham, 82
Brinker, Fannie J., 82
Brinker, Jessie B, 82
Brinker, John B., 82
Brinker, John D. (J. D.), 82, 119, 125, 182, 220, 223, 224
Brinker, Martha G., 82
Brinker, Robert, 82
Brinker, Sarah B., 82
Brinker, William Hugh, 82
Brown, Egburt, 219
Brown, John, 10, 11, 72
Brunswick, Missouri, 180, 200
Brush Creek, 73
Bryan, Rebecca, 163
Buel, James T., 110, 152, 211
Bull Run, 7
Burges, W M, 88
Burges, William I., 88
Burgess, Edward, 88
Burgess, Francis Marion, 88
Burgess, Garland A. Reverend, 88, 89
Burgess, Henrietta Elizabeth, 88
Burgess, Henrietta H. McCown, 88
Burgess, Julia A., 88
Burgess, Mary Jane, 88
Burgess, William M., 174, 223, 224
Burgess, William Mc., 128
Burgess, William McCown, 88
Burk, Mary McCown and Margaret, 191
Burnett, G N, 93
Burns, Catherine H., 86
Burns, Crittenden, 86
Burns, Dennis, 86
Burns, Dick, 70, 87
Burns, Felix J., 86
Burns, John T., 86
Burns, Nancy F., 86
Burns, Richard F., 86, 222, 224, 227, 228, 229
Burns, Serilda, 86
Burns, Wesley, 86

Burns, William T., 86
Burns, William W., 86
Burris, Missouri Ann, 163
Burt, George, 145, 202
Bush, Alisa, 193
Butler, Benjamin F., 214
Butler, Missouri, 42
Butler, William H., 92, 224, 230, 232
Byrd and Snodgrass Funeral Home, 94
Callaway County, Missouri, 150, 170
Camden County, Missouri, 127
Campbell, Alexander A., 122
Campbell, Colin C., 118
Campbell, Doc, 145
Campbell, Lucy Ann, 118
Campbell, Mary A., 122
Campbell, William H., 118, 144, 167, 204, 224, 229, 231
Canada, 63
Canadian River, 160
Canal Dover, Ohio (See also, Dover, Ohio), 53, 60, 93
Cane Hill, Arkansas, 129, 159
Cape Girardeau, Missouri, 15, 167
Carmichael Cemetery, 104
Carmichael, Pleasant, 105
Carroll County, Missouri, 169, 224
Carrollton, Missouri, 169
Carson, Kit, 133
Carthage, Missouri, 12, 151, 163, 209, 210, 212
Cass County, Missouri, 24, 145, 146, 154, 165, 166, 168, 170, 198, 209, 213, 224
Cat Island Plantation, 176
Cave, William, 220
Center Township, 164
Centerview, Missouri, 32, 88, 132, 133, 135, 139
Centralia, Missouri, 1, 2, 3, 5, 59, 63, 64, 65, 68, 74, 78, 86, 93, 146, 154, 159, 170, 174, 179, 186, 187, 196, 204, 210
Chadwell, Bill, 214
Chamblin, William, 113, 224, 230
Champion Hill, Mississippi, 197
Chariton County, Missouri, 144, 224
Cheatham, W. F., 108, 117, 223, 224
Cherokee Nation, 100, 157
Chester County, Pennsylvania, 162
Chiles, Christopher Lillard, 110, 211, 223, 224, 227, 228
Chiles, Henry Clay, 150
Chiles, Jim, 87
Chiles, Rachael Davis, 110
Chiles, Richard Ballinger, 110

282

QUANTRILL'S THIEVES By: Joseph K. Houts, Jr.

Chiles, William H., 110
Chilton, Shade, 196
Chilton, Tho., 196
City Cemetery, 216
City Hotel, 130, 161
Clay County, Missouri, 81, 108, 109, 224
Clay, Henry, 31, 150
Clayton, George, 107
Clements, Archie, 3, 72, 111, 222
Clifton, Joe, 112
Clifton, Samuel L., 63, 78, 79, 80, 112, 220, 224, 229, 231
Cobb, Thomas M., 85
Cockrell, Francis Marion, 37, 114, 116, 134, 162
Cockrell, Jeremiah Vardaman, 77, 83, 90, 91, 114, 115, 120, 151, 162
Cockrell, Joseph, 114
Cockrell, Mary H., 162
Cockrell, Nancy, 114
Cockrell, Simon N., 114
Cockrell, Syrus, 37, 114, 134, 224, 229, 232
Coffee, John T., 151
Coffeeville, Kansas, 208
Coffman, Eleanor, 181
Colclasier, Lidia, 108, 109
Colclasier, Thomas, 108, 109
Colclasier, W., 108
Colesure, Thomas, 224, 230
Colesure, William, 224, 230
Collesure, Thomas, 109
Collesure, W, 108
Colonel John B. Clark Jr.'s Regiment Missouri Infantry, 84
Colonel Rosser's Regiment, Rains Division, 65
Columbia, 181
Columbus, Missouri, 120, 132
Combs, Samuel R., 114
Company A, Seventh Cavalry, Missouri State Militia, 34
Company I., Shank's regiment, 66
Company L, First Iowa Cavalry, 45
Concord Graveyard, 72
Concord, Missouri, 207
Confederate Army, 52, 77, 82, 83, 96, 102, 105, 106, 123, 147, 163, 173, 175, 176, 196, 211
Confederate Camp No. 751, 197, 199
Confederate Cemetery, Higginsville, Missouri, 97, 161
Confederate Home, Ardmore, Oklahoma, 94
Confederate Memorial Home, Ardmore, Oklahoma, 94

Confederate Memorial Home, Higginsville, Missouri, 60, 84, 85, 94, 96, 161, 168, 232
Confederate Partisan Rangers Act, 18, 56, 61, 152
Confederate Partisan Rangers Act of April 21, 1862, 18, 61, 152
Confederate Veterans, Shelby's Camp, 130
Conn, Patience, 126
Connelley, William E., 5, 6, 49, 60
Constitution, 16, 27, 222
Cooper County, Missouri, 131
Copeland, Levi, 57, 71, 152
Corinth, Mississippi, 197
Corsicana, Texas, 167
Coryrell County, Texas, 116
Cottage Grove Cemetery, 177
Council Grove, Kansas, 205, 218
Coyville, Kansas, 94
Crandall, Colonel, 199
Crawford, Armenia, 22
Crittenden, Thomas T., 36, 37
Cuba, 214
Cuban Revolution, 118, 231
Cumberland Presbyterian Church, 135
Cummins, 77
Cunningham, A L, 106, 122, 147, 179, 224, 228, 230
Cunningham, Elizabeth B, 104, 106
Cunningham, Henry G., 104, 106
Cunningham, James Hamilton, 90, 104, 106, 122, 147, 201, 224, 228, 230
Cunningham, John H., 104, 106
Cunningham, Julia A., 104, 106
Cunningham, Lewis A., 90, 104, 106, 201
Cunningham, Mary Hammond, 104, 106
Cunningham, Nancy J., 104, 106
Cunningham, Pelina, 104, 106
Cunningham, Susan Jeannette (Carmichael), 104
Cupp, Sarah J., 78
Curtis, Samuel R., 20, 21, 116
Cypress Lodge No. 89 F. and A.M, 176
Dallas, Texas, 114
Dalton Gang, 208
Dalton, Bob, 208
Dalton, Emmett, 208
Dalton, Grat, 208
Daughters of the American Revolution, 29
Davenport, Anne, 120
Davenport, Lawrence, 120
Davenport, Rebecca F., 120

283

QUANTRELL'S THIEVES By: Joseph K. Houts, Jr.

Davenport, Robert, 90, 120, 201, 224, 230
David, Daniel, 110
Davidson, T. J., 157
Davis, Ada Cleveland, 94
Davis, J. D., 141
Davis, Jefferson, 18
Daws, Uncle, 33
Dean, John, 199
Declaration of Independence, 19, 163, 233
Dejarnett, James R. (J.J.R.), 119, 125, 182, 224, 230
DeSoto, Missouri, 105
Diamond Springs, 218
Dickers, J N, 123
Dickey, Elizabeth, 123
Dickey, John B., 123, 223, 224
Dickey, Thomas, 123
Dickson, J. C., 177
Dillingham, Evans, 147
Dillingham, Joshua, 148
Dillingham, Mary Elizabeth, 148
Dillingham, Sally, 147
Dillingham, Susan Walker, 148
Doak, Francis, 122
Doak, Henry, 122
Doak, Josephine, 122
Doak, Martha, 122
Doak, N. F., 122
Doak, Samuel, 122
Doak, William T., 122, 223, 224
Doake, N. F., 90
Doake, N. T., 90, 201
Dodge, Grenville M., 187
Doke, N F, 122
Doore, Jerre (J. F. Doores), 45, 126, 173
Doores, Amanda, 125
Doores, Emma, 125
Doores, F., 125, 126
Doores, James, 125
Doores, Jeremiah F., 45, 125, 126, 143, 173, 195, 223, 224, 228
Doores, M. H., 224, 229, 231
Doores, Sarah O., 125, 126
Doores, W. M., 125
Doores, William E., 119, 125, 182
Doors, M H, 125
Doors, W. M., 125
Douglas County, Kansas, 55, 145, 171, 202
Dover Historical Society, 60
Dover, Ohio (see also Canal Dover, Ohio), 60
Drake Constitution, 27, 222
Drake, Charles D., 27

Eads, James D., 33, 133
Edmonson Creek, 124
Edwards, John N., 83, 106, 143, 161
Edwin, Jacob, 32
Elk Creek, Virginia, 185
Ellis, Nancy, 114
Elmwood Cemetery, 194
Emiline Barnett, 94
Eminence, Shannon County, Missouri, 196
Emporia, Kansas, 218
Enfield Rifles, 3, 73
Ersey, Pauline Hays, 153
Estes, Alvis, 127
Estes, Daniel, 127
Estes, Noah, 127, 223, 224
Eutonia, Arkansas, 207
Evans, Esculania, 95
Evans, Levi, 95
Evans, Narcissus Christian, 95
Ewing, Jr, Thomas J., 21, 22, 23, 24, 58, 146, 213, 222
Ewing, Jr, Thomas W., 57
Ewing, Thomas E. Jr., 21, 22, 23, 24, 57, 58, 146, 212, 213, 222, 235, 237, 238
F M Scott Commissary, 73
F. M. Robertson/Robinson, 128
Fayette, Missouri, 5, 64, 179, 186, 203
Ferguson, 36
First National Bank of Northfield, Minnesota, 214
Fisher County, Texas, 116
Fishpool, E. I., 164
Flanagan, Harris, 163
Flannery house, 219
Flannery, Ike, 87
Fletcher, Thomas C., 26, 164
Floyd, Kentucky, 114
Forbes, Floy Hays, 153
Ford, Robert, 27
Fort Leavenworth, Kansas, 15, 152, 204, 206, 219, 237
Fort Scott, Kansas, 31, 130
Fort Sumter, 7
Foster, 34, 37, 42, 82, 83, 120, 152, 211, 215
Foster, Emery S., 34, 39, 120
Fourth Amendment, 19
Frank James, 14, 73, 155, 215
Frankfort, Kentucky, 141
Frederick County, Virginia, 162
Freebooters, 13, 225
Freeman, James G., 128, 191, 224, 230
Freeman, Missouri, 163
Freeman, Sarah C., 128
Freemasonry, 68

284

QUANTRILL'S THIEVES By: Joseph K. Houts, Jr.

Frémont, James C., 15, 26
Fulton County, Arkansas, 199
Gains, Elizabeth F., 198
Gains, John M., 198
Gallatin, Missouri, 213
Gamble, Hamilton R., 15
Gardner, 218
Gates, Elijah, 79
General Order No. 1, 16, 18, 22, 23, 57, 58, 212, 238
General Order No. 10, 21, 22, 57, 212, 238
General Order No. 11, 21, 23, 24, 58, 219, 222
General Order No. 18, 18
General Order No. 19, 19
General Order No. 2, 16, 17, 18, 20, 38, 134, 234
General Order No. 24, 16, 20
General Order No. 30, 20
General Order No. 32, 15
General Order No. 35, 20
General Order No. 48, 21
General Order No. 9, 19, 25, 235, 236
General Order No. 96, 25
George Cemetery, 130
George Family Cemetery, 130, 175
George, David C., 129, 173
George, Frances Fitzhugh, 173
George, Gabriel W., 173
George, Hicks, 43
George, Hiram James, 173, 175
George, J. H., 224, 225, 228, 229
George, John Hicks, 129, 165, 173, 175, 224, 225, 228, 229
George, Lavisa Adeline, 129
George, Martha E., 175
George, Moore, Frances, 173
George, N. B., 173
George, Nancy E. Bass, 173
George, Nancy E. Bates, 129
Georgetown, Missouri, 169
Gettysburg, PA, 23
Gilchrist, Gregg, 71
Gilchrist, Joseph, 56, 71, 156, 211
Gilkeson, Shanklin, 33
Gillet, Martha Jane McFarland, 132
Gilvey, Armenia, 212
Golden City, Colorado, 157
Goode, M. W., 140
Gower, Bill, 74, 170
Gower, James D., 42, 46
Gower, Missouri, 42, 43, 44, 45, 46, 48, 49, 74, 170
Grand Gulf, Mississippi, 197
Grand Junction, Colorado, 181

Grant, Ulysses S., 52
Gratiot Street Prison, 127, 158, 205
Gray, Barbary Jane, 72
Greater Lew Nicholas Show, 216
Gregg, Ellen, 157
Gregg, Jacob, 65
Gregg, Nancy Lewis, 65
Gregg, William H., 44, 46, 56, 58, 61, 64, 65, 66, 69, 71, 73, 75, 138, 152, 156, 157, 165, 186, 187, 211, 215, 224, 227, 228, 229
Gross, George P., 85
Haden, Robert, 132
Hall, E. B., 154
Hall, Isaac, 146, 154
Hall, J J, 146
Hall, John, 154
Hall, Joseph, 154
Hall, Margaret, 154
Hall, Nora, 216
Hall, Robert, 154, 224
Hall, Robert H., 146, 154, 224
Hall, Robert J., 230
Hall, Thomas J., 146, 154, 224, 230
Hallar, Wm, 61
Halleck, Henry W., 15, 16, 17, 18, 20, 21, 38, 48, 56, 134, 151, 234
Haller, George Washington, 61
Haller, William M., 46, 61, 63, 119, 125, 143, 156, 182, 220, 223, 224, 227
Halleran, O., 127
Halley, Lucinda Halley, 141
Halley, Samuel, 140
Halley, William R., 140, 141, 224, 229, 231
Hally, Elizabeth, 141
Hally, Emily, 141
Hally, Marie, 141
Hally, Samuel, 141
Hally, W, 140
Halterman, Lydia G. Halterman, 157
Hamilton, James H., 106
Hampton, David, 144
Hampton, Dorcas, 144
Hampton, John, 44, 126, 143, 173, 195, 223, 224, 228
Hampton, Mary C., 143
Hampton, Oscar L., 144, 167, 204, 224, 229
Hampton, Susan Gaines, 144
Hannibal, Missouri, 99
Harding, B. F., 130, 173
Harding, Chester, 187
Harding, J. M., 173
Harkins, Elizabeth Ann, 185
Harriet McFarland, 131

QUANTRELL'S THIEVES By: Joseph K. Houts, Jr.

Harris, A., 78, 79, 80, 107, 144, 148, 167, 220, 224, 227, 228, 229
Harris, Jane Hall, 148
Harris, John, 155
Harris, Margaret Ann Alexander, 148
Harris, Mary Elizabeth, 148
Harris, Nannie, 22
Harris, Nealy A., 149
Harris, R. A., 78, 79, 80, 220
Harris, Samuel, 148
Harris, Selvey, 22
Harrison, Charley (Ki), 61
Harrisonville, Missouri, 209
Harrodsburg, Kentucky, 76
Hart, Joe, 73
Hartville, Missouri, 159
Harvey Douglass Funeral Home, 94
Haun, Alfred, 207
Haun, Ann, 207
Haun, Nancy, 207
Hayes, Amanzon, 150
Hayes, Margaret J., 150
Hays, Boone, 150
Hays, Upton, 42, 43, 57, 61, 70, 71, 82, 127, 129, 130, 150, 153, 165, 167, 207, 223, 224, 227
Heaton, Bowman, Smith and Sidenfaden Chapel, 140
Heaton-Begole Funeral Home, 140
Helena, Arkansas, 77, 96, 104, 106, 121
Helena, Montana, 157
Hendricks, Arthur J., 157
Hendricks, Bessie, 157
Hendricks, Carrie E., 157
Hendricks, Charles J., 157
Hendricks, Clarence E., 157
Hendricks, Henry C., 157
Hendricks, James A, 56, 156, 167, 228
Hendricks, John, 56
Hendricks, Peter, 156
Hendricks, Riley E., 157
Hendricks, Sarah Land, 156
Hendrickson, J. G., 156
Hendrix, James A., 67, 75, 144
Henry County, Missouri, 24
Hickman Mills, Missouri, 167
Higbee, Charles, 71
Higgins, William, 36, 37
Higginsville Confederate Home Cemetery, 60
Higginsville, Missouri, 84, 96, 130, 161, 168, 207, 232
Hilton, Dave, 155
Hindman, Thomas C., 57, 115, 151, 152
Hindman, Thomas L., 57, 115
Hippocratic Oath, 231

Hodges, Louisa, 118
Holden, 96, 104, 122, 181
Holden, Missouri, 96, 104, 122, 181
Hollowly, Hester, 149
Hook, Elizabeth Eleanor, 67
Horn, Given N., 145, 224, 230
Horn, Mattie F., 145
Horn, Richard, 145
Hornsby Farm, 43
Horse Shoe, 70
Horton, Sarah, 114
Houston, M. F., 147
Houston, Nathan, 224, 228, 230
Houston, Sam, 114
Houts, Christopher G., 30
Houts, George Wilson, 30, 31
Houts, Thomas Dawson, 33
Houts, Thomas W., 29, 30, 31, 34, 35, 36, 37, 39, 40, 48, 50, 52, 82, 88, 89
Houts, William L., 31, 39
Houx, Catherine Elizabeth, 40
Houx, Dorothy, 131, 133
Houx, George Washington, 32
Houx, Jacob, 31, 32, 133
Houx, James Henry, 138, 162, 208
Houx, Jim Henry (Reverend), 139
Houx, John Jacob, 131
Houx, Margaret Hutchison Morrow, 32, 138
Houx, Martha Jane McFarland, 132
Houx, Mary, 38
Houx, Mat, 39, 135
Houx, Matthias, 30, 31, 33, 37, 38, 39, 40, 43, 90, 114, 120, 131, 133, 134, 135, 138, 224, 229
Houx, Michael Morningstar, 30, 31, 39, 90, 131, 138, 224, 230
Houx, Philip Simons, 32, 138
Houx, Robert, 30, 40, 43, 125, 131, 132, 138, 139, 224, 225, 230
Houx, Robert Washington Kavanaugh, 30, 32, 39, 40, 43, 90, 119, 125, 129, 131, 138, 182, 224, 225, 230
Houx, Susan Morningstar, 31, 32
Howard County, Missouri, 92, 149, 181, 224
Howard, Thomas (see, Jesse James), 214
Hoy, Perry, 18, 56, 57, 71, 152, 156
Hudspath, Babe, 59
Hudspath, Rufus, 59
Hudspeth, Rufus, 76, 159
Hudspeth, William Napoleon, 59, 76, 202
Hughes and Wasson Bank, 86
Hulse, Bill, 155
Hunt, Sally, 114

QUANTRILL'S THIEVES By: Joseph K. Houts, Jr.

Hurst's, 37, 133
Independence, Missouri, 19, 40, 45, 56, 61, 62, 63, 64, 65, 68, 70, 71, 73, 74, 76, 86, 87, 99, 104, 110, 112, 123, 129, 141, 148, 149, 151, 152, 158, 159, 163, 167, 169, 186, 192, 210, 211, 217, 219, 227
Indian Head Penny, 163
Ironton, Missouri, 200
Iuka, Mississippi, 105
Jackman, D. A., 77, 83, 90, 104, 117, 120, 162, 189, 201
Jackson County Cavalry, 70, 144, 165, 167, 195, 204, 205, 207
Jackson County United Confederate Veterans Roster of 1895, 215
Jackson County, Missouri, 24, 42, 56, 65, 66, 67, 68, 70, 73, 78, 79, 80, 82, 97, 98, 99, 101, 110, 112, 123, 125, 126, 127, 129, 143, 148, 149, 150, 151, 152, 156, 159, 165, 167, 168, 170, 175, 192, 197, 204, 207, 208, 209, 215, 217, 219, 224, 225, 226, 227, 228, 238
Jackson, Andrew, 208
Jackson, Claiborne F., 10, 11
Jacksonport, Arkansas, 199
James, Frank, 14, 73, 86, 155, 187, 213, 214, 215, 216
James, Harrison, 199
James, Hiram, 130
James, Jesse, 27, 59, 69, 76, 86, 87, 140, 159, 187, 213, 214, 216
James-Younger Gang, 69, 213
Jarrette, John, 68, 70, 111, 144, 165, 167, 176, 178, 187, 204, 210, 217, 224, 225, 229
Jarrette, Josephine, 22, 68, 69, 122, 163
Jarvis, Dr. W. M., 85
Jasper County United Confederate Veterans Camp #52, 163
Jayhawkers, 5, 10, 13, 15, 17, 21, 55, 56, 66, 72, 91, 93, 120, 123, 143, 148, 150, 154, 171, 182, 183, 189, 209, 217, 222, 225, 226
Jefferson Barracks National Cemetery, St. Louis, Missouri, 127, 158
Jefferson City, Missouri, 24, 35, 48, 129, 172, 200
Jefferson County, Tennessee, 162
Jennison, Charles R., 10, 13, 24, 36, 146, 150, 151, 154, 167, 209, 217
Jewell, J. M., 88
John B. Clark Jr.'s Regiment Missouri Infantry, 84

Johnson County, Missouri, 28, 30, 31, 32, 43, 77, 82, 83, 88, 89, 90, 91, 96, 104, 106, 114, 115, 118, 120, 122, 125, 128, 131, 134, 138, 141, 147, 162, 170, 174, 178, 179, 181, 182, 183, 189, 191, 201, 202, 224, 225, 227, 228
Johnson, A.V.E., 3, 159
Johnson, Albert Sidney, 54
Johnson, Hiram, 164
Johnson, Ol, 179
Johnson, Richard M., 114
Jones, Payne, 87, 155
Jordan Lowe house, 56, 71, 148
Judd, William F., 158, 223, 224
Kabrick, Francis Fitzhugh (George) Moore, 173
Kalmer Nyckel, 162
Kanawha County, Virginia, 88
Kansas City Star & Times, 188
Kansas City, Missouri, 22, 24, 41, 57, 63, 73, 74, 99, 107, 110, 112, 146, 154, 161, 168, 170, 171, 188, 194, 209, 212, 219, 235, 236, 238
Kansas Militia, 218
Kansas State Historical Society, 60
Kansas Tribune, 171
Kansas-Nebraska Act of 1854, 7, 8, 9, 11, 12, 27, 50, 54
Kehoe, Martin, 42, 138, 143
Kelley, C. H., 141
Kelly, James, 143
Kerr, Charity McCorkle, 22, 168
Key, Gacy, 96
Key, Martha Ann, 96
Keytesville, Missouri, 64, 84, 144
Kile, Jas., 196
King, Kate, 57, 163
Kingsville, Missouri, 162
Kinyoun, Joseph James, 40
Koger, Edward, 56, 143, 159
Koger, John H., 78, 79, 80
Koger, John William, 46, 56, 59, 76, 100, 143, 156, 159, 161, 169, 224, 228, 229, 232
Koller, Krist, 112
Lafayette County, Missouri, 24, 32, 64, 68, 72, 81, 95, 102, 106, 138, 147, 185, 186, 195, 210, 224
Laffite, Jean, 53
Lane, James H., 10, 13, 23, 24, 64, 66
Lathrop, C. H., 46
Laughlin, E. M., 177
Lawrence, Amos, 8
Lawrence, Kansas, 8, 10, 13, 22, 23, 25, 39, 54, 55, 57, 63, 64, 65, 66, 68, 71,

287

QUANTRELL'S THIEVES By: Joseph K. Houts, Jr.

72, 74, 81, 86, 93, 94, 99, 112, 129, 132, 135, 139, 141, 145, 146, 159, 168, 170, 171, 179, 182, 183, 202, 210, 211, 212, 216, 217, 219, 231
Lawther, Robert R., 82, 220
Lea, Joseph C., 70, 187, 194, 211, 218
LeCompton, Kansas, 10
Lee, Robert E., 26, 52, 59, 76, 159, 208, 211
Lewis, Warren, 77, 151
Lexington, Missouri, 12, 13, 33, 37, 41, 55, 76, 78, 79, 80, 85, 93, 102, 133, 134, 135, 169, 173, 187, 194, 197, 210, 220, 222
Liberty, Missouri, 69, 73, 86, 110
Lilly, Jim, 155
Lincoln Ford on Big Creek, 43
Lincoln, Abraham, 11, 15, 20, 21, 50, 59, 76, 160
Linn Creek, Missouri, 127
Little Rock, Arkansas, 77, 90, 104, 106, 121, 122
Little, James, 58, 66, 73, 156
Little, John, 143, 156, 159
Little, Tom, 87
Loan, Benjamin, 20, 210
Lobb, John, 81
Lone Jack, Missouri, 35, 61, 65, 70, 71, 77, 78, 86, 90, 99, 104, 106, 115, 122, 127, 141, 152, 154, 158, 159, 162, 167, 169, 174, 189, 195, 202, 203, 207, 210, 220
Long, B L, 164
Long, Benjamin F., 164, 224, 229
Long, Peyton, 72, 74, 170
Longacre, Ann Burris, 163
Longacre, Charles A., 90, 122, 162, 224, 229, 231
Longacre, Charles L., 202
Longacre, Ida, 163
Longacre, James Barton, 163
Longacre, John, 162
Longacre, Joseph D., 162
Longacre, Josephine, 163
Longacre, Martha Jane Oldham, 162
Longacre, Nancy, 163
Longacre, Phoebe B. Thurlton, 162
Longacre, Richard Ireson, 162
Longacre, Susan E, 163
Los Angeles, California, 69, 211
Lotspeich farm, 42
Louisville, Kentucky, 59, 86
Lowe, Jordan, 56, 71, 148
Lowe, Sandy, 120
Lumford, Bennie Lee, 145
Lyon, James, 165, 166, 224, 230

Lyon, Nathaniel, 11
Lyons, Cynthia A, 165
Lyons, Daniel, 165
Lyons, Martha J., 165
Lyons, James, 165, 166, 224, 230
Lyons, John, 165
Lyons, Laura A., 165
Lyons, Martha J., 165
Lyons, Peter, 165
Lyons, William, 165
Maddox, George M., 44, 56, 74, 143, 145, 170, 195, 224, 229, 231
Maddox, George W., 170
Maddox, Jane Estill Power, 74, 170
Maddox, Larkin, 74, 170
Maddox, Estill Power, 74, 170
Maddox, Mary, 170
Maddox, Richard, 67, 70, 74, 144, 157, 165, 167, 204, 213, 223, 224
Madelia, Minnesota, 215
Madison Township, Missouri, 91, 118, 147, 174, 189, 190, 228
Mann, Jack, 100, 171
Mansfield, Louisiana, 77, 84, 96, 104, 107
Marias des Cygnes River, 54
Marmaduke, John S., 65, 68, 73, 134
Marshall, John, 208
Martin, Roger, 141
Martin, William A., 42, 45, 46
Marysville, Montana, 157
Mason, 176
Masonic, 68, 168, 177
Masonic Home, 168
Maximillian, Generalissimo, 118, 231
McAdam, Alice Hays, 153
McClellan, John W., 200
McCorkle, Jabez, 168
McCorkle, John, 14, 22, 57, 146, 160, 168, 212
McCormack, M., 81
McCormack, Rufus, 81
McCown, James, 115, 134
McCown, Mary, 191
McCown, William, 88, 191
McCulloch, Henry, 58
McDermott, Lieutenant John, 45
McDowell, James L., 218
McFarland, Harriet, 131
McFerran, Union Colonel, 198
McGuire, Andy, 87, 155
McGuire, William, 72, 171, 206
McIntyre, Lieutenant, 45
McMillan, Nelson, 60
McMurty, Lee, 155
McSpadden, Texas, 132

Melton, Mabel, 99
Memphis, Tennessee, 59
Mendota, Illinois, 54
Methodist Episcopal Church, 88
Mexican War, 7, 31, 114, 133, 162
Mexico, Missouri, 194
Miami, Missouri, 123
Micah, 221, 222, 232, 233
Micajah, 127
Miller, Clell, 214
Mineral Creek, 58
Mississippi River, 18, 59, 70, 84, 103, 187, 194, 211
Missouri 1st Infantry unit, 169
Missouri City, Missouri, 73
Missouri Compromise of 1820, 7, 9
Missouri Confederate Army, 102
Missouri Constitution, 27
Missouri Drake Constitution, 222
Missouri Federal Census, 81, 98, 101, 102
Missouri Republic, 171
Missouri Seventh Cavalry, 48
Missouri State Guard, 12, 18, 37, 52, 55, 63, 65, 133, 167, 196, 209
Missouri State Militia, 2, 25, 31, 82, 83, 93, 96, 120, 169, 179, 195
Missouri State Penitentiary, 172
Missouri State Treasurer, 24
Missouri Unionists, 14, 15, 17, 143, 205, 226
Mockbee, Cutbert, 209
Monroe, James, 95, 185
Montgomery, 10, 13
Montgomery, James, 10
Monticello, Arkansas, 83
Montrey, Elizabeth Hays, 153
Moore, Ezra, 45, 126, 129, 143, 173, 195, 223, 224, 225, 228
Moore, Frances Fitzhugh, 173
Mormon Uprising, 31, 133
Morris, Burilda L., 169
Morris, James L., 46, 70, 169, 223, 224
Morris, Thomas W., 169
Morrison, C. M., 169
Morrow, Ben, 159
Morton, John, 163
Mount Mora Cemetery, 141
Muir, Boone Traveler, 144, 165, 167, 168, 204, 217, 224, 225, 227, 230, 232
Muir, James F., 167
Muir, Louisa, 167
Muir, Lucinda, 167
Muir, Maria, 167
Muir, Martha J., 167, 217

Muir, Mary E., 167
Muir, Matilda, 167
Muir, Sally A., 167
Muir, Samuel D, 167
Muir, William, 167
Murrey, Wm. W., 121
N. B. Forest Camp of Confederate Veterans, 157
Nevada, Missouri, 163, 172, 181
New England Emigrant Aid Society, 8
New Orleans, Louisiana, 84, 92, 149, 166, 207, 214
New Santa Fe, 204, 227
Newtonia, Missouri, 153
Nickolls, Governor, 176
Niger Stealers, 10
Noland, John, 81
Norman, George, 196
North Carolina, 123, 127, 128, 145, 150, 220
Nyckel, Kalmer, 162
Oak Grove, Missouri, 72, 129, 130, 173, 175, 227
Odessa, Missouri, 67, 179
Odgen, Harry, 176
Offutt, Mary M., 181
Offutt, Otho, 90, 102, 179, 224, 229
Offutt, Otto, 90, 102, 179, 180, 181, 224, 229
Ogden, Beverly J., 176
Ogden, Elias, 176, 178
Ogden, Frank M., 176, 177, 178, 224, 230
Ogden, Harry, 176
Ogden, Henry, 70, 229, 231
Ogden, Henry Warren, 90, 176, 202
Ogden, Louie, 177
Ogden, Louisa, 176
Ogden, Mariah L., 176, 178
Ogden, Mary S., 176
Ogden, Mary Scott, 177
Ogden, Newton, 176
Ohio, 8, 53, 60, 73, 93, 159, 173, 194, 224, 232
Oklahoma, 75, 94, 194
Olathe, Kansas, 57, 63, 153, 210
Old Lobb Cemetery, 193
Old Smyrna Cemetery, 88, 89
Oldham, Martha Jane, 162
Oliphant, James S., 125, 174
Oliphant, John Newton, 174, 201, 223, 224, 228
Oliphant, M. D., 174
Oliphant, M. J. C., 174
Oliphant, Margaret M., 174
Olliphant, J N, 174

QUANTRELL'S THIEVES By: Joseph K. Houts, Jr.

Oregon Treaty, 7
Osage River, 13, 145
Osawatomie, Kansas, 10
Osceola, Missouri, 13
Oshwatowie, Kansas, 10
Ottawa, Kansas, 171
Overstreet, Margaret, 153
Owings, J, 175
Owings, Joshua, 175, 224, 225
Owings, Martha E., 175
Owings, Mary J., 175
Owings, Richard, 175
Owings, Winifred, 175
Ownings, Joshua, 228, 229
Palo Pinto County, Texas, 131, 132, 139
Paris, Missouri, 200
Parker County, Texas, 186
Parker, B. F., 110
Parker, Ben, 206
Parmer, Allen, 74, 87, 116, 155, 170
Partisan Rangers Act, 18, 19, 56, 61, 152
Patrick County, Virginia, 148
Patterson, J., 156
Pea Ridge, Arkansas, 12, 13, 14, 17, 37, 104, 134, 151, 196
Peach Creek, 181
Pemberton, D. C., 90, 122, 189, 202, 223, 224, 228
Pemberton, Henry C., 90, 122, 189, 202, 223, 224
Pemberton, William C., 228
Pence, Bud, 155
Penick, W. R., 110
Perdee, Andrew J., 182
Perdee, Franklin, 182
Perdee, George W., 182
Perdee, James P., 183, 224, 230
Perdee, James R., 90, 132, 135, 182, 183
Perdee, Jefferson, 182
Perdee, Mary, 182, 183
Perdee, Thomas D., 90, 182, 224, 230
Perry, A. M., 115
Perry, C. A., 142
Perry, Nathan Washington, 37, 40
Perry, Noble County, Oklahoma, 94
Perry, Susan Elizabeth, 40
Petersburg, Tazewall County, Virginia, 114
Philadelphia Mint, 163
Philips, John F., 36
Philpott, Addison, 173
Pindalls, Sharp Shooters, Missouri Volunteers, 162
Pink Hill, 70, 71, 101, 227
Pink Hill M. E. Church, 101
Pink Hill, Missouri, 70, 71

Pinkerton Agency, 214
Plattsburg, Missouri, 73
Pleasant Hill, Louisiana, 84, 96
Pleasant Hill, Missouri, 39, 40, 41, 56, 61, 65, 70, 71, 73, 77, 78, 79, 80, 81, 82, 86, 88, 90, 93, 98, 99, 101, 108, 109, 110, 113, 117, 118, 119, 123, 125, 126, 128, 129, 131, 132, 134, 138, 141, 143, 144, 145, 146, 148, 152, 154, 158, 159, 165, 169, 170, 171, 173, 174, 175, 176, 178, 182, 183, 186, 189, 191, 192, 193, 194, 195, 198, 199, 202, 204, 207, 210, 220
Pocahontas, Arkansas, 59, 155, 159
Pool, Amanda Powell, 185
Pool, Catherine, 185
Pool, D M, 185
Pool, Elizabeth Ann, 185
Pool, Francis Marion, 4, 44, 46, 78, 79, 80, 106, 185, 197, 219, 220, 222, 224, 229
Pool, Jane Thompson, 185
Pope, John, 26
Port Gibson, Mississippi, 197
Portland, Oregon, 94
Post Oak Creek, 39, 134
Post Oak Township, 88, 128
Pottawatomie Creek, 10
Pottowatamie River, 10
Power, Michael, 59
Prairie Grove, Arkansas, 77, 90, 96, 104, 106, 121, 122, 129, 156, 159, 167, 186, 189, 202
Price, Sterling, 2, 11, 12, 13, 14, 15, 16, 17, 18, 35, 37, 55, 57, 63, 64, 77, 83, 90, 96, 104, 106, 115, 118, 120, 122, 133, 144, 174, 180, 189, 191, 196, 200, 209, 234
Pukes, 10
Quantrell, W C, 53
Quantrill, Caroline Clarke, 53, 54, 60, 130, 161
Quantrill, Thomas Henry, 53, 54
Quantrill, William Clarke, 14, 17, 18, 19, 22, 23, 25, 29, 30, 31, 37, 39, 40, 41, 42, 43, 44, 45, 46, 47, 48, 49, 50, 52, 53, 54, 55, 56, 57, 58, 59, 60, 61, 62, 63, 64, 65, 66, 67, 68, 69, 70, 71, 72, 73, 74, 76, 77, 78, 79, 80, 81, 82, 84, 86, 88, 89, 91, 93, 95, 96, 99, 101, 102, 103, 106, 108, 110, 112, 113, 116, 117, 118, 119, 120, 122, 123, 125, 126, 127, 128, 129, 130, 131, 132, 134, 138, 141, 142, 143, 144, 146, 147, 148, 151, 152, 154, 155,

QUANTRILL'S THIEVES By: Joseph K. Houts, Jr.

156, 157, 158, 159, 160, 161, 162, 163, 164, 165, 167, 168, 169, 170, 171, 172, 173, 174, 175, 176, 179, 181, 182, 183, 186, 187, 189, 191, 192, 193, 194, 195, 196, 198, 199, 201, 202, 203, 204, 205, 206, 210, 211, 213, 215, 217, 218, 220, 222, 223, 224, 226, 229, 230
Ragan, Stephan, 161, 215
Ragan, Stephen, 67
Raker, David M., 77, 83, 90, 91, 96, 104, 106, 120, 122, 162, 189, 201
Reaser, J. B., 199
Red River, 58, 157, 187
Redlegs, 94, 120
Reed, Jim, 212
Republican Party, 11
Republication, 116
Revolutionary War, 19, 104, 106, 208
Rich, John A., 85
Rich, Judge John A., 85
Richfield (Missouri City), Missouri, 73
Richmond, Missouri, 86
Richmond, Virginia, 57, 65, 68, 71, 73, 130
Ricketts, Mary J., 175
Rider, Alfred Tralle, 192
Rider, Alisa, 193
Rider, Charles Quantrell (sic), 192
Rider, Eliza Jane, 193
Rider, Elizabeth, 192, 193
Rider, George W., 148, 192, 193, 224, 227, 228, 229
Rider, John Winiard, 148, 192, 193, 224, 228, 229
Rider, Mary Ann, 193
Rider, Mary Eliza, 192
Rider, Miley, 193
Rider, Nellie, 192
Rider, Oliver J., 193
Rider, Samuel B., 193
Rider, Walter, 192
Rider, William E., 193
Rider, Winiard Martin, 192
Roane County, Tennessee, 162
Robertson, F. M., 128, 191, 224, 230
Robertson, Mary M., 181, 191
Robertson, Wealthy J., 191
Robinson, F M, 191
Rocheport, Boone County, Missouri, 92
Rock Island, Illinois, 130
Rock Springs, 218
Rodewald, W. H., 110
Rogers, E. E., 78, 79, 80, 194, 197, 220
Roll of Quantrell's Company Guerllars, 29

Roll of Quantrell's Company of Thieves, 29
Rose Hill in Johnson County, 43
Rose Hill, Missouri, 43, 91, 94, 122, 189, 190
Ross, John, 155
Russellville, Kentucky, 69, 133
Saline County, Missouri, 123, 191
Saline River, Arkansas, 84
Saline, Missouri, 84
Salt Lake City, Utah, 141
Samuel, Archie, 214
San Jacinto, 114
Santa Fe Trail, 217, 218
Santa Fe, New Mexico, 150
Savannah, Missouri, 111
Schofield, John M., 18, 19, 20, 21, 23, 25, 35, 48, 49, 151, 152
Scotland, 63, 195
Scotland County, Missouri, 195
Scott County, Kentucky, 74, 207
Scott, Al, 145
Scott, Fernando M., 73, 74, 144, 167, 204, 223, 224
Scott, William W., 60
Sears Farm, 43, 126, 143, 173
Second Creek Baptist Church Cemetery, 202
Selvey, Armenia Crawford, 22, 168
Seventh Missouri State Militia, 120
Seward, William H., 8
Shank's Regiment, 70, 144, 165, 167, 195, 204, 205, 207
Shanks, David, 70
Shannon County, Missouri, 196, 197, 199, 200
Shaw, John B., 86
Shawnee, Kansas, 63
Shawneetown, Kansas, 57, 210, 213
Shelby, Joseph O., 10, 35, 58, 66, 68, 70, 95, 117, 130, 141, 151, 156, 162, 167, 175, 181, 187, 207
Sheldon, James A., 57
Shelly, Bridgett, 60
Shepard,, 76, 111, 159, 170
Shepard, George, 67, 70, 75, 111, 188
Shepard, Ol, 76, 159, 170
Sherman, Texas, 64, 66, 72, 74, 132, 135, 139, 155, 182, 183, 187, 218
Sherman, William Tecumseh, 2, 21, 57, 58, 64, 66, 72, 74, 132, 135, 139, 154, 182, 183, 187, 188, 218
Shirley, John, 212
Shreveport, Louisiana, 77, 92, 95, 96, 104, 107, 121, 130, 149, 166, 176, 207, 211

QUANTRELL'S THIEVES   By: Joseph K. Houts, Jr.

Sibley, Missouri, 110
Sidenfaden, O. F., 140
Sieffart, Edward, 141
Siloam, Arkansas, 163
Slack, Thomas, 77
Smart, Robert G., 123
Smith Cemetery, 73, 168
Smith, E. Kirby, 92, 189
Smith, Francis, 69
Smith, Frank, 64, 112, 217
Smith, Jehu, 179
Smith, Joseph, 31, 133
Smith, Kirby, 211
Sni-A-Bar River, 219
Sni-A-Bar Township, 101
South Carolina, 11, 130
South Yuba River, 156
Southampton County, Virginia, 11
Southern Cross of Honor, 76
Spiebuck, Golightly, 55
Springfield, Louisiana, 77, 104, 107, 121
Springfield, Missouri, 152, 159, 167
St. Francis County, 82
St. Joseph, Missouri, 27, 99, 140, 141, 214
St. Louis, Missouri, 9, 17, 37, 41, 82, 92, 96, 127, 130, 158, 168, 205, 219
St. Mary's Catholic Cemetery, 59, 60
Stanton, Edwin, 20
Starr, Belle, 212
Starr, Tom, 212
State Hospital Insane Asylum No. 2, 140
Stephenson, Robert, 78, 79, 80, 194, 220, 224, 229
Stewart, Bill, 180
Stewart, James, 145
Stierlin, Henry J., 43, 46, 48, 91
Stillwater Penitentiary, 215
Stone, 63, 112
Stone, Joseph, 63, 112
Stony Point, 65, 79, 80, 156, 227
Strange, Mary Frances Strange, 93
Sturgeon, Missouri, 3
Sugar Creek, MO, 42
Talley, Thomas, 169
Tate, David, 56
Taylor, Fletch, 56, 58, 66, 73, 100, 107, 170
Taylor, Simon, 88
Teague, A B, 199
Teague, Ab, 106, 192, 193, 196, 197, 198, 199, 224, 229, 232
Teague, John H., 78, 79, 80, 196, 197, 198, 220, 224, 230, 232
Teague, Thomas F., 192, 193, 196, 198, 224, 230

Tecumseh, 21, 150
Terrell, Edwin, 59
Terry, Ellen, 220
Terry, John H., 78, 79, 80, 119, 125, 182, 220, 224, 230
Terry, William, 220
Texas, 7, 38, 39, 57, 58, 59, 64, 66, 67, 69, 72, 74, 75, 76, 100, 114, 116, 121, 131, 132, 135, 139, 141, 155, 157, 159, 167, 168, 171, 173, 182, 183, 186, 187, 188, 212, 213, 218, 219, 222, 224, 229
Texas Revolution, 114
Thayer, Eli, 8
Thompson, Gideon W., 56, 61, 65, 151
Thompson, J. D., 34
Thompson, James, 122, 201, 223, 224
Thompson, Oliver P., 201, 202
Thompson, Oscar, 202
Thomson, 201
Thrailkill, John, 2, 200
Tigue, Nat or Neal, 196
Todd and Thrailkill's bands, 2
Todd, George A., 63
Todd, George W., 2, 42, 56, 58, 61, 63, 66, 69, 73, 76, 78, 79, 80, 99, 107, 112, 151, 154, 156, 159, 171, 186, 187, 200, 203, 208, 211, 219, 223, 224, 230
Todd, Margaret, 63
Toler, 70
Topeka Daily, 94
Topeka, Kansas, 94
Torrey, Henry, 54
Totten, James, 37, 39
Traber, Zach, 107
Trace, Harrison, 56
Treaty of Versailles, 26
Triplett Township, Chariton County, Missouri, 144
Tucker, James L., 70
Tucker, James S., 70, 195, 224, 230
Tucker, William D., 44, 143, 164, 165, 173, 195, 223, 224
Turner, Nat, 11
Union Cemetery, 112
United Confederate Veterans Camp, 130, 163, 172
United Daughters of the Confederacy, 76, 153, 189
United States Congress, 37, 54, 176, 229
United States Constitution, 16, 27, 222
United States Constitution, Bill of Rights, 16, 19
United States House of Representatives, 178

United States Senate, 9, 176
United States Supreme Court, 208
Van Alstyne, Texas, 100
Van Dorn, General, 104
Vandever, Susan Crawford, 22, 168, 212
Vaughan, James, 70, 144, 165, 167, 204, 205, 219, 223, 224, 228
Vaughan, Joseph H., 156
Vaughan, Josiah, 205
Vaughan, Mary, 205
Vaughan, Nancy Jane, 205
Vaughan, William H., 144, 165, 204, 224, 228, 230
Vaughn, Daniel, 205
Vaughn, David, 35
Vaughn, James, 70, 167, 205, 219
Vaughn, Joe, 56
Vaughn, Margaret, 205
Vaughn, Mary, 205
Vaughn, Robert T., 205
Vaughn, Sarah L., 205
Vaughn, Susan E., 205
Vaughn, Thomas, 205
Vaughn, Wm, 204
Venable, Ran, 155
Vera Cruz, Missouri, 200
Vernon County, Missouri, 24, 164, 224
Vicksburg Campaign, 197
Vicksburg, Mississippi, 23, 32, 197
Vicksburg, MS, 23, 32, 197
Wadesburg, MO, 42
Wakefield, James H., 59
Walker, Andrew, 93, 143
Walker, Morgan, 55, 93, 143, 146, 148, 149, 154, 192, 193, 230
Walker, Samuel, 22
Walley, Irvin, 209
War Eagle, 166
War of 1812, 104, 106, 150
Warrensburg, Missouri, 28, 33, 36, 42, 77, 82, 89, 116, 133, 135, 176, 178, 179
Washington Creek, 156
Watson, Frank, 141
Watts, John S., 150
Watts, Margaret J., 150
Waverly, Missouri, 210
Weekly Standard, 116
Wells, J. A., 198
West Virginia, 88

West, George, 199
Westphalia, Anderson County, Kansas, 163
Westport, Missouri, 12, 59, 64, 73, 78, 79, 80, 84, 146, 150, 153, 154, 155, 167, 187, 206, 235, 238
White River, 83
White, John, 129
White, Lavisa Adeline, 129
Whitesides, Jennie Upton Hays, 153
Wichita Banner, 94
Wigfall, Louis T., 57
Wilkinson, James W., 72
William Scott, 60
Williamson, Ann, 207
Williamson, Charles F., 224
Williamson, Charles T., 165, 207, 230
Williamson, James, 207
Williamson, Johnson, 207
Williamson, Lizzie, 207
Williamson, Lula, 207
Williamson, Susan, 207
Williamson, Thomas, 207
Williamson, William, 207
Willow Swamp, Arkansas, 96
Wilson, Adeline, 208
Winona, Missouri, 197
Woodford County, Kentucky, 104
Woodlawn Cemetery at Independence, Missouri, 62, 64
Woodside, J. R., 197, 199
Woodson, C. A., 141
Wyandotte, Kansas, 205
Wyeth County, Virginia, 185
Yeager, James B., 217
Yeager, Martha J., 217
Yeager, Mary J., 217
Yeager, Richard E., 69, 205, 211, 217, 223, 224, 225, 227
Younger, Busheba Fristoe, 208
Younger, Charles Lee, 208
Younger, Cole, 22, 46, 57, 68, 69, 70, 107, 110, 162, 167, 168, 169, 208, 209, 210, 211, 212, 213, 214, 215, 216, 218, 224, 225, 229, 232
Younger, Henry, 107, 208, 209
Younger, James Henry (Jim), 208
Younger, Josephine, 69
Younger, Robert Ewing (Bob), 213
Zeiger, W. H., 177

Printed in the United States
16705LVS00002B/5

9 780971 992931